Evangelical Theology

DOING THEOLOGY

Doing Theology introduces the major Christian traditions and their way of theological reflection. The volumes focus on the origins of a particular theological tradition, its foundations, key concepts, eminent thinkers, and historical development. The series is aimed at readers who want to learn more about their own theological heritage and identity: theology undergraduates, students in ministerial training, and church study groups.

Evangelical Theology

Uche Anizor
Rob Price
Hank Voss

t&tclark

LONDON • NEW YORK • OXFORD • NEW DELHI • SYDNEY

T&T CLARK
Bloomsbury Publishing Plc
50 Bedford Square, London, WC1B 3DP, UK
1385 Broadway, New York, NY 10018, USA
29 Earlsfort Terrace, Dublin 2, Ireland

BLOOMSBURY, T&T CLARK and the T&T Clark logo are trademarks
of Bloomsbury Publishing Plc

First published in Great Britain 2021

Cover design: Terry Woodley
Cover image © Paul Biris /Getty

A catalogue record for this book is available from the British Library.

Library of Congress Cataloging-in-Publication Data
Names: Anizor, Uche, 1976– author. | Price, Robert B., author. |
Voss, Hank, 1976– author.
Title: Evangelical theology / Uche Anizor, Robert B. Price, Hank Voss.
Description: London ; New York : T&T Clark, 2021. | Series: Doing theology
Identifiers: LCCN 2020045374 (print) | LCCN 2020045375 (ebook) |
ISBN 9780567677136 (hb) | ISBN 9780567677129 (pb) | ISBN 9780567677143
(ebook) | ISBN 9780567677150 (epdf)
Subjects: LCSH: Reformed Church–Doctrines. | Evangelicalism.
Classification: LCC BX9422.3 .A55 2021 (print) | LCC BX9422.3 (ebook) |
DDC 230/.04624–dc23
LC record available at https://lccn.loc.gov/2020045374
LC ebook record available at https://lccn.loc.gov/2020045375

ISBN: HB: 978-0-5676-7713-6
PB: 978-0-5676-7712-9
ePDF: 978-0-5676-7715-0
eBook: 978-0-5676-7714-3

Series: Doing Theology

Typeset by Newgen KnowledgeWorks Pvt. Ltd., Chennai, India

To find out more about our authors and books visit www.bloomsbury.com
and sign up for our newsletters.

To the late J. I. Packer
Evangelical theologian par excellence

CONTENTS

List of Illustrations ix
Acknowledgments xi
List of Abbreviations xiii

Introduction—What Is Evangelical Theology? 1

Foundations 11

1 "According to the Scriptures": The Bible 13
2 "Go and Make Disciples": Mission 39

Themes 69

3 "Christ Died for Our Sins": Atonement 71
4 "You Must Be Born Again": Conversion 95
5 "You Have Been Saved by Grace": Justification 121
6 "Be Holy as I Am Holy": Sanctification 145

Developments 175

7 "You Will Receive Power": The Holy Spirit 177
8 "In the Name of the Father, Son, and Holy
   Spirit": Trinitarian Theology 201

Conclusion—*Quo Vadis?* The Promise of Evangelical
   Theology 221

Index 231

ILLUSTRATIONS

Figure

6.1 Wesleyan understanding of sanctification 167

Tables

2.1 Global Summary of Christian Mission and the Poor 47
2.2 Global Summary of Unreached People Groups 48
2.3 Impact of 1900s Missionary Movement on Global
     Evangelical Populations 51
2.4 2020 Global Distribution of Evangelicals 62
6.1 Human Participation in Sanctification 148
6.2 The Study of Sanctification and Christian Spirituality 151
6.3 Owen's Ten Preparation Steps for Killing Sin 155
6.4 Historical Development of the Triple Way 161

ACKNOWLEDGMENTS

Uche would like to thank Talbot School of Theology and Biola University for the gift of a research leave that gave me the time and space to write. Dan Treier and Kelly Kapic, thank you for encouraging me (and helping open the door) to write this book. I'm grateful to Kyle Strobel and Fred Sanders for connecting me with valuable resources, and to Jeremy Treat for taking the time out of a busy pastoral schedule to provide helpful feedback. To my coauthors, Rob and Hank, thank you for your excellent work and careful (and gracious) comments on mine. You are wonderful colaborers. Sincerest thanks to my wife, Melissa, and kids, Zoe, Eli, and Ezra, for never begrudging me taking time away to write *another* theology book. Writing this book was a surprising joy. My love and appreciation of the evangelical tradition only deepened as a result of tracing the story of our theology.

Rob would like to thank the students from his fall 2016 seminar in evangelical theology: Michael Andreas, Dale Chamberlain, Joshua Coffey, P. J. Davis, Job Garcia, Jon Garcia, Joshua Kim, Stan Klapauszak, James Klein, Ryan Landes, Carlos Pamplona, Elius Pribadi, H. B. Sim, and Scott Visser. Gentlemen, the biblical insight and the passion for ministry that you brought to our discussions wonderfully enriched my own thinking and, I trust, this book as well.

Hank would like to thank students and friends who have read and commented on parts of this work including Isaiah Swain, Kiersten Mackintosh, Caleb Model, Jeanette Voss, and Nathan Esela. He also thanks Taylor University's provost, Mike Hammond; dean, Tom Jones; and fellow faculty, especially Jenny Collins, Phil Collins, Greg Magee, Ed Meadors, Bill Heth, May Young, Joseph Pak, Phil Collins, Mike Severe, and Bob Priest, for encouragement and constructive criticism at various points. Charles White of Spring Arbor College was kind to respond to several questions related to Phoebe Palmer. Hank is especially appreciative of the many hours

Uche and Rob spent reading and commenting on his chapters. The above saved me from many errors; remaining faults are mine alone. Last, but not least, I am deeply thankful to Johanna, Samuel, David, Reneé, Isaiah, and Darriona. Each of you is a good gift from God, and I appreciate your patience as I disappeared from family life for far too many hours in order to complete this project. May the fruit of this work be many more laborers for the harvest (Matt 9:36–38).

As an authorial team we deeply appreciate our editors, Anna Turton and Veerle Van Steenhuyse. They have shown an extraordinary amount of patience through various delays and challenges. Finally, we dedicate this book to the memory of J. I. Packer. Dr. Packer died as this book was reaching its final stages. For more than seventy years he embodied much of what is best in the global evangelical movement.

ABBREVIATIONS

AF³	*The Apostolic Fathers: Greek Texts and English Translations*, edited by Michael Holmes. 3rd ed. Grand Rapids: Baker Academic, 2007.
ANF	*Ante-Nicene Fathers*. Electronic ed. Edited by Alexander Roberts and James Donaldson. Buffalo, 1885–96. 10 vols. Reprint. Peabody: Hendrickson, 1994.
CCEL	*Christian Classics Ethereal Library*, www.ccel.org.
CD	Karl Barth, *Church Dogmatics*. Edited by G. W. Bromiley and T. F. Torrance. 4 vols. In 13 parts. Edinburgh: T&T Clark, 1956–75. Reprint. Peabody: Hendrickson, 2010.
CTC	*Cape Town Confession*. Rose Dowsett, ed. *The Cape Town Commitment: Study Edition*. Peabody: Hendrickson, 2012.
CTHDD	Jaroslav Pelikan. *The Christian Tradition: A History of the Development of Doctrine*. 5 vols. Chicago: University of Chicago Press, 1971–89.
DTIB	Kevin Vanhoozer, Craig Bartholomew, Daniel Treier, and N. T. Wright, eds. *Dictionary for Theological Interpretation of the Bible*. Grand Rapids: Baker, 2005.
EDT	Daniel Treier and Walter A. Elwell, eds. *Evangelical Dictionary of Theology*. 3rd ed. Grand Rapids: Baker Academic, 2017.
ET	English Translation
GAMEO	*Global Anabaptist Mennonite Encyclopedia Online*, www.gameo.org.
GDT	*Global Dictionary of Theology*. Edited by William Dryness et al. Downers Grove: InterVarsity, 2008.
IET	Daniel Treier. *Introducing Evangelical Theology*. Grand Rapids: Baker, 2019.

Inst.	John Calvin. *Institutes of the Christian Religion.* Edited by John Thomas McNeill. Translated by Ford Lewis Battles. 2 vols. LCC 20. Philadelphia: Westminster, 1960.
JIDRR	*Junius Institute for Digital Reformation Research,* www.juniusinstitute.org.
LC	*Lausanne Covenant*
LOP	*Lausanne Occasional Paper*
LW	*Luther's Works.* Edited by Jaroslav Pelikan and Helmut T. Lehmann. 56 vols. St. Louis: Concordia; Philadelphia: Fortress, 1955–86.
NDBT	*New Dictionary of Biblical Theology: Exploring the Unity and Diversity of Scripture.* Edited by T. Desmond Alexander et al. Downers Grove: InterVarsity, 2000.
NPNF [1]	*Nicene and Post-Nicene Fathers,* Series 1. Electronic ed. Edited by Philip Schaff. New York, 1886–9. Reprint, Peabody, 1994.
NPNF [2]	*Nicene and Post-Nicene Fathers,* Series 2. Electronic ed. Edited by Philip Schaff and Henry Wace. New York, 1890. Reprint, Peabody, 1994.
NWDCS	Philip Sheldrake, ed. *The New Westminster Dictionary of Christian Spirituality.* Louisville: Westminster John Knox, 2005.
PWCM	*Perspectives on the World Christian Movement: Reader.* Edited by Ralph D. Winter et al. 3rd ed. Pasadena: William Carey Library, 1999.
WJE	*Works of Jonathan Edwards.* 26 vols. New Haven: Yale University Press, 1957–2008.
WJO	John Owen. *The Works of John Owen.* Orig. 1850–3. 16 vols. Edinburgh: Banner of Truth, 2013.
WJW	*Wesley, John. Works of John Wesley.* Vol. 14. Kansas City: Beacon Hill, 1978.
ZDCS	*Zondervan Dictionary of Christian Spirituality.* Edited by Glen G. Scorgie et al. Grand Rapids: Zondervan, 2011.

Introduction—What Is Evangelical Theology?

This is a book about evangelical theology. Precisely what counts as evangelical theology takes a little explaining.[1] For one thing, while various denominations and institutions are rightly described as evangelical, there is no denomination or institution that can claim to represent evangelical theology in any official capacity. For another, evangelical theology can be found alongside nonevangelical theology in many denominations and institutions that have their own particular identities. For instance, other books in this *Doing Theology* series address Lutheran theology, Reformed theology, Anglican theology, Baptist theology, and Methodist theology. Each of these theologies has certain characteristic teachings that mark its particular identity. And yet, with all of these traditions, evangelical theology shares a commitment to orthodox Protestant teaching. To be orthodox is to confess, with the universal Christian church, the triune nature of God the Creator and the incarnation, crucifixion, and resurrection of his Son, Jesus Christ, as summarized in the Apostles' Creed and the Nicene Creed. To be Protestant is to confess that we are justified by faith not works and that God's authority over the church comes ultimately through Scripture. Orthodox Protestant belief is the least common denominator to these various traditions.

What then distinguishes evangelical theology as evangelical? Historians of the evangelical movement have identified four

---

[1]Thomas S. Kidd, *Who Is an Evangelical? The History of a Movement in Crisis* (New Haven: Yale University Press, 2019).

distinguishing marks of evangelical theology.[2] These marks can be found in varying degrees in all of these orthodox Protestant traditions. They can be found especially in the non-denominational, free church, and charismatic traditions. First, evangelical theology emphasizes the Bible as the word of God, true and authoritative and life-giving, to be preached and taught, read and memorized, pondered and prayed. Second, evangelical theology emphasizes the atoning work of Christ on the cross, his death in place of sinners, and his resurrection in power and glory. Third, evangelical theology emphasizes the experience of the Holy Spirit in conversion and in ongoing transformation in the Christian life. Fourth, evangelical theology emphasizes the mission of proclaiming the good news about Jesus to all the world. These marks are by no means absent from any orthodox Protestant tradition. They are basic elements of all biblical Christianity. What distinguishes evangelicals, even from within these specific traditions, is the central importance assigned to these elements in an overall vision of Christianity. It is not unique doctrines, but unique doctrinal *emphases*, that mark evangelical theology. Bible, cross, conversion, and mission are the emphases that animate evangelical theological reflection and often delimit it from other theological traditions.

In each of these emphases we see that evangelical theology is a theology oriented around the personal—personal faith, personal conversion, personal experience, and personal mission. The Bible is no mere catalog of things to believe and ways to behave. It is what God says to me personally. It is the big story that makes sense of my own life story. The cross is not just something that happened to Jesus. It is where my own sins were punished and taken away. It is the pattern of suffering to which I was personally committed in baptism. Conversion is not only joining a local congregation of Christians. It is my own, personal choice, made possible by the Holy Spirit and renewed as often as need be, to reject my sinful self-absorption and to commit myself to loving Jesus, following

---

[2]D. W. Bebbington, *Evangelicalism in Modern Britain: A History from the 1730s to the 1980s* (London: Routledge, 1989), 1–19; Timothy Larsen, "Defining and Locating Evangelicalism," in *The Cambridge Companion to Evangelical Theology*, ed. Timothy Larsen and Daniel J. Treier (Cambridge: Cambridge University Press, 2007), 1–14; Mark Noll, "What Is 'Evangelical'?" in *The Oxford Handbook of Evangelical Theology*, ed. Gerald R. McDermott (Oxford: Oxford University Press, 2010), 19–32.

his ways, and serving others. Mission is not just an organizational goal for my denomination or local congregation. It includes my personal responsibility to tell others of the forgiveness, salvation, and healing that Jesus offers to them. These four defining emphases of evangelical Christianity—Bible, cross, conversion, and mission— they each express aspects of the personal experience of salvation.

The History of Evangelical Theology

These distinguishing marks of evangelical theology developed over the course of a history. As a set of emphases within Protestant theology, evangelical theology hearkens back to major Protestant Reformers like Martin Luther and John Calvin, who indeed will appear in this volume. As a variant within basic orthodox Christianity, however, evangelical theology also finds at least partial representatives across the history of the church. The *Confessions* of the great church father Augustine (354–430) has been described as "the earliest adequate expression of that type of religion which has since attached to itself the name of 'evangelical'."[3] The *Confessions* brilliantly narrates Augustine's personal experience of salvation in imagery and language drawn extensively from the Bible, climaxing in the famous conversion scene in the garden in Milan, and issuing in Augustine's vision of his mission as a bishop. Nevertheless, Augustine and the Reformers are more on the order of presuppositions to evangelical theology. They are there in the background, but they do not explain the uniqueness of the evangelical movement.

That uniqueness begins to emerge in a variety of movements in seventeenth-century European Christianity, most clearly in what is broadly designated Pietism.[4] Pietists emphasized piety. Piety, the personal practice of religion, is what many felt was lacking in the nominal Christianity surrounding them.[5] So pietists called

---

[3]B. B. Warfield, "Augustine and His *Confessions*," in *The Works of Benjamin B. Warfield*, vol. 4, *Studies in Tertullian and Augustine* (New York: Oxford University Press, 1932; reprint Grand Rapids, MI: Baker, 2003), 250.

[4]Mark Hutchinson and John Wolffe, *A Short History of Global Evangelicalism* (Cambridge: Cambridge University Press, 2012), 25–32.

[5]Carter Lindberg, "Introduction," in *The Pietist Theologians: An Introduction to Theology in the Seventeenth and Eighteenth Centuries*, ed. Carter Lindberg (Malden: Blackwell, 2005), 1–20.

not for new doctrines, but for renewed emphasis on doctrines and practices they believed had fallen into neglect. Philipp Jakob Spener (1635–1705) is one of the most broadly representative of the pietist leaders. His *Pious Desires* (1675) summarized many of the central aims of the movement.[6] Spener called first and foremost for a more prominent role for the Bible in the Christian life. He wanted all Christians to be regularly reading and studying the Bible, and he wanted Christian leaders better equipped with knowledge of the Bible and with skills in preaching and teaching it. Spener called for all Christians to exercise their spiritual priesthood. He wanted every believer to take responsibility for their own and others' growth in Christianity, not only for the initial "rebirth" or conversion to Christianity, but especially for the new life of transformation into the likeness of Christ into which we are born again. Spener called for a practical faith that was active in loving service toward others. He wanted not only right doctrine but also right practice. In terms of evangelical distinctives, Spener—with the broad Pietist movement—clearly emphasized the centrality of Bible, conversion, and mission. But while Pietists loved the cross, it was not for them the preoccupation that it would be for the evangelical movement, nor did Pietists broadly seek the kind of religious revivals, with the kind of interdenominational cooperation, that later evangelicals did.

With the great revivals of the eighteenth century, the evangelical movement finally emerges in its distinctive identity. These revivals were led by figures like Jonathan Edwards (1703–1758), George Whitefield (1714–1770), John Wesley (1703–1791), and Charles Wesley (1707–1788).[7] Although the so-called Great Awakening was focused around events in New England in 1739–42, it was part of "an international series of revivals that stretched from Germany to Nova Scotia to the Caribbean," and from the 1730s to the 1780s.[8] Central to these revivals was the preaching of the "new birth." Simply being born into a Christian society was not enough. Every individual needed to be born again (Jn 3:3), by the power of the Holy Spirit, into a life of joyful obedience that is pleasing to God. This new birth was made possible by the cross. There Christ died

---

[6]Philipp Jakob Spener, "*Pia Desideria*," in *Pietists: Selected Writings*, ed. Peter C. Erb, Classics of Western Spirituality (New York: Paulist, 1983), 31–49.
[7]Mark A. Noll, *The Rise of Evangelicalism: The Age of Edwards, Whitefield and the Wesleys* (Downers Grove: InterVarsity, 2003).
[8]Kidd, *Who Is an Evangelical?* 21.

in place of sinners, receiving the punishment their sins deserved, so that a holy God could justly forgive all who trust Jesus for salvation. With supreme confidence in the Bible as God's word, evangelicals prayed and labored intensely to expand the reach of the Bible's good news and bring revival to more and more people. For example, John Wesley, over the course of his long ministry, traveled an estimated 250,000 miles and preached some forty thousand sermons.[9] Huge crowds gathered in the open air to hear the gospel. A flood of publishing documented and furthered the revivals' reach: pamphlets, newspaper stories, evangelical magazines, sermon collections, hymnals, and conversion narratives.[10] Evangelicalism thus began as an international, interdenominational movement of revival, unified around a core set of theological emphases.

It was in the nineteenth century that the evangelical movement extended its reach across the globe. It did so as the expansionist impulse of the evangelical revivals flowed into international missionary work. Evangelical commitment to mission includes not only personal evangelism and social activism. It also includes preaching the gospel where Christ is not known (Rom 15:20) and making disciples of all nations (Mt 28:19). This international dimension of evangelical zeal for mission began in earnest in the 1790s with the foundation of major missionary societies. By the time of the landmark World Missionary Conference in Edinburgh in 1910, evangelical missions had made such progress that leaders could speak—in the optimism of the era, though not without reason—of "the evangelization of the world in this generation."[11] At the beginning of the century (1800), roughly 1 percent of Protestants globally lived outside Europe and North America. By the end of the century (1900), roughly 10 percent did.[12] (Today roughly 80 percent or more do.[13]) Herculean efforts of Bible translation accompanied missionary endeavors. The century after 1815 saw a fivefold increase in the number of languages (estimated at 572) into which at least a portion of Scripture had been translated, mostly by

---

[9]Mark A. Noll, *Turning Points: Decisive Moments in the History of Christianity*, 3rd ed. (Grand Rapids: Baker, 2012), 220.

[10]Hutchinson and Wolffe, *Global Evangelicalism*, 35–6, 47–54.

[11]Hutchinson and Wolffe, *Global Evangelicalism*, 138.

[12]Philip Jenkins, *The Next Christendom: The Coming of Global Christianity*, 3rd ed. (Oxford: Oxford University Press, 2011), 49.

[13]Hutchinson and Wolffe, *Global Evangelicalism*, 242.

Protestants.[14] Throughout the century, Bible, cross, conversion, and mission continued to identify the evangelical movement even as it expanded into cultures across the globe.[15]

Finally, of the various twentieth-century developments in evangelical theology, three stand out. First, evangelicalism expanded to include much of the new charismatic movement. The century began with a remarkable series of international revivals: "Melbourne (1902), Wonsan, Korea (1903), Wales (1904), Mukti, India (1905), Los Angeles (1906), Pyongyang, Korea (1907), [and] The Heart of Africa Mission in the Belgian Congo (1914), Ivory Coast and Ghana (1914–15)."[16] Some of these, such as the Azusa Street Revival in Los Angeles, included intensely personal experiences of salvation that involved speaking in tongues, prophecy, and physical healings. Explosive growth has brought membership in these Pentecostal and charismatic churches to some 644 million believers as of 2020, roughly a quarter of the world's Christians.[17] Though often only distantly connected to the evangelical history summarized here, most of these churches share some form of the evangelical theological emphases.[18]

Second, the churches planted by the Western-led evangelical missionary movement in the nineteenth century shifted to indigenous leadership in the twentieth.[19] As ties to Western theological training grew weaker, these new churches began to reflect their own cultures more fully. This helps to explain the relative independence of many Pentecostal and charismatic churches today. As these majority world churches matured theologically, they have pressed evangelical theology to be more aware of its rootedness in Anglo-American

---

[14]Matthias Gerner, "Why Worldwide Bible Translation Grows Exponentially," *Journal of Religious History* 42, no. 2 (June 2018): 153–9.

[15]Kelly Cross Elliott, "The Bebbington Quadrilateral Travels into the Empire," in *Evangelicals: Who They Have Been, Are Now, and Could Be*, ed. Mark A. Noll, David W. Bebbington, and George M. Marsden (Grand Rapids: Eerdmans, 2019), 127.

[16]Hutchinson and Wolffe, *Global Evangelicalism*, 149.

[17]"Global Pentecostalism," Center for the Study of Global Christianity at Gordon-Conwell Theological Seminary, accessed July 23, 2020, https://www.gordonconwell.edu/center-for-global-christianity/research/global-pentecostalism.

[18]Mark A. Noll, "World Cup or World Series?" in *Evangelicals: Who They Have Been, Are Now, and Could Be*, ed. Mark A. Noll, David W. Bebbington, and George M. Marsden (Grand Rapids: Eerdmans, 2019), 305–6.

[19]Noll, *Turning Points*, 261–85.

and European cultures and to welcome the theological insights of evangelicals from Africa, Asia, and Latin America.[20]

Third, the evangelical movement achieved more formal expressions of its global, theological coherence. Representatives from twenty-one nations were involved in the global expansion of the World Evangelical Alliance beginning in 1951.[21] In 1974, the first International Congress on World Evangelization was held in Lausanne, Switzerland, under the leadership of John Stott and Billy Graham. Evangelical representatives from over 150 nations—more than the membership of the United Nations at the time[22]—signed the Lausanne Covenant, one of the most beautifully crafted confessions in the history of Christianity and quintessentially evangelical.[23] The 2010 meeting of the Congress produced The Cape Town Commitment, signed by representatives of 198 nations, a stunning evangelical-ecumenical achievement.[24]

This brief sketch of the history of the evangelical movement has sought to highlight its coherence around personal experience and doctrinal emphasis. From its revivalist and expansionist beginnings, evangelicalism has been on a trajectory of increasing cultural diversity. This diversity has always been something of a puzzle. From the beginnings of the movement to the scholarly debates of today, plausible objections have been raised against speaking of evangelicalism as single movement. What the most recent history of the movement has shown is that, right alongside increasing cultural diversity, there has emerged also a striking confessional unity. For all the variety of evangelicalism, confessions like the Lausanne

---

[20]See, e.g., the chapters dedicated to evangelical theology in each of these contexts in Larsen and Treier, eds., *Cambridge Companion to Evangelical Theology*; Timothy C. Tennent, *Theology in the Context of World Christianity: How the Global Church Is Influencing the Way We Think about and Discuss Theology* (Grand Rapids: Zondervan, 2007); Gene L. Green, Stephen T. Pardue, and K. K. Yeo, eds., *Majority World Theology*, 6 vols. (Carlisle: Langham Global Library, 2015–9).

[21]"Our History," World Evangelical Alliance, accessed July 23, 2020, https://worldea.org/en/who-we-are/our-history.

[22]"Growth in United Nations membership, 1945–Present," United Nations, accessed July 24, 2020, https://www.un.org/en/sections/member-states/growth-united-nations-membership-1945-present/index.html.

[23]"The Lausanne Covenant," Lausanne Movement, accessed July 23, 2020, https://www.lausanne.org/content/covenant/lausanne-covenant.

[24]"The Cape Town Commitment," Lausanne Movement, accessed July 23, 2020, https://www.lausanne.org/content/ctcommitment.

Covenant have given formal, public acknowledgment to what has always been at the pulsing center of every evangelical heart: the personal experience of the salvation that Jesus offers to all and a vision of the Christian life centered on Bible, cross, conversion, and mission.

Chapter Overview

This book attempts to describe and commend the unique emphases of evangelical theology. Each chapter addresses a particular doctrine by examining its biblical roots, historical developments, ongoing challenges, and future prospects. Readers are introduced in each chapter to a key figure in evangelical theology, whose work helps to guide our exposition.

Part 1, "Foundations," presents two foundational commitments of evangelical theology. Evangelical theology is committed to the Bible and to mission. If the work of Jesus Christ on the cross and the work of the Holy Spirit in conversion are the center of evangelical theology (Part 2), then the Bible and mission could be described as its origin and goal. Evangelical theology is biblical theology, rooted in exegesis and confident in the inspiration, authority, and trustworthiness of God's written words (Chapter 1). Evangelical theology therefore aspires to bring the message of Scripture to all nations through its mission of embodying, proclaiming, and defending the gospel (Chapter 2). Together, the Bible and mission determine the overall feel of evangelical theology—its texture and orientation—more strongly than do the central doctrines covered in Part 2. They are guiding principles, determining the overall ethos of the movement. By arranging the material in this sequence, we intend to highlight the unique roles that the Bible and mission have played in shaping the general character of evangelical theology.

Part 2, "Themes," takes up the core of evangelical theology: the work of Christ on the cross and the work of the Holy Spirit in conversion. On the cross, Christ died for our sins (Chapter 3). At the very center of the vast significance of the crucifixion is Christ's bearing the penalty our sins deserve—namely, death—and his doing so in our place, as a substitute for us. The salvation thus accomplished for us by Christ must also be applied to us by the Holy Spirit. With the work of the Holy Spirit in the individual soul, evangelical theology reaches the center of the personal experience of salvation. The following three chapters address the primary aspects of this experience. Conversion is being born again from spiritual death into spiritual life, a radical personal reorientation from self to God, and from sin to holiness (Chapter 4). In justification, God reckons my sins to Jesus and his righteousness to me, incorporating believers into the "wondrous exchange" of the cross and issuing in God's gracious pardon and acceptance (Chapter 5). Sanctification is the lifelong process of inner transformation, spiritual renewal, and growth in holiness that begins the moment of justification (Chapter 6). In conversion, justification, and sanctification, believers experience the special work of the Holy Spirit in conviction and repentance, comfort and assurance, empowerment and hope.

Part 3, "Developments," then turns attention to two promising and closely related developments within evangelical theology. The first is renewed reflection on the role of the Spirit in evangelical experience (Chapter 7). The second is an increasing awareness of evangelicalism's trinitarian depth (Chapter 8). By highlighting these trends, we do not mean to suggest that the evangelical theology of previous generations was in any way sub-trinitarian. Rather, we want to show how evangelicals today have begun devoting more sustained attention to the person and work of the Holy Spirit and to the doctrine of the Trinity. We conclude with a reflection on the promise of evangelical theology in this twenty-first century.

Foundations

1

"According to the Scriptures": The Bible

We affirm the divine inspiration, truthfulness and authority of both Old and New Testament Scriptures in their entirety as the only written word of God, without error in all that it affirms, and the only infallible rule of faith and practice.

LAUSANNE COVENANT §2

Evangelicals love the Bible. We gather to hear the Bible preached and taught. We read it and talk about it in our homes. We hang its promises on our walls. We strive to obey its commands. We give money to support the free distribution of the Bible and its translation into more and more languages. There is a simple reason why evangelical devotion to the Bible runs so deep. We believe that the Bible is the word of God.

To confess that the Bible is the word of God is to say that the words of the Bible are God's own. The Bible's words are God's words. This is true not merely because God spoke them long ago through prophets and apostles. More than history is involved here. The Bible's words are also what God is saying to us right now. God remains just as committed to his words today as when he first spoke them. God stands ever ready to bless the hearing and reading and doing of his words. Evangelical love for the Bible is simply an extension of our love for God.

In this chapter we highlight the work of American churchman Benjamin Breckinridge Warfield (1851–1921), professor of theology at Princeton Seminary. Warfield's spirited essays on the doctrine of Scripture have exerted a profound influence on contemporary English-speaking evangelicals' understanding of the Bible.[1] Evangelicals hold the same basic Protestant view of Scripture that was championed by Luther and Calvin, and both Luther and Calvin continue to inform evangelical thinking about Scripture. Yet it was Warfield as much as anyone else who put this classic Protestant doctrine into a contemporary idiom and defended it convincingly against modern critics.[2]

The Doctrine of Scripture

In order to explain how it is that the Bible is the word of God, evangelical theology emphasizes a series of attributes of the Bible: its inspiration, authority, and truthfulness. To affirm these attributes of the Bible is a crucial step toward a fully biblical account of the Bible as the means by which God speaks to us today. This section will survey these attributes of Scripture. The following section will turn to the history of the interpretation of Scripture.

Inspiration

God talks. God is verbal. From the beginning of the Bible to the end, God comes to his people in words. He declares blessings and he issues commands. He questions and he rebukes. He promises to be with us. He speaks the world into existence and summons Lazarus from the grave. He pronounces judgment and tells of time to come. The doctrine of inspiration includes Scripture among the words that God has spoken.

---

[1]Warfield is cited more than any classic theologian besides Luther and Calvin by the thirty-seven authors in D. A. Carson's 1,200-page, edited volume, *The Enduring Authority of the Christian Scriptures* (Grand Rapids: Eerdmans, 2016). Warfield's essays will be cited from *The Inspiration and Authority of the Bible*, ed. Samuel G. Craig (Phillipsburg: Presbyterian and Reformed, 1948). They are also collected in *The Works of Benjamin B. Warfield*, vol. 1, *Revelation and Inspiration* (New York: Oxford University Press, 1932; reprint Grand Rapids: Baker, 2003).
[2]Fred G. Zaspel, *The Theology of B. B. Warfield: A Systematic Summary* (Wheaton: Crossway, 2010), 111–75.

"All Scripture is inspired by God" (2 Tim 3:16, CSB). That is, the words of the Bible are God's words. This is the simple claim made by the doctrine of inspiration. Some have thought that God "inspires" the prophets, or the prophets' ideas. But God did not merely motivate the human authors to write, nor did he merely suggest ideas to them. Inspiration is not primarily about authors and ideas. Rather, according to Scripture, God authored a text. It is "Scripture" that is "inspired by God." In a brilliant essay, Warfield showed that "inspired" could just as well be translated "God-breathed."[3] Warfield's insight is reflected in the English Standard Version's "All Scripture is *breathed out* by God." In other words, Scripture is "not so much *in*-spired as *ex*-spired," as J. I. Packer explains it.[4] Clearly, what God "breathes out" is words—not prophets or wordless ideas! It is the words of the Bible that have their origin in God.

The words of the Bible are also, obviously, human words. "No prophecy of Scripture comes from someone's own interpretation. For no prophecy was ever produced by the will of man, but men spoke from God as they were carried along by the Holy Spirit" (2 Pet 1:20–21). Though God is the primary author of Scripture—its words do not originate in the prophets' will or interpretation—nevertheless, "men spoke." The doctrine of inspiration does not deny the conscious, deliberate involvement of human authors and editors in the production of Scripture.[5] Isaiah's style is different than Jonah's, and Luke's style is different than John's. It was not Moses who wrote the account of Moses's death (Deut 34), and someone collected and arranged the Book of Psalms. At the same time, all of these people did their work "as they were carried along by the Holy Spirit." Their human words are also God's words.

Authority

The doctrine of inspiration is closely associated with two further characteristics of Scripture: authority and truthfulness. As the words of the God who made us, Scripture has God's own authority

---

[3]Warfield, "God-Inspired Scripture" (1900): 245–96.
[4]J. I. Packer, *"Fundamentalism" and the Word of God* (Leicester: InterVarsity, 1958), 77.
[5]Warfield, "The Biblical Idea of Inspiration" (1915): 150–3.

to tell us what to believe and how to live. And as the words of the God "who never lies" (Titus 1:2), Scripture always speaks truthfully. The *Westminster Confession of Faith* 1.4 explains the connection between God as the inspiring author of Scripture and Scripture's authority and truthfulness: "The authority of the Holy Scripture, for which it ought to be believed and obeyed, depends ... wholly upon God (who is truth itself), the author thereof; and therefore it is to be received, because it is the Word of God." If God is the author of Scripture, it follows logically that Scripture is authoritative and true.

It is not simply as a logical deduction, however, that evangelicals affirm these characteristics of Scripture. We do so because Scripture itself says that it bears God's authority and truthfulness. Scripture itself teaches that it is authoritative and true. It does so explicitly, repeatedly, and comprehensively.

Jesus himself constantly relies on the authority of Scripture.[6] When tempted by Satan, Jesus does not appeal directly to the Father's authority or to his own authority. He appeals to the authority of Scripture (Mt 4:1–11; Lk 4:1–13). Three times he responds to Satan, "It is written." Again, when Jesus explains why he submits to arrest and crucifixion, he does not appeal directly to the Father's authority or to his own authority. Jesus appeals to the authority of Scripture (Mt 26:47–56; Mk 14:43–50; cf. Lk 22:37). "Let the Scriptures be fulfilled" (Mk 14:49). Even before an angry mob in the temple, Jesus confidently relies on subtle implications of Old Testament and insists that "Scripture cannot be broken" (Jn 10:35). Jesus states categorically in the Sermon on the Mount: "Do not think that I have come to abolish the Law or the Prophets; I have not come to abolish them but to fulfill them. For truly, I say to you, until heaven and earth pass away, not an iota, not a dot, will pass from the Law until all is accomplished" (Mt 5:17–18). Jesus delighted in the authority of Scripture: "I delight to do your will, O my God; your law is within my heart" (Ps 40:8; cf. Heb 10:5–7). Jesus believes that Scripture bears God's own authority. Evangelicals follow.

The authors of the New Testament naturally take Jesus's view of Scripture's supreme authority as their own.[7] They rely on its

---

[6]John Wenham, *Christ and the Bible*, 3rd ed. (Grand Rapids: Baker, 1994), 16–44.
[7]Packer, *Fundamentalism*, 62–3.

grammatical details (Gal 3:16). They boldly proclaim that the word of God is "living and active" (Heb 4:12; cf. 1 Pet 1:23), that it is "able to save your souls" (Jas 1:21; cf. 2 Tim 3:15), and that it is the foundation on which the church is built (Eph 2:19–20; cf. Mt 7:24–25) and for which faithful martyrs are beheaded (Rev 20:4; cf. Rev 6:9).

Warfield notes the curious way in which the New Testament often makes no distinction between words that are attributed to God in the Old Testament and those that are not.[8] For example, it is God himself who says to Abraham, "In you all the families of the earth shall be blessed" (Gen 12:3). When Paul quotes this passage, however, he says that "Scripture" says these words (Gal 3:8; cf. Exod 9:16 in Rom 9:17). On the other hand, it is not God but David who asks, "Why do the nations rage and the peoples plot in vain?" (Ps 2:1). When Peter quotes this passage, however, he says that it is "God" who says these words (through David and by the Spirit) (Acts 4:24–25; cf. Gen 2:24 in Mt 19:4–5 and Ps 95:7 in Heb 3:7). These patterns of citation show that the New Testament authors make "an absolute identification ... of 'Scripture' with the speaking God" so that "in point of directness of authority no distinction was made between them."[9] This is why Paul can refer to the entire Old Testament as "the oracles of God" (Rom 3:2), that is, as the "high, authoritative, sacred utterances" of God himself.[10]

Truthfulness

Scripture also teaches that it is true. "Every word of God proves true" (Prov 30:5). False words come from the devil (Jn 8:44), but God's word is truth (Jn 17:17). The longest chapter in the Bible, Psalm 119, is a "love poem" about the Bible itself: about its truth and goodness, its beauty and authority, its power and perfection.[11]

Christians have always believed in the truthfulness of Scripture. In the controversy leading up to the Diet of Worms (1521), Martin Luther appealed to the supreme truthfulness of Scripture to explain

---

[8]Warfield, "'It Says:' 'Scripture Says:' 'God Says'" (1899).

[9]Warfield, "'It Says:' 'Scripture Says:' 'God Says'" (1899): 299–300.

[10]Warfield, "The Oracles of God" (1900): 403 (see esp. 403–7).

[11]Kevin DeYoung, *Taking God at His Word: Why the Bible is Knowable, Necessary, and Enough, and What That Means for You and Me* (Wheaton: Crossway, 2014), 11–25.

his criticism of what had been taught by certain leaders. "Everyone, indeed, knows that at times they have erred, as men will; therefore I am ready to trust them only when they give me evidence for their opinions from Scripture, which has never erred."[12] Only a completely true Bible can be completely trusted. Luther goes on to quote a famous letter of Augustine (354–430), whose passionate defense of the truthfulness of Scripture became a standard point of reference in all subsequent debate. Augustine wrote of the books of Scripture, "Of these alone do I most firmly believe that the authors were completely free from error."[13] This is a clear statement of basic Christian conviction: Scripture is completely free from error. Thomas Aquinas (1225–1274) quotes this same letter and later says, "It is unlawful to hold that any false assertion is contained either in the Gospel or in any canonical Scripture, or that the writers thereof have told untruths."[14] The Bible contains no false assertions. Warfield is right to affirm that, with the exception of critical churches in the modern West, this "Augustinian inerrancy"[15] has been "the settled faith of the universal church of God ... from the first planting of the church until today."[16] In March 2020, Henry C. Ndukuba was installed as the fifth (Anglican) Primate of

---

[12]Martin Luther, "Defense and Explanation of All the Articles, 1521," in *LW* 32.11; cf. 112.

[13]Augustine, *Letter* 82.3, in *Nicene and Post-Nicene Fathers*, First Series, ed. Philip Schaff (Peabody: Hendrickson, 1994), 1.350. See also the earlier *Letter* 28 (1.251–3). Cf. Packer, *Fundamentalism*, 107–10.

[14]Thomas Aquinas, *Summa Theologiae* 1.1.8 ad 2 and 2.2.110.3 ad 1, trans. Fathers of the English Dominican Province (Notre Dame: Ave Maria Press, 1948), 1.6, 3.1660.

[15]Kevin J. Vanhoozer, "Augustinian Inerrancy: Literary Meaning, Literal Truth, and Literate Interpretation in the Economy of Biblical Discourse," in *Five Views on Biblical Inerrancy*, ed. J. Merrick and Stephen M. Garrett (Grand Rapids: Zondervan, 2013), 199–235.

[16]Warfield, "The Church Doctrine of Inspiration" (1894): 106. Cf. Mark Noll, "A Brief History of Inerrancy, Mostly in America," in *The Proceedings of the Conference on Biblical Inerrancy 1987* (Nashville: Broadman, 1987), 9–10: "The conviction that God communicates in Scripture a revelation of himself and of his deeds, and that this revelation is entirely truthful, has always been the common belief of most Catholics, most Protestants, most Orthodox, and even most of the sects of the fringe of Christianity." Daniel J. Treier, *Introducing Theological Interpretation of Scripture: Recovering a Christian Practice* (Grand Rapids: Baker, 2008), 167–78; Peter A. Lillback and Richard B. Gaffin Jr., *Thy Word Is Still Truth: Essential Writings on the Doctrine of Scripture from the Reformation to Today* (Philadelphia: P&R, 2013), xx.

All Nigeria. When asked in an interview how he would approach certain theological controversies in the Church of Nigeria, he stated,

> Our desire is to stand by the Word of God … [The] revisionist agenda will not stand. … I have seen Jesus prove Himself over and over again and protecting me. … Will I now, in the new context God has called me, begin to deny Him because I want some goodies from the White people or because I want to please somebody or a group? … It is Jesus or nothing; it is the Word of God or nothing. If we will die, let us die for the real thing; let us die believing Him. When we suffer, let it be because of our faith in Him, and there is no going back.[17]

Christians historically and globally, and evangelicals in particular, have firmly believed of the entire Bible, "These words are trustworthy and true" (Rev 21:5).[18]

But what about the words of the Bible that appear not to be true? What do we do with passages that seem to conflict with history or science? What about passages that appear inconsistent with each other—or, more to the point, inconsistent with our own moral intuitions? Both the theological and the practical implications here are momentous.

Theologically, evangelical confidence in Scripture's truthfulness would seem sturdy enough to handle a few dozen minor errors of fact. However, it is not just a question of whether an exhausted census worker flubbed a few figures (Ezra 2 vs. Neh 7), or whether

---

[17]Ngozi Adighibe, "Revisionist Agenda Has No Place in Church of Nigeria, Anglican Communion Says Primate Ndukuba," Church of Nigeria (Anglican Communion) website, accessed July 3, 2020, https://anglican-nig.org/revisionist-agenda-has-no-place-in-church-of-nigeria-anglican-communion-says-primate-ndukuba; Philip Jenkins, *The New Faces of Christianity: Believing the Bible in the Global South* (Oxford: Oxford University Press, 2006), 35: "Whether in the global North or the global South, belief in the absolute authority of scripture shapes the ways in which biblical texts are read." With reference to Ndukuba's predecessor once removed, see Philip Jenkins, "Defender of the Faith: Why All Anglican Eyes in London Are Nervously Fixed on a Powerful African Archbishop," *The Atlantic*, November 2003, 46–9.

[18]See, e.g., Pope Leo XIII's encyclical "On the Study of Holy Scripture," *Providentissimus Deus* (1893), §21 (which also quotes Augustine); and *The Chicago Statement on Biblical Inerrancy* (1978), in *Inerrancy*, ed. Norman L. Geisler (Grand Rapids: Zondervan, 1980), 493–502.

Jesus's travel itinerary actually took him through Sidon before Tyre (Mk 7:31), or whether Joseph leaned on his bed rather than his staff (Gen 47:31, Heb 11:21). These apparently trivial details can mask what Warfield describes as "the real problem of inspiration." The real problem is this: if the Bible speaks falsely anywhere, then the Bible's claim to inspiration, authority, and truthfulness is false.[19] If there are false words in the Bible, either God speaks false words or the false words are not his, that is, not inspired. If there are false words in the Bible, they cannot bear authority. And if we cannot trust what Jesus and the apostles say about the Bible, why should we trust what they say about anything else? With good reason does Augustine advise a policy of self-doubt. "If in these [biblical] writings I am perplexed by anything which appears to me opposed to truth, I do not hesitate to suppose that either the manuscript is faulty, or the translator has not caught the meaning of what was said, or I myself have failed to understand it."[20] This is not because Augustine is unwilling to face the evidence. It is because a crucial piece of the evidence, in fact the decisive piece of evidence, is that Jesus and the apostles clearly teach that the Bible is inspired, authoritative, and true.[21] Are they right or not?

Practically, the doctrine of Scripture's complete truthfulness is one of the most frustrating, humbling, and life-giving doctrines of Christianity. Every time we feel the allure of disobedience, every time some rule in the Bible is not to our liking, sin asks us, as the serpent asked Adam and Eve, "Did God really say?" Did God really say that sex belongs only in marriage? Did God really say that I must love my enemies? Did God really say that Jesus will return in judgment to send unbelievers to eternal damnation? The evangelical doctrine of Scripture stubbornly insists, "Yes, he did." What Scripture says, God says. On the other hand, if the Bible is not God's own word—inspired, authoritative, and true—its rules will seem arbitrary, stingy, oppressive, and ultimately negotiable, just as God's command seemed to Adam and Eve. But God's commands are good. God's words give life to the soul, joy to the heart, and light to the eyes: "In keeping them there is great reward" (Ps 19:7–11; cf. Gen 3:6). Confident in this good reward, Augustine urges us

---

[19]Warfield, "The Real Problem of Inspiration" (1893): 169–226, esp. 180–1.
[20]Augustine, *Letter* 82.3.
[21]Warfield, "Biblical Idea of Inspiration," 139–40; cf. Packer, *Fundamentalism*, 160–1.

not [to] contradict holy Scripture—whether we understand it (as when it hits at some of our vices) or fail to understand it (as when we feel that we could by ourselves gain better knowledge or give better instruction)—but rather ponder and believe that what is written there, even if obscure, is better and truer than any insights that we can gain by our own efforts.[22]

In such trust, we will bear the cost of discipleship and taste the goodness of what is written in the Bible.

A Brief History of the Interpretation of Scripture

Christians have always held that Scripture is God's own word to us, divinely inspired, fully authoritative, and perfectly true. Evangelicals across the globe continue to hold these beliefs about Scripture today. The history to be told about evangelicals' understanding of Scripture is not one of change and development in doctrine. The change and development have come not in doctrine, but in practice: the practice of interpretation. Given that the Bible is God's authoritative and true word to us, how do we interpret it?

In this section, Martin Luther will set the stage for the story of evangelical interpretation of Scripture. We will then trace two deforming trends in academic and liberal interpretation of Scripture: historical criticism and general hermeneutics.[23] These trends pushed evangelical theology into a narrowing emphasis on the historicity and inerrancy of Scripture and a devaluation of the role of theology and tradition in interpretation. Two re-forming— but not unproblematic—trends followed. First, postmodernism unmasked the illusion of pure objectivity in interpretation. This freed evangelicals to acknowledge and assess their subjective (theological) biases in reading of Scripture, expanding the narrow focus on historicity and inerrancy. Second, narrative theology

---

[22]Augustine, *On Christian Teaching*, trans. R. P. H. Green (Oxford: Oxford University Press, 1997), 2.16–17 (33–4).

[23]Daniel J. Treier, "Scripture and Hermeneutics," in *Mapping Modern Theology: A Thematic and Historical Introduction*, ed. Kelly M. Kapic and Bruce L. McCormack (Grand Rapids: Baker Academic, 2012), 67–96.

highlighted the role of community in interpretation. This raised evangelical esteem for the Christian community throughout history for providing wisdom in interpretation.

Just as evangelicals share with classical Christianity a doctrine of Scripture, so we also share much in our interpretation of Scripture. Nevertheless, the roots of distinctively evangelical interpretation of Scripture go back especially to Martin Luther.[24] Like others before him, Luther was concerned with the literal sense of Scripture. He achieved an astounding mastery of Hebrew and Greek and explained that his goal as an interpreter was to discern "the grammatical, historical meaning" of the biblical text.[25] He appealed to the intentions of the Bible's human authors and also interpreted the Bible as the words that God is speaking to us today. For our purposes, two elements of Luther's interpretation of Scripture are of particular interest. First, Luther interpreted Scripture as a single, coherent story about Jesus. Second, Luther drew deeply on the Christian tradition in his own interpretation of the Bible.

Jesus Christ is the center of Luther's interpretation of Scripture. That is, Luther believes that it is the nature of every book of the Bible to "show us Christ."[26] And so Luther interprets every book of the Bible as doing precisely this. In a lovely image, he describes the Old Testament as "the swaddling cloths and the manger in which Christ lies."[27] In his very first lectures on the Bible, Luther notes Jesus's description of the Old Testament as "the Scriptures ... that bear witness about me" (Jn 5:39). Then Luther announces, "Every prophecy and every prophet must be understood as referring to Christ the Lord, except where it is clear from plain words that someone else is spoken of."[28] Luther's strong convictions here never mellowed. Thirty years only added spice to the sauce: "Whoever does not have ... Jesus Christ ... must keep

---

[24]Robert Kolb, *Martin Luther and the Enduring Word of God: The Wittenberg School and Its Scripture-Centered Proclamation* (Grand Rapids: Baker Academic, 2016), 98–131.

[25]Luther, *Answer to the Hyperchristian Book (1521)*, in *LW* 39.181.

[26]Luther, *Preface to the Epistles of St. James and St. Jude 1546 (1522)*, in *LW* 35.396.

[27]Luther, *Preface to the Old Testament 1545 (1523)*, in *LW* 35.236.

[28]Luther, *First Lectures on the Psalms I*, in *LW* 10.7.

his hands off the Bible"![29] For Luther, and so for the evangelical tradition that has followed him, Christ is the key that unlocks the meaning of the whole Bible.

A second aspect of Luther's legacy to evangelical theology is his reliance on the wisdom of Christians who had gone before him. Luther is sometimes portrayed as having made a clean break with the squalid medieval church. In fact, Luther was deeply indebted to the Christian tradition, and he was happy to admit it.[30] "There is much that is Christian and good under the papacy ... and has come to us from this source."[31] It was especially the writings of Augustine that helped Luther as he wrestled with Scripture.[32] But Luther had no interest in merely reproducing the teachings of previous theologians, and he rejected certain elements even of Augustine's teaching.[33] For Luther, the role of tradition is not to define the Bible's teaching, but to help us understand it. "Our dear fathers"—that is, the great doctors and theologians of the church—"wanted to lead us to the Scriptures by their writings."[34] For Luther, the supreme authority of Scripture is in no way opposed to the subordinate wisdom of the past.[35]

But if Luther set evangelical theology off in the right direction in the interpretation of Scripture, we have not always kept to the path. In the centuries since Luther, two movements in particular have attracted but ultimately vexed evangelical interpreters of the Bible: historical criticism and general hermeneutics.

[29]Luther, *Treatise on the Last Words of David (2 Samuel 23:1–7)*, in *LW* 15.268.

[30]Erik Herrmann, "Luther's Absorption of Medieval Biblical Interpretation and His Use of the Church Fathers," in *The Oxford Handbook of Martin Luther's Theology*, ed. Robert Kolb, Irene Dingel, and L'ubomír Batka (Oxford: Oxford University Press, 2014), 71–90.

[31]Luther, *Concerning Rebaptism, 1528*, in *LW* 40.231.

[32]Because of Augustine's influence on Luther, Warfield famously described *Luther's* Reformation as "the triumph of *Augustine's* doctrine of grace." "Augustine," in *The Works of Benjamin B. Warfield*, vol. 4, *Studies in Tertullian and Augustine* (New York: Oxford University Press, 1932; reprint Grand Rapids: Baker, 2003), 130.

[33]Luther, *Preface to the Complete Edition of Luther's Latin Writings, 1545*, in *LW* 34.337.

[34]Luther, *To the Christian Nobility of the German Nation Concerning the Reform of the Christian Estate, 1520*, in *LW* 44.205.

[35]Timothy George, *Theology of the Reformers*, rev. ed. (Nashville: B&H Academic, 2013), 80–3.

Historical Criticism

Historical criticism is a way of interpreting the Bible that focuses on the historical setting in which a text was authored or edited. The idea is that the meaning of a text emerges from its historical context. The word "criticism" sounds grumpy. But here it simply means literary analysis, which is of course enormously valuable. The Bible was written by real people in real cultures using real languages. Understanding this history is vital to understanding the Bible.

Several factors help to explain why evangelicals value historical context so highly in biblical interpretation. In the sixteenth century, the early Reformers were inspired by Renaissance humanists, who were eager to get back to the sources of classical culture. Luther and those who followed him wanted to read the Bible in the Hebrew and Greek directly, not just the Latin Vulgate. They wanted to meet Augustine and the church fathers in person, and not just through anthologies and textbooks. They soon found that this more historical approach to Scripture and tradition exposed mistranslations in the Latin Vulgate and misrepresentations of the church fathers. And this had the electrifying effect of exposing the historical inadequacy of some Roman Catholic claims. History supported Protestants.

Then, beginning in the seventeenth century, Enlightenment critics of traditional Christianity attacked any appeal to miracle, mystery, or authority, and they also attacked the historical reliability of Scripture and the historical particularity of its claims.[36] Christians broadly responded with renewed emphasis on history. Christians were glad to have, in the historical dimensions of the faith, what seemed a more objective, more "scientific," and thus more culturally credible basis for Christianity than anything supernatural. History supported traditional Christianity.

Finally, since the latter eighteenth century, Western scholars have assembled an astounding and ever-increasing abundance of historical knowledge.[37] Biblical scholars have found this wealth of historical knowledge irresistibly suggestive and often wonderfully

---

[36] Jaroslav Pelikan, *Christian Doctrine and Modern Culture (since 1700)*, vol. 5 of *The Christian Tradition: A History of the Development of Doctrine* (Chicago: University of Chicago Press, 1989), 61–74.

[37] Jacques Barzun, *From Dawn to Decadence: 500 Year of Western Cultural Life: 1500 to the Present* (New York: HarperCollins, 2000), 481–3.

illuminating for biblical interpretation.[38] History enriches biblical interpretation. For all these reasons, evangelicals remain rightly committed to interpreting Scripture in historical terms.

But if historical criticism is vital as one element of biblical interpretation, it is anemic as the only element.[39] It's a strong voice in the choir, but a sad soloist. Christian interpreters have always paid attention—often not enough!—to what they knew of the historical context of the Bible. But at least until recent centuries, they have always seen the most important context for interpretation as the biblical context.[40] That is, we interpret any given passage of the Bible primarily in light of the rest of the Bible. "Scripture interprets Scripture," as the saying goes, and as supplemented by what we can gather from historical context. To Christian interpreters today, however, there beckons a vast body of reliable, extra-biblical knowledge of the ancient world. This provides an alternative primary context for interpreting individual passages of Scripture. When this extra-biblical historical context comes to dominate interpretation, to the exclusion of the biblical context, individual passages are drained of their meaning and detached from Christian beliefs.

Take Psalm 110 for example. Psalm 110 is one of the most frequently cited passages in the New Testament. It contains the famous verses, "The LORD said to my Lord" (Ps 110:1) and "You are a priest forever, after the order of Melchizedek" (Ps 110:4). Understood in whole-Bible context, in light of its use in the New Testament, Psalm 110 speaks of Jesus's relation to the Father (Mt 22:44; Mk 12:36; Lk 20:42–43; Acts 2:34–35), his ascension and enthronement (Heb 1:13; 1 Pet 3:22), and his heavenly, priestly session (Heb 5:5–10; 7:15–22) until the Second Coming (Heb 10:12–13). On the other hand, understood exclusively in its historical context, in light of ancient Near Eastern enthronement

---

[38]Pelikan, *Christian Doctrine and Modern Culture*, 75–89.

[39]Carl F. H. Henry, "The Uses and Abuses of Historical Criticism," in *God, Revelation, and Authority*, vol. 4, *God Who Speaks and Shows: Fifteen Theses, Part Three* (Waco: Word, 1979), 385–404; Darian R. Lockett, "'Necessary but Not Sufficient': The Role of History in the Interpretation of James as Christian Scripture," in *Explorations in Interdisciplinary Reading: Theological, Exegetical, and Reception-Historical Perspectives*, ed. Robbie F. Castleman, Darian R. Lockett, and Stephen O. Presley (Eugene: Pickwick, 2017), 69–90.

[40]Augustine, *On Christian Teaching* 2.24–31, trans. R. P. H. Green (Oxford: Oxford University Press, 1997), 35–7.

rituals, Psalm 110 voices the confidence of a postexilic prophet that, despite the collapse of the monarchy, Israel had in God himself an even better king than David.

The differences are stark. Ideally, of course, interpretation would synthesize insights from both biblical and historical contexts. But this synthesis does not always occur. And when it does not, it is usually the biblical context that is ignored. A recent, evangelical commentary develops this narrowly historical reading of Psalm 110. It notes in conclusion that the New Testament uses this psalm extensively, but then says precisely zero about what the New Testament suggests about the meaning of Psalm 110. The doctrines of the Trinity and of Christ's ascension, heavenly session, and Second Coming do not inform its interpretation of Psalm 110. What the rest of the Bible says about the meaning of Psalm 110 has been lost.

As this example shows, when historical criticism walks out to center stage, two things often go wrong. First, what the rest of the Bible tells us about a given passage can fade into the background. As the spotlight of attention falls tightly on the immediate historical context of a passage, the connections between this passage and the rest of Scripture can be overlooked. Second, when interpretation is not merely occupied, but preoccupied with history, the nonhistorical dimensions of the passage's own meaning—spiritual, theological, pastoral—can be missed.[41] When it comes to interpreting the Bible, history is absolutely necessary and wonderfully helpful. Left to itself, however, it isolates texts and obscures and limits their meaning. There's no fixing a car without a good wrench. But you need more than a wrench.

General Hermeneutics

A second major trend that has influenced evangelical biblical interpretation is the rise of what is called general hermeneutics. General hermeneutics are universal theories about how texts bear meaning. For example, one of the most sensible of these theories claims that the meaning of a text lies in what its author intended to communicate. Others claim that meaning lies not in the intention of the author but in the way the text is used. A delicate, ancient

---

[41]Hans W. Frei, *The Eclipse of Biblical Narrative: A Study in Eighteenth and Nineteenth Century Hermeneutics* (New Haven: Yale University Press, 1974), 1–16.

poem might supply the menacing lyrics of a battle song. Historical criticism itself can be a form of general hermeneutics. That is, historical criticism can be the expression of a general theory of how texts bear meaning: the meaning of texts lies in what their original authors intended in their historical contexts.

As with historical criticism, when any theory of general hermeneutics makes true claims about textual meaning, it can be wonderfully helpful for biblical interpretation. Because the Bible itself often refers to what its human authors meant, the hermeneutics of authorial intention has been especially welcome in evangelical interpretation. When skeptical scholars insist that all texts are actually about money (Marx) or sex (Freud) or power (Nietzsche) or maybe nothing objective at all, evangelicals rightly rejoiced at the publication of a brilliantly sophisticated "defense of the author."[42]

As also with historical criticism, the problems arise when a vitally important aspect of interpretation comes to be seen as the only aspect of interpretation. The human authors of the Bible are not the only authors of the Bible. The Bible is the word of God. But no general theory of interpretation offers guidelines for texts whose author is God. General hermeneutics has no need of that hypothesis in order to understand Homer and Shakespeare. So, under the pressure of securing a place at the table of skeptical, elite scholarship, evangelicals who love the Bible as the word of God, and who also follow general hermeneutics, can grow strangely forgetful of Scripture's divine author.

The effect is a twofold isolation. First, without a divine author carrying the human authors of Scripture, each book of the Bible is interpreted as if it stood on its own, with no necessary connection to or coherence with other books of the Bible. The result here parallels that of a narrowly historical approach to interpretation. Less and less attention is paid to how the teachings of each book of the Bible fit together into a single, God-authored story about Jesus.[43] We grasp this intuitively with other writings by a single author. If J. K. Rowling wrote the whole Harry Potter series, then the astonishing denouement of the final book can reveal things that she had hidden

---

[42]E. D. Hirsch Jr., *Validity in Interpretation* (New Haven: Yale University Press, 1967), 1–23; cf. 121–2; cf. Kevin J. Vanhoozer, *Is There a Meaning in This Text? The Bible, the Reader, and the Morality of Literary Knowledge* (Grand Rapids: Zondervan, 1998), 74–7.

[43]Frei, *Eclipse*, 6–7.

years before in the first book. But when biblical interpreters focus exclusively on the human authors of the Bible, they have little reason to think that Matthew, for example, could tell us any more about what Hosea intended than Hosea's own words would indicate. When Hosea reports God as saying, "Out of Egypt I called my son" (11:1), it appears as if Hosea is referring to Israel's Exodus from Egypt. But Matthew says that Hosea's words were fulfilled when Joseph and Mary return with the child Jesus from their flight to Egypt (Mt 2:13–15). If God is understood as the coauthor with both Hosea and Matthew, then God can tell us through Matthew what he meant by Hosea's words. This should hardly be surprising. Even at a human level, if "all the prophets who have spoken"— presumably this would include Hosea—"proclaimed these days" (Acts 3:24), and if Hosea himself was trying to figure out how the Spirit in him was predicting "the sufferings of Christ" (1 Pet 1:10–11), then Hosea must have known that there were messianic implications of his words.[44] But if Hosea's words are interpreted without reference to God or to the New Testament, then it must be that Matthew "takes those words out of their original context and gives them a whole new meaning," as claimed by a popular evangelical textbook on interpretation.[45] If Matthew's meaning is wholly new, it cannot tell us what Hosea meant. Hosea must be interpreted in isolation from the other authors of Scripture.

Second, if we ignore the divine author of the Bible, we will interpret it in isolation from centuries of Christian exposition. Christians have traditionally valued prior expositions of Scripture in the conviction that the same Spirit who inspired Scripture also actively guides Christians' understanding of Scripture (Eph 1:18). On the other hand, interpreters who overlook God's direct role in inspiring the Bible often overlook God's indirect role in illumining Christian readers of the Bible. If we cannot trust even Matthew to tell us what Hosea meant, why bother with Augustine? Oxford professor Benjamin Jowett famously described the ideal interpreter of the Bible as one who was perfectly indifferent to Christian

---

[44]G. K. Beale, "The Use of Hosea 11:1 in Matthew 2:15," in *The Inerrant Word: Biblical, Historical, Theological, and Pastoral Perspectives*, ed. John MacArthur (Wheaton: Crossway, 2016), 210–30.

[45]Gordon D. Fee and Douglas K. Stuart, *How to Read the Bible for All Its Worth: A Guide to Understanding the Bible* (Grand Rapids: Zondervan, 1982), 166.

tradition: "The history of Christendom is nothing to him … All the after-thoughts of theology are nothing to him … The simple words of that book he tries to preserve absolutely pure from the refinements or distinctions of later times."[46] This same suspicion of "the refinements of Christendom" lingers in evangelical interpretation. For example, an acclaimed two-volume evangelical commentary on Genesis never engages Augustine's widely influential works on Genesis, or Luther's brilliant lectures, or the writings of any other major interpreter of the Christian church before the year 1800, Calvin alone excepted.

Postmodernism and Narrative Theology

Thankfully, the days of the dominance of historical criticism and general hermeneutics are coming to an end. In the past few generations, two movements in the broader academy have helped restore evangelical interpretation to its own better insights: postmodernism and narrative theology.

Postmodernism includes a range of cultural and philosophical movements that began in the 1960s and that share two basic convictions: we cannot know anything with pure objectivity, and so everything we do know has been colored by our particular contexts.[47] Evangelicals cannot accept these claims as they stand. The Bible knows some things with objective, transcultural certainty. Evangelicals can, however, acknowledge that perspective does affect how we see things. For evangelical biblical interpretation, postmodernism has had two important effects. First, postmodernism gleefully discredited historical criticism's claim to pure objectivity.[48] For evangelicals, the most welcome accomplishment of postmodernism is to have shoved historical criticism off of its pretended throne of interpretation. Second, postmodernism has

---

[46]Benjamin Jowett, "On the Interpretation of Scripture," in *Essays and Reviews: The 1860 Text and Its Reading*, ed. Victor Shea and William Whitla (Charlottesville: University Press of Virginia, 2000), 481–2.

[47]Craig G. Bartholomew, "Postmodernity and Biblical Interpretation," in *Dictionary for Theological Interpretation of the Bible*, ed. Kevin J. Vanhoozer et al. (Grand Rapids: Baker, 2005), 600–7.

[48]Richard E. Burnett, "Historical Criticism," in *Dictionary for Theological Interpretation of the Bible*, ed. Kevin J. Vanhoozer et al. (Grand Rapids: Baker, 2005), 291.

invited careful consideration of the influence of our particular contexts on interpretation. The context of the interpreter, it turns out, can not only obscure our attempts at understanding, as many postmodernists would maintain. Context can also clarify our attempts at understanding. In other words, bias is not all bad. A bias in favor of traditional Christian beliefs can actually make us better readers of the Bible. And if one biblical scholar can offer separate "formalist, structuralist, feminist, materialist, and deconstructionist" readings of Esther, and decide that all of them are at least sort of valuable, what is to prevent an evangelical from attempting the novelty of a Christian reading of Esther?[49] Christians have always believed that some things are "spiritually discerned" (1 Cor 2:14) and that the road to understanding begins with faith. Postmodernism has given this old belief a degree of plausibility once again in secular culture. Proper interpretation does not require that we abandon our beliefs, but that we examine them. Theology and exegesis can play on the same team.

Narrative theology, or postliberal theology, gained prominence in the 1980s and has drawn the attention of evangelicals to the importance of narrative for biblical interpretation.[50] It is the genius of narrative both to depict the character of its protagonists and to shape the character of its readers. Narrative theology thus highlights two particular contexts in which narrative works its charm: the context of the canon and the context of local interpretative communities.

First, narrative theology highlights the way that God's character is revealed in the unified canon of Scripture. God's identity is revealed largely through stories of his dealings with Israel and the church, and especially through the Gospel accounts of Jesus. And just as a story cannot be understood in fragments, so the narrative of God's identity cannot be cobbled together from sixty-six books each understood in isolation from the others. God's story must be read whole, from beginning to end, with all of its turns and surprises, crises and resolutions, and as-yet unresolved tensions. Narrative theology has helped evangelicals see more clearly that the

---

[49]Bartholomew, "Postmodernity," 604.
[50]Treier, *Theological Interpretation*, 79–85; T. R. Phillips, "Postliberal Theology," in *Evangelical Dictionary of Theology*, 3rd ed., ed. Daniel J. Treier and Walter A. Elwell (Grand Rapids: Baker, 2017), 682–5.

Bible is a single, dramatic unfolding of God's character, with Jesus as the narrative key to God's identity.

Second, narrative theology is deeply aware of how Christian understanding of Scripture is shaped, for good and ill, by the narrative, the lived experience, of a local church community. While postmodernism recognizes the importance of context generally for interpretation, narrative theology pays particular attention to the context of the church. Through proclamation and prayer, praise and confession, service and suffering and fellowship, the narratives of our local congregations are joined with Scripture's metanarrative. We come to see ourselves as part of God's story, and our hearts grow attuned in particular ways to God's grace. But our hearts are also hardened in particular ways as we are simultaneously shaped by the counter-narratives of culture.[51] Narrative theology has helped evangelicals see that interpreters have contexts just like their texts do. Evangelicals have realized that, if interpretation is not to be merely contextual and therefore relative, but also to reach universally valid truth, we will have to distinguish good bias from bad. This will involve comparing our ecclesially embodied, local interpretation of Scripture with those of other communities, communities from other cultures and from other times, whose insights and confusions can provide clarifying foil for our own. Narrative theology has thus helped push evangelicals beyond enlightenment suspicion of tradition to a renewed esteem for the interpretive insights of Christian communities throughout history and across the globe.[52]

Postmodernism and narrative theology have helped evangelicals begin to see once again how theology, the whole Bible, the Christian tradition, and the worldwide Christian church can make us better readers of Scripture. In this way they have begun to reverse the two historically deforming trends of historical criticism and general hermeneutics. Evangelicals are returning to classically Christian and specifically Protestant ways of reading the Bible.

---

[51]For analysis of five prominent counter-narratives, see Tim Keller's "Preaching and the (Late) Modern Mind," in *Preaching: Communicating Faith in an Age of Skepticism* (New York: Penguin, 2015), 121–56.

[52]E.g., Tokunboh Adeyemo, ed., *Africa Bible Commentary: A One-Volume Commentary Written by 70 African Scholars* (Grand Rapids: Zondervan, 2010).

Challenges to Doctrine and Interpretation

The church is never without its challenges. God wants faith to be exercised. When it comes to the Bible, what are the challenges that face evangelicals today? In general, we might say that the challenges facing our *doctrine* of Scripture have more the character of external threats, while for our *interpretation* of Scripture they have more the character of internal opportunities.

Doctrine

The threats to our doctrine of Scripture are the usual suspects, even if armed with the latest weapons. The inspiration, authority, and truthfulness of Scripture will always be attacked—especially when this will sell a lot of books! So, the church will always be in need of champions of the Bible.[53] The challenge for evangelicals, now as in generations past, is to defend the Bible without reducing it to what is culturally or academically defensible. It is true that the right books made it into the canon, and that they form a coherent whole. Each is indeed inerrant, historically reliable, and well attested by the manuscripts. And we praise God that we can make so strong a case for these claims. But we cannot allow our heroic apologetics to give the wrong impression. The Bible is no mere damsel in distress, waiting helplessly to be rescued by a church in shining armor. The Bible is living and active. The Bible, in the power of the Holy Spirit, judges and sanctifies, puts to death and makes alive.[54] The Bible is God's primary means of creating and sustaining the church. Challenges to our doctrine of Scripture threaten to draw our attention away from the most glorious thing about it: that in

---

[53]D. A. Carson is a strong claimant to the mantle of Warfield in spirited and tireless defense of Scripture. See D. A. Carson and John D. Woodbridge, eds., *Scripture and Truth* (Grand Rapids: Baker, 1983); D. A. Carson and John D. Woodbridge, eds., *Hermeneutics, Authority, and Canon* (Grand Rapids: Zondervan, 1986); D. A. Carson, *Collected Writings on Scripture* (Wheaton: Crossway, 2010); and Carson, *Enduring Authority*.

[54]John Webster, *Holy Scripture: A Dogmatic Sketch* (Cambridge: Cambridge University Press, 2003), 87–91.

Scripture, by the power of the Spirit, we behold the glory of God in the face of Jesus Christ (2 Cor 3:18; 4:6).

One particular challenge concerns precisely that relation between the text of Scripture and the power of the Spirit. It is a standing task of the Christian church always to think these two together. In the twentieth century, one episode of their falling apart came from the theology of Karl Barth, whose doctrine of Scripture emphasized the subjective experience of the Spirit's power. Revelation, for Barth, was the direct work of the Spirit in our experience. The text of Scripture, on the other hand, was merely "a witness to" revelation.[55] The Bible would only become "revelation" in the full sense in the "event" of the Spirit's activity. "The Bible ... becomes God's Word in this event."[56] Calvin himself had said that "the Word will not find acceptance in men's hearts before it is sealed by the inward testimony of the Spirit."[57] But in the battle-for-the-Bible environment of mid-century, it was hard for evangelicals to hear Barth other than as devaluing Scripture. Many evangelicals rushed to counter-emphasize the objective truthfulness of the Bible's text. One such evangelical was the influential American churchman and theologian Carl F. H. Henry, whose six-volume *God, Revelation, and Authority* (1976–83) was a herculean exposition and defense of classic evangelical theology, particularly the doctrine of Scripture.

When Barth visited America in 1962, Henry attended a question-and-answer luncheon. Many journalists were present. Henry took an early spot at the mic. "Identifying myself as 'Carl Henry, editor of *Christianity Today*', I continued: 'The question, Dr. Barth, concerns the historical factuality of the resurrection of Jesus.' ... If these journalists had [been present], was the resurrection of such a nature [as] to have fallen into their area of responsibility?" Henry wanted to know if the resurrection, as Barth understood it, was an objective, historical fact. Barth responded, "Did you say Christianity *Today* or Christianity *Yesterday*?" Laughter erupted. Barth later apologized. Henry's assessment was this: "For Barth, the

---

[55]Karl Barth, *Church Dogmatics*, ed. G. W. Bromiley and T. F. Torrance (Edinburgh: T&T Clark, 1956–75), I/2, 457–72, 506–14; cf. Timothy Ward, *Words of Life: Scripture as the Living and Active Word of God* (Downers Grove: IVP, 2009), 60–7.

[56]Barth, *Church Dogmatics* I/1, 110.

[57]John Calvin, *The Institutes of the Christian Religion*, trans. Ford Lewis Battles, ed. John T. McNeill (Philadelphia: Westminster, 1960), 1.7.4 (79).

resurrection of Jesus did not occur in the kind of history accessible to historians."[58] Carl was right, and so was Karl. Henry rightly insists that Scripture records objective, knowable, historical facts—the kind that journalists can record in their notebooks and that four Evangelists did record in their Gospels. Henry was also right to challenge Barth's unwillingness to affirm the historical objectivity of the resurrection—at least in this context.[59] But Barth was right that, while journalists might have been able to document a dead man's return to life, something on the order of the raising of Lazarus, they could not have caught on camera the working of Father, Son, and Spirit, for instance, or the effect of the resurrection on the church or the "rulers and authorities" (Col 2:13–15). In other words, a dichotomy between objective Word (Henry) and subjective Spirit (Barth) can only be false. Evangelical theology must face the challenge of holding them in intimate connection. The charismatic among us will have to guard against underplaying the text of Scripture. The confessional among us will have to guard against underplaying the power of the Spirit.

Interpretation

The challenges facing our interpretation of Scripture, on the other hand, involve remarkable opportunities. Holy Scripture is an unfathomable treasure, overflowing with wonders new and old (Mt 13:52). So, the church always stands at a moment of fresh discovery of the riches of Scripture. And evangelicals today are indeed in the midst of such a rediscovery. Christian theology and the long Christian tradition are helping to refocus our scattered vision on the Bible as a whole, as it bears witness to Jesus Christ. Two challenges in particular face evangelical interpretation of the Bible today.

---

[58]Carl F. H. Henry, *Confessions of a Theologian: An Autobiography* (Waco: Word, 1986), 211.

[59]Barth's *Church Dogmatics* IV/1 had appeared in English translation six years before (1956). In that context, Barth was happy to affirm the objective historicity of the resurrection of Jesus. "If Jesus Christ is not risen—bodily, visibly, audibly, perceptibly, in the same concrete sense in which He died, as the texts themselves have it—if He is not also risen, then our preaching and our faith are vain and futile; we are still in our sins." Christ's resurrection is "just as real, just as concrete, just as visible, audible, perceptible, just as historical as the death which He took upon Himself." *Church Dogmatics* IV/1, 351–2, 555.

First, evangelicals are wrestling with how to combine both theological and grammatical-historical insight in interpreting Scripture.[60] Grammatical-historical procedures "are no longer given the kind of objective and final weight in our interpretation of Scripture that they once were."[61] So how does theology fit in? How, for example, do the doctrines that the New Testament sees in Psalm 110 fit in with the implications of the historical context of the psalm? Abstract answers are hard to give. Interpretation has to commend itself passage by passage. Thankfully, scores of theologically minded interpreters are now at work on full-scale biblical commentaries.[62] If varied success may be expected to attend new endeavors, so also, we may hope, will increased evangelical insight into the depths of God's word.

Second, evangelicals are learning once again how to take counsel from tradition in interpreting Scripture.[63] If tradition rarely got invited over to dinner in previous generations, it now has a seat at the table again.[64] Even as we delight in its company, we are having to make sure that tradition does not dominate the conversation. As Protestants, we believe that Scripture is our ultimate authority in belief and practice. Tradition's proper role is to help us hear

---

[60]R. Michael Allen, ed., *Theological Commentary: Evangelical Perspectives* (London: T&T Clark, 2011); Michael Allen and Scott R. Swain, *Reformed Catholicity: The Promise of Retrieval for Theology and Biblical Interpretation* (Grand Rapids: Baker Academic, 2015); Craig G. Bartholomew and Heath A. Thomas, *A Manifesto for Theological Interpretation* (Grand Rapids: Baker Academic, 2016); Craig A. Carter, *Interpreting Scripture with the Great Tradition: Recovering the Genius of Premodern Exegesis* (Grand Rapids: Baker Academic, 2018).

[61]Douglas J. Moo and Andrew David Naselli, "The Problem of the New Testament's Use of the Old Testament," in Carson, *Enduring Authority*, 746.

[62]At least five series of theological commentaries are currently in production: Concordia Commentary: A Theological Exposition of Sacred Scripture (1996–), the Two Horizons New Testament Commentary (2005–), the Brazos Theological Commentary on the Bible (2005–), Belief: A Theological Commentary on the Bible (2010–), and the T&T Clark International Theological Commentary (2016–).

[63]Gavin Ortlund, *Theological Retrieval for Evangelicals: Why We Need Our Past to Have a Future* (Wheaton: Crossway, 2019); Matthew Y. Emerson, Christopher W. Morgan, and R. Lucas Stamps, eds., *Baptists and the Christian Tradition: Toward an Evangelical Baptist Catholicity* (Nashville: B&H Academic, 2020).

[64]Witness InterVarsity Press's twenty-nine-volume Ancient Christian Commentary on Scripture (1998–2014), which has been so well received that they are now fifteen volumes in to a parallel Reformation Commentary on Scripture (2011–).

Scripture more clearly.[65] But tradition can muffle Scripture, too. How do we tell the difference? For example, Paul's impassioned argument in Romans 9–11 crescendos with the denouement of salvation history and a climactic, threefold exaltation of God: "For from him and through him and to him are all things. To him be glory forever. Amen." The Christian tradition hears Trinitarian echoes in this verse, but most contemporary interpreters do not. Attending to this tradition may attune our ears to wonders to which we have grown somewhat deaf. But older is not necessarily better. "The one who states his case first seems right, until the other comes and examines him" (Prov 18:17). We must not succumb to the nostalgia of imagining that ancient traditions are intrinsically superior to today's.[66] Acknowledging the unique insight of every Christian tradition, we will perhaps find that "in an abundance of counselors there is safety" in interpretation (Prov 11:14).

Forward: Loving the Bible Better

For evangelicals and the Bible, the way forward will involve maintaining doctrine and refining practice. The classic Protestant doctrine of Scripture—that it is God's own gracious word to us, fully authoritative, and perfectly true—this is what evokes our love for the Bible. We need to celebrate the truth of this doctrine, embrace its guidance, and defend it against attack. In our practice of interpretation, two strategic adjustments could yield still richer understanding of Scripture.

First, evangelical interpretation must recapture an awareness that God is the primary author of Scripture. This does not mean that we suddenly ignore the human authors of Scripture, with all their unique concerns and contexts and styles. It does mean that we attend more carefully to the single Mind that gave us all of Scripture. To focus interpretation on God as the primary author of Scripture will press us to see the Bible as the unified whole that it is. If we see Scripture as the words of the one God, we will not only allow the

---

[65]Michael Allen and Scott R. Swain, *Reformed Catholicity: The Promise of Retrieval for Theology and Biblical Interpretation* (Grand Rapids: Baker Academic, 2015), 49–70.
[66]D. A. Carson, "Theological Interpretation of Scripture: Yes, But …," in *Theological Commentary*, 196–8.

Old Testament to shed light on the New Testament. We will also allow the New Testament to shed light on the Old Testament. We will relearn the ancient practice of "reading backwards."[67] Figural or typological reading will find its place once again as part of our engagement with Scripture. Further, to see God as the author of all Scripture will also help us acknowledge his unified intention in all Scripture: to testify to Jesus that we might be saved.

Second, evangelical interpretation must renew its zeal for the literal sense of Scripture. Historical criticism often assumes that the literal meaning of Scripture is opposed to Christian theology. But that is not the case. Luther insisted that it is not speculative allegorical symbolism that yields real theological insight, but the literal sense of Scripture, the "grammatical, historical meaning." Luther is right. It is widely acknowledged that the path to the theological significance of Scripture runs straight through its literal sense.[68] Grammar and history should not be faulted for their abuse by historical criticism, but rather turned toward more evangelical ends.[69] When this happens, lexical research and word-by-word analysis can achieve stunning confirmations of long-standing theological intuitions.[70] As evangelicals, the only interpretations of Scripture we will find enduringly convincing are those that can be shown to reside in the actual words of Scripture.

Finally, as we move forward in our practice of interpretation, we may have to remind ourselves of our confidence in the clarity of Scripture. Change is disorienting. Unless it has been our custom, we will struggle to interpret the Bible as a whole, in light of the Christian tradition, for its literal-theological meaning. As we adjust, reading the Bible may feel harder than before. But we cannot let ourselves think, and we dare not communicate in our preaching or teaching, that the Bible is too hard for even the simplest believer to

---

[67]Richard B. Hays, *Reading Backwards: Figural Christology and the Fourfold Gospel Witness* (Waco: Baylor University Press, 2014).

[68]Frei, *Eclipse*, 37; Peter J. Leithart, *Deep Exegesis: The Mystery of Reading Scripture* (Waco: Baylor University Press, 2009), vii; Hays, *Reading Backward*, 15; Mark S. Gignilliat, *Reading Scripture Canonically: Theological Instincts for Old Testament Interpretation* (Grand Rapids: Baker, 2019), 97.

[69]Carson, "Theological Interpretation of Scripture," 189–92.

[70]See, e.g., the articles by Charles Lee Irons, "A Lexical Defense of the Johannine 'Only Begotten'," and D. A. Carson, "John 5:26: *Crux Interpretum* for Eternal Generation," in *Retrieving Eternal Generation*, ed. Fred Sanders and Scott R. Swain (Grand Rapids: Zondervan, 2017).

understand. The Bible is God's word, and he is able to make himself understood. God is his own interpreter, and he takes particular delight in revealing himself "to little children" (Mt 11:26). As Mark Thompson writes, "The Scriptures are not the private possession of an ecclesiastical or scholarly elite, with the rest of us dependent upon them to clarify a text we have no hope of understanding otherwise. They can be approached with confidence, following the example of Jesus himself, as the generous gift of a gracious heavenly Father."[71] We never read the Bible alone. God is with us always, and he will open our eyes to its wonders.

Recommended Reading

D. A. Carson, ed., *The Enduring Authority of the Christian Scriptures* (Grand Rapids: Eerdmans, 2016).

Kevin DeYoung, *Taking God at His Word: Why the Bible Is Knowable, Necessary, and Enough, and What That Means for You and Me* (Wheaton: Crossway, 2016).

John Piper, *Reading the Bible Supernaturally: Seeing and Savoring the Glory of God in Scripture* (Wheaton: Crossway, 2017).

Timothy Ward, *Words of Life: Scripture as the Living and Active Word of God* (Downers Grove: IVP, 2009).

---

[71] Mark D. Thompson, "The Generous Gift of a Gracious Father: Toward a Theological Account of the Clarity of Scripture," in Carson, *Enduring Authority*, 643.

2

"Go and Make Disciples": Mission

We believe the gospel is God's good news for the whole world, and we are determined, by his grace, to obey Christ's commission to proclaim to all mankind and to make disciples of every nation.

LAUSANNE COVENANT

Evangelicals live as if Acts is our story. John Stott explains, "We evangelical Christians are naïve enough to believe what Jesus and his apostles taught."[1] We embrace Jesus's command in Acts 1:8: "be my witnesses." We are commissioned as ambassadors for Jesus (2 Cor 5:17) who go so that the "gospel of the kingdom will be proclaimed throughout the whole world as a testimony to all nations" (Matt 24:14). Like Moravian missionaries (1734) willing to sell themselves into slavery, our passion for Christ's glory can be summarized in their motto, "Our Lamb has conquered; let us follow Him!"[2]

In this chapter, you will meet women and men who followed Jesus to the ends of the earth so that the Lamb might receive the glory he purchased on the cross. They often suffered greatly, "some

---

[1]John Stott, "The Bible in World Evangelization," in *PWCM*, 25.
[2]Note the personal pronoun in the motto, "our" Lamb. Augustus Charles Thompson, *Moravian Missions: Twelve Lectures* (New York: Charles Scribner's Sons, 1882), 73.

were tortured, refusing to accept release, so that they might rise again to a better life" (Heb 11:35b). Despite caricatures in many movies, textbooks, and popular media, there can be no doubt that the evangelical missionary movement has radically changed both the global South and North America for good. Sociologist Robert Woodberry has persuasively shown that evangelicals, whom he calls "conversionary Protestants," have "heavily influenced the rise and spread of stable democracy around the world..." and that they "were a crucial catalyst initiating the development and spread of religious liberty, mass education, mass printing, newspapers, voluntary associations, and colonial reforms, thereby creating the conditions that made stable democracy more likely."[3] In a similar way, the thousands of evangelical missionaries sent out from the United States between the 1890s and the 1960s profoundly impacted their home country. They returned home with new awareness of racism, nationalistic imperialism, and what René Padilla calls "culture Christianity."[4]

Why would many thousands of evangelicals leave their homes and families behind—often to never return? Where does this evangelical zeal for the glory of the Lamb come from? Rather than try to be exhaustive, we focus on a few "compelling biographies" and important events to tell the story of what evangelicals believe about evangelism and mission.[5] We have to leave many stories untold—the amazing work of mission agencies like Wycliffe Bible translators, World Vision, Youth With A Mission (YWAM), and hundreds of others. To understand the missionary emphases and doctrine of evangelicals we begin with Rev. John Stott (1921–2011), who, together with Rev. Billy Graham (1918–2018), is remembered as the architect of the global evangelical missionary network known as the Lausanne Movement. We then overview four centuries of missional highlights, before identifying current challenges and

---

[3]Robert Woodberry, "The Missionary Roots of Liberal Democracy," *American Political Science Review* 106, no. 2 (2012): 212. For an excellent introduction to Woodberry's work see Andrea Palpant Dilley, "The World the Missionaries Made," *Christianity Today*, January 2014.

[4]C. Rene Padilla, *Mission between the Times: Essays on the Kingdom* (Grand Rapids: Eerdmans, 1985), 15; David A. Hollinger, *Protestants Abroad: How Missionaries Tried to Change the World but Changed America* (Princeton: Princeton University Press, 2017).

[5]James McClendon, *Biography as Theology: How Life Stories Can Remake Today's Theology* (Nashville: Abingdon, 1974).

future opportunities as evangelicals move into a fifth century of missionary activity.

Doctrine: John Stott, the *Lausanne Covenant*, and the Good News of the Kingdom

Who are twenty-first-century "evangelicals"? "Evangelical" is a term often used in a truncated way to describe a small portion of the world's evangelicals as if they were the whole. The vast majority of evangelicals are neither of European descent nor members of a particular North American political party. In reality, as Table 2.3 illustrates, some 80 percent of evangelicals live in the global South while those living in Europe and North America make up the remaining 20 percent.[6] Perhaps the best way to explore the beliefs of this globally diverse group is with the *Lausanne Covenant*. While the *Lausanne Covenant* is not without controversy, like Vatican II among Roman Catholics, it remains a turning point for the global evangelical movement.[7]

On July 24, 1974, Rev. Billy Graham stood before some 2,400 evangelical leaders gathered from 135 denominations and 150 nations to give the closing address for the Lausanne International Congress on World Evangelization. *Time Magazine* called the delegates gathered in Lausanne, Switzerland, "possibly the widest ranging meeting of Christians ever held."[8] Over half of these leaders came from Christian communities in the global South, and many would be returning to churches facing severe persecution and grave suffering. Among the group were many of the most influential evangelical thinkers of their generation: Kwame Bediako and

---

[6]The United Nations designates the global South as consisting of Asia, Africa, Latin America, and Oceania. Population statistics are adapted from the Center for the Study of Global Christianity, "Christianity in Its Global Context, 1970–2020 Society, Religion, and Mission" (South Hamilton: Gordon-Conwell Theological Seminary, 2013), 17, www.globalchristianity.org/globalcontext.

[7]Brian Stanley, *The Global Diffusion of Evangelicalism: The Age of Billy Graham and John Stott* (Downers Grove: IVP Academic, 2013), 179.

[8]Timothy Dudley-Smith, *John Stott, a Global Ministry: A Biography: The Later Years* (Downers Grove: InterVarsity, 2001), 209.

Bishop Festo Kivengere from Africa; Samuel Escobar, René Padilla, and Orlando Costas from South America; Saphir Athyil, Jonathan Chao, Vinay Samuel, and B. V. Subamma from Asia; Carl F. H. Henry, J. I. Packer, Ron Sider, Howard Snyder, Ralph Winter, and Os Guinness from North America; Henri Blocher, Francis Schaeffer, and Corrie ten Boom from Europe.

Graham began his address with a text George Ladd calls "the most important single verse in the Word of God for God's people today."[9] It reads, "This gospel of the kingdom will be proclaimed throughout the whole world as a testimony to all nations, and then the end will come" (Matt 24:14). From his exposition of Matt 24:14 and the necessity of the whole world hearing the good news about Christ's kingdom, Graham went on to describe eight challenges for Lausanne's delegates: know that you have been converted; remember that God is with you; embrace the loneliness of the gospel; carry a burden for souls; allow the Word of God to burn within you; pray; be bold; and finally, embrace the simplicity of a disciplined life.[10] Few have embodied these eight challenges better than John Stott, the chairman of Lausanne's Theology Working Group, a man who modeled the "spirit of Lausanne" for the remainder of his life.[11] Stott was the primary author and the authoritative interpreter of the *Lausanne Covenant*, the conciliar document drafted by members of the congress.[12] It provides a window into evangelicals' love for the good news about Jesus Christ.

Lausanne Covenant: A Missionary God and a Missionary Bible

In John's version of the "Great Commission" the resurrected Jesus states, "As the Father has sent me, even so I am sending you"

---

[9]Ladd begins the sentence with "Perhaps." George Ladd, "The Gospel of the Kingdom," in *PWCM*, 68.

[10]Graham Billy, "The King Is Coming: Closing Address of the First Lausanne Congress," in *The Lausanne Legacy: Landmarks in Global Mission*, ed. Julia Cameron (Peabody: Hendrickson, 2016), 58-9.

[11]Chris Wright, *John Stott: Pastor, Leader and Friend: A Man Who Embodied "the Spirit of Lausanne"*, Didasko Files (Peabody: Hendrickson, 2012), 6.

[12]Hereafter abbreviated as *LC*. The fifteen clauses of the *Lausanne Covenant* are referred to as sections (e.g., §1 for clause 1). Most Lausanne documents, including the *Lausanne Covenant*, can be read at the Lausanne Content Library (https://www.lausanne.org/category/content).

(John 20:21b). This verse is foundational to the first section of the *Lausanne Covenant*, "The Purpose of God" (*LC* §1). For Stott, the Trinitarian God revealed in the Bible is a missionary God. At his first plenary address at Lausanne, he defined mission as "an activity arising out of the very nature of God. The living God of the Bible is a sending God."[13] Since Lausanne, support for mission as an attribute of God, like love or holiness, has gained wide acceptance among evangelicals.[14] Section 3 emphasizes that Jesus, sent by the Father, is the unique Savior before whom every knee must one day bow (Isa 45:23; Phil 2:10). Section 14 adds further clarification about God's missional activity in the present. Mission today must be pursued in the power of the Holy Spirit as "the Holy Spirit is a missionary Spirit; thus evangelism should arise spontaneously from a Spirit-filled church" (*LC* §14).

Bible and mission are the orienting commitments for evangelical theology. Thus, it is not surprising to discover that Section 2 is entitled, "The Authority and Power of the Bible." Evangelicals have a commitment to mission because the Bible is a "missionary document."[15] David Bosch, a South African evangelical deeply engaged with the Lausanne Movement from 1974 until his tragic death in 1992, calls attention to over ninety different New Testament Greek expressions used for various aspects of mission.[16] More recently, N. T. Wright insists the purpose of the New Testament is "to sustain and direct the missional life of the early church."[17] Since Lausanne, evangelicals have become increasingly articulate about the necessity of reading God's Word with an attentive ear to the missionary Spirit speaking in Scripture. Work from Chris Wright and Michael Goheen has especially helped the church read Scripture with a consciousness of their participation in

---

[13]John Stott, "The Biblical Basis of Evangelism," Lausanne Movement, July 17, 1974, https://www.lausanne.org/content/john-stott-biblical-basis-of-evangelism.

[14]Stephen Holmes, "Trinitarian Missiology: Towards a Theology of God as Missionary," *International Journal of Systematic Theology* 8 (2006): 72–90; Michael Goheen, *The Church and Its Vocation: Lesslie Newbigin's Missionary Ecclesiology* (Grand Rapids: Baker Academic, 2018).

[15]David Bosch, *Transforming Mission: Paradigm Shifts in Theology of Mission* (Maryknoll: Orbis, 1995), 15–55.

[16]Bosch, *Transforming Mission*, 16.

[17]N. T. Wright, "Reading the New Testament Missionally," in *Reading the Bible Missionally*, ed. Michael Goheen, Gospel and Our Culture Series (Grand Rapids: Eerdmans, 2016), 125.

God's mission.[18] Scripture is a single story describing God's mission and an invitation to every generation to participate in it.

In addition to its emphasis on the power and authority of the Bible, Section 2 broke new ground for many evangelicals in the area of biblical interpretation. John Stott was convinced that Christian mission required a "double listening," by which he meant careful listening to God's Word and God's world in order to "avoid the opposite pitfalls of unfaithfulness and irrelevance."[19] Listening to God's Word helps us understand God's world, but Lausanne made it equally clear that listening to God's world helps us understand God's Word. While explaining Section 2, Stott calls attention to René Padilla's insight that much North American evangelical biblical interpretation is not "biblical Christianity" but actually "culture-Christianity."[20] Other evangelicals were just as direct. Lausanne delegate Jonathan Chao, dean of a seminary in Hong Kong, described evangelicals in the global South as having been locked in "prisons of western confinement, particularly Anglo-American, evangelical confinement."[21]

Stott address these concerns by drawing attention to three phrases in Section 2.[22] First, the Holy Spirit actively speaks through the Bible—an insight Bernard Ramm called the "Protestant Principle."[23] Second, with a rebuke to Western individualism, the *Lausanne Covenant* challenges North American and European believers to recognize that the Holy Spirit reveals truth to "the whole church" (*LC* §2). The Spirit's truth is comprehended with "all the saints" (Eph 3:18). Third, the Holy Spirit is continually

---

[18]Christopher Wright, *The Mission of God: Unlocking the Bible's Grand Narrative* (Downers Grove: InterVarsity, 2006); Goheen, *Reading the Bible Missionally*.

[19]John Stott, *Authentic Christianity: From the Writings of John Stott*, ed. Timothy Dudley-Smith (Downers Grove: InterVarsity, 1995), 323; Dudley-Smith, *John Stott*, 228.

[20]John Stott, "The Authority and Power of the Bible," in *The New Face of Evangelicalism: An International Symposium on the Lausanne Covenant*, ed. C. René Padilla (Downers Grove: InterVarsity, 1976), 44.

[21]Jonathan Chao, "Education and Leadership," in *The New Face of Evangelicalism*, 194.

[22]Stott, "Authority and Power of the Bible," 45–7.

[23]Cited in Kevin Vanhoozer, "'One Ring to Rule Them All?' Theological Method in an Era of World Christianity," in *Globalizing Theology: Belief and Practice in an Era of World Christianity*, ed. Craig Ott and Harold A. Netland (Grand Rapids: Baker, 2006), 107. Bernard Ramm's "Protestant Principle" is not Paul Tillich's version.

revealing "ever more of the many-colored wisdom of God" (*LC* §2). As John Robinson saw in 1620, there is "more truth and light yet to break forth" from Holy Scripture.[24] When the Bible enters new contexts, generations, and cultures, the Holy Spirit progressively clarifies "the church's mind on the great doctrines of Scripture."[25] Kevin Vanhoozer calls this the principle of "Pentecostal plurality," explaining, "it takes many interpretive communities spanning many times, places and cultures in order fully to appreciate the rich, thick meaning of Scripture."[26]

Lausanne Covenant: Do the Work of an Evangelist for the King Is Coming

The *Lausanne Covenant* begins and ends with an emphasis on a missionary God who speaks in a missionary Bible. Between these bookends, the vast majority of the document calls God's people to be a missionary people. Thus, the *Lausanne Covenant* affirms "that Christ sends his redeemed people into the world as the Father sent him, and that this calls for a similar deep and costly penetration of the world" (*LC* §6). Reflecting on Lausanne after the conference, Stott identified several ways in which the global evangelical understanding of evangelism had been advanced.[27]

First, evangelicals clarified that all believers are called to participate in God's mission, and that this responsibility is wider than evangelism. Stott cites Samuel Escobar's call for evangelicals to repent of "a false and anti-biblical dichotomy between evangelism and social action."[28] Evangelism and social concern are both integral to the gospel of the kingdom. "When people receive Christ they are born again into his kingdom and must seek not only to exhibit but also to spread its righteousness in the midst of an unrighteous world"

---

[24]William Wallace Fenn, "John Robinson's Farewell Address," *Harvard Theological Review* 13 (1920): 236.
[25]Stott, "Authority and Power of the Bible," 47.
[26]Vanhoozer, "Theological Method," in *GDT*, 896; Hank Voss, "From 'Grammatical-Historical Exegesis' to 'Theological Exegesis': Five Essential Practices," *Evangelical Review of Theology* 37 (2013): 149–51.
[27]John Stott, "The Significance of Lausanne," in *The Study of Evangelism: Exploring a Missional Practice of the Church*, ed. Paul Chilcote and Laceye Warner, orig. 1975 (Grand Rapids: Eerdmans, 2008), 305–12.
[28]Stott, *Significance of Lausanne*, 306.

(*LC* §5). Lausanne clearly articulated that "gospel" and "kingdom" belong together: "the salvation we claim should be transforming us in the totality of our personal and social responsibilities" (*LC* §5).

René Padilla has often described the relationship of evangelism and social action as the left and right wings of a plane or a bird. Neither wing can be removed without serious consequences.[29] In an essay circulated to delegates in six languages prior to Lausanne, Padilla noted that "there is no place for statistics on 'how many souls die without Christ each minute' if they do not take into account how many of those souls are dying of hunger."[30] One result of this challenge from the global South is that the *Lausanne Covenant* did not exclusively focus on those without knowledge of Christ; it also included a challenge to remember the poor (Gal 2:10). When evangelical David Barrett began publishing the annual report on global Christianity in the *International Bulletin of Missionary Research* some ten years after Lausanne, it included statistics on those living in abject poverty. A recent version reports that there are some 2.5 billion people living in urban poverty with 1.3 billion lacking access to basic necessities like clean water, adequate shelter, and food. John Holmes, an undersecretary at the United Nations, reports that twenty-five thousand people die from hunger every day—more than ten thousand of which are children.[31]

Lausanne emphasized that the model for Christian mission is the Suffering Servant who came to sacrificially serve. The Servant's mission included evangelism (*kerygma*), ethical instruction (*didache*), and service (*diakonia*; Matt 4:23; 9:35).[32] The 1974 Covenant affirmed that feeding the thousands who will die tomorrow from hunger is part of the servant mission to which God has called evangelicals.

A second point of clarity at Lausanne was an acknowledgment of the priority of evangelism (John 9:4; Matt 9:35–38; Rom

---

[29]For an introduction to Padilla see his *Mission between the Times*; Tetsunao Yamamori, C. René Padilla, and Brian Cordingly, *The Local Church, Agent of Transformation: An Ecclesiology for Integral Mission* (Buenos Aire: Kairós, 2004); C. René Padilla, "My Theological Pilgrimage," *Journal of Latin American Theology* 4 (2009): 91–111.

[30]Padilla, *Mission between the Times*, 24–5. For a North American perspective see works by Ron Sider.

[31]John Holmes, "Losing 25,000 to Hunger Every Day" (New York: The United Nations, 2009), https://www.un.org/en/chronicle/article/losing-25000-hunger-every-day.

[32]Padilla, *Mission between the Times*, 22.

TABLE 2.1 *Global Summary of Christian Mission and the Poor*

Population	2020	Percentage	2050	Percentage
Global	7,795,482,000		9,771,823,000	
Urban Poverty	2,580,000,000	33%	4,100,000,000	42%
Urban Slums	1,360,000,000	17%	1,900,000,000	19%

Source: Adapted from Todd Johnson and Gina Zurlo, "Status of Global Christianity, 2020, in the Context of 1900–2050" (Hamilton: Center for the Study of Global Christianity, 2020), https://www.gordonconwell.edu/center-for-global-christianity/resources/status-of-global-christianity/.

9:1–3; 10:14–15; 1 Cor 9:19–23). While evangelism and social action are the responsibility of every individual Christian, "in the church's mission of sacrificial service evangelism is primary" (*LC* §6). If Stott's previous point called evangelicals to prioritize care for the poor, this one calls evangelicals to prioritize reaching the unreached. In 1974, the *Lausanne Covenant* reported that 2.4 billion, or nearly two-thirds of the world's population at that time, had not had the opportunity to hear, understand, or respond to the gospel of the kingdom. In 2020, the situation has improved, but the need is still urgent. According to the Joshua Project, an unreached or "least-reached" people group is one in which there is either no indigenous Christian community or where the evangelical population is less than 2 percent.[33] As Table 2.2 shows, while the percentage of unreached people in the world has gone down since 1974, there are still approximately 7,400 unreached people groups with a population of around 3.2 billion who have never heard the name of Jesus in a way they could understand or to which they might respond.

Both evangelism and social action are integral to the church's mission. Evangelicals must resist polarization of the two aspects of God's mission without denying that there are specializations

---

[33]"Global Summary of Unreached Peoples," Joshua Project, accessed August 10, 2020, https://joshuaproject.net/.

TABLE 2.2 *Global Summary of Unreached People Groups*

Global People Groups	17,413
Unreached People Groups	7,402
Percentage in Unreached People Groups	42.5%
Global Population	7.75 billion
Population of People in Unreached Groups	3.22 billion
Percentage of People in Unreached Groups	41.6%

Source: "Global Summary of Unreached Peoples," Joshua Project, accessed August 10, 2020, https://joshuaproject.net/.

Notes: "Global Summary of Unreached Peoples." Using a different methodology, Johnson and Zurlo arrive at 2.2 billion unevangelized or 28 percent of global population ("Status of Global Christianity, 2020").

within Christ's body. Some are especially called and gifted for the work of evangelism and others for the work of addressing social needs.[34]

Perhaps the most important contribution of Lausanne was the wakeup call it provided to North American evangelicals regarding the extent to which their proclamation of the gospel had been polluted by winds of worldliness, especially North American nationalism. Stott especially identifies René Padilla and Orlando Costas with this fourth contribution, although he also could have pointed to work by African evangelicals like David Bosch, Kwame Bediako, or John Gato. Padilla's paper, written in preparation for Lausanne, identified how worldliness had seeped into the global mission movement through what he called "Culture Christianity." Just as the nationalistic interests of European colonialism had infected

---

[34]In contrast to Chris Wright, Jonathan Leeman, John Franke, and Peter Leithart are typical of North American evangelicals when they interact almost exclusively with North American and European scholarship in *Four Views on the Church's Mission*, ed. Jason S. Sexton (Grand Rapids: Zondervan, 2017). Their work would be enriched with greater engagement in the global evangelical discussion as reflected in the Lausanne and Langham literature. See especially *Evangelism and Social Responsibility: An Evangelical Commitment (LOP 21)* and related publications.

much missionary thinking and practice in the 1800s, Americanism had infected much missionary thinking and practice in the 1900s.[35] Padilla showed how the "American Way" had become confused with Christ's "Way" (Acts 9:2) in the minds of many American missionaries. America's role as a global superpower combined with cultural blind spots in its largely white missionary force meant that "the gospel that is preached today in the majority of countries of the world bears the marks of 'the American Way of Life.'"[36] In places like Latin America "the identification of Americanism with the gospel" was a major barrier to people hearing and responding to the New Testament's gospel of the kingdom.[37]

Stott names other advances as well, but these four in particular would powerfully shape the future of global evangelical missions. In sum, Lausanne offered clarity on (1) the relationship between "mission" and "evangelism"; (2) the relationship between evangelism and social action; (3) the priority of evangelism; and (4) the necessity for humble openness and ready repentance from the ever-present worldliness infiltrating the church. In 1975, Stott penned another important work entitled *Christian Mission in the Modern World*. He concludes the chapter on evangelism by citing Section 4 of the *Lausanne Covenant* entitled "The Nature of Evangelism." We follow his example here.

To evangelize is to spread the good news that Jesus Christ died for our sins and was raised from the dead according to the Scriptures, and that as the reigning Lord he now offers the forgiveness of sins and the liberating gift of the Spirit to all who repent and believe. Our Christian presence in the world is indispensable to evangelism, and so is that kind of dialogue whose purpose is to listen sensitively in order to understand. But evangelism itself is the proclamation of the historical, biblical Christ as Savior and Lord, with a view to persuading people to come to him personally and so be reconciled to God. In issuing the Gospel invitation we have no liberty to conceal the cost of discipleship. Jesus still calls all who would follow him to deny themselves, take up their cross, and identify themselves with his

---

[35]Padilla, *Mission between the Times*, 15.
[36]Padilla, *Mission between the Times*, 16.
[37]Padilla, *Mission between the Times*, 16.

new community. The results of evangelism include obedience to
Christ, incorporation into his church and responsible service in
the world. (*LC* §4)

History: Four Hundred Years of Evangelical Mission

The global evangelical movement began with the missionary
outreach of Puritans and Pietists in the 1600s. Some two hundred
years later, around 1800, less than 1 percent of evangelicals
lived outside Europe and North America.[38] Over the next two
hundred years, the situation changed rapidly. Today, eight out
of ten evangelicals live in the global South (Table 2.3). To better
understand how the evangelical world turned upside down, this
section explores evangelism and mission through representative
events and figures from the past four centuries.

With rare exceptions, none of the major Reformation churches
(Lutheran, Reformed, Anglican) engaged in mission outside of
Christendom for their first two hundred years. While Luther's and
Calvin's doctrine was missionary in its core, it took centuries to break
the strong Christendom paradigm that held captive the imagination
of most believers. Thus, the Anabaptists were the only churches for
nearly two hundred years that taught that the Great Commission,
Matt 28:19–20, applied to all church members. More typical of
Reformation churches was the 1652 Wittenberg statement issued
by the theology faculty explicitly denying that the Lutheran church
had any responsibility for mission and that this responsibility rested
solely with the state; similarly Theodore Beza (d. 1605), Calvin's
successor, "fiercely opposed" the idea that the "Great Commission"
applied to all believers.[39] Like Wittenberg's faculty and Beza, most
Lutheran and Reformed churches taught a cessationist version of
the Great Commission, arguing that the missionary imperative only
applied to the apostles in the first century. They concluded that
if Christian mission was to be done at all, it should be done by
the state and not the church. Thus, the Magisterial Reformation

---

[38]Philip Jenkins, *The Next Christendom: The Coming of Global Christianity*, 3rd ed.
(Oxford: Oxford University Press, 2011), 49.
[39]Bosch, *Transforming Mission*, 251, 247.

TABLE 2.3 *Impact of 1900s Missionary Movement on Global Evangelical Populations*

	1600	1700	1800	1900	2020
Global North Europe and North America	99.9%	99.9%	99%	90%	20%
Global South Africa, Asia, South America, Oceana	>0.01%	>0.01%	1%	10%	80%

Sources: "Global Summary of Unreached Peoples," Joshua Project, accessed August 10, 2020, https://joshuaproject.net/; Todd Johnson and Gina Zurlo, "Status of Global Christianity, 2020, in the Context of 1900–2050" (Hamilton: Center for the Study of Global Christianity, 2020), https://www.gordonconwell.edu/center-for-global-christianity/resources/status-of-global-christianity/; Donald Lewis and Richard Pierard, eds., Global Evangelicalism: Theology, History & Culture in Regional Perspective *(Downers Grove: IVP Academic, 2014).*

churches generally opposed church-based missionary activity in Africa, Asia, or the New World.[40]

Christendom, with many of its strengths, had also left a significant missional blind spot that would take generations to recognize.[41] Martin Luther's world was vastly different than the world we know—as a contemporary of Christopher Columbus—lands beyond the Turks were difficult to imagine. Thus, for Luther the world as he knew it was almost entirely baptized—he met fewer than two dozen unbaptized adults in his entire life.[42] Luther's focus was on survival and the reform of the church. Practical difficulties to engaging in mission also existed since the closing of monastic orders left the Protestant church without a vehicle for mission for some two hundred years until the formation of the missionary

---

[40]Bosch, *Transforming Mission*, 243–52.
[41]Bosch, *Transforming Mission*, 243–52; George Huntston Williams, *The Radical Reformation* (Philadelphia: Westminster, 1962), 271.
[42]Ingemar Öberg, *Luther and World Mission: A Historical and Systematic Study with Special Reference to Luther's Bible Exposition*, trans. Dean Apel (St. Louis: Concordia, 2007), vii.

societies in the late 1700s. The Peasants War of 1525 and Luther's conflicts with the more missionary-minded Anabaptists led him to take precautions against Christian laity proclaiming their faith in public. Luther eventually emphasized that all public offices of proclamation should be tied to a geographic parish and require the permission of a local magistrate. Luther's disciple, Philip Melanchthon, would teach a reified version of this principle, namely the religion of the ruler should also be the religion of the ruled (*cuius regio, eius religio*).[43]

Evangelism and Missions in the 1600s

The first significant Protestant missionary activity outside Christendom began in North America. Within thirty years of the Mayflower's arrival in America, Puritan pastor John Eliot began preaching to the North American Algonquin tribe in their own language. In 1650 through a partnership with Cockenoe, a Native American member of the Algonquin tribe, Eliot planted Natick Church, the first indigenously led church in North America. Together Eliot and Cockenoe published a catechism, which would be the first book published in a Native American language in North America. Eliot completed translation of the Bible into the Algonquin language in 1663. The Algonquin Bible was the first complete Bible printed in North America. There would eventually be more than thirteen Algonquin churches before they were destroyed and the members killed or forced to flee during conflicts between European settlers and warring indigenous tribes. Edward Andrews has identified by name 275 black and Native American missionaries who planted churches, proclaimed the gospel of the kingdom, and worked for justice in the 1600s and 1700s.[44] Many of Eliot's coworkers are represented on this list.

Evangelism and Missions in the 1700s

In 1706 Bartholomäus Ziegenbalg and Heinrich Plutschau were the first of more than fifty missionaries sent out by the Pietist Missionary

---

[43]Cf. *LW* 13:64–65.
[44]Edward Andrews, *Native Apostles: Black and Indian Missionaries in the British Atlantic World* (Cambridge: Harvard University Press, 2013), 231–61.

Training Center established in Halle. They planted a church in India and translated the Bible into Tamil.[45] Their example inspired a 15-year-old boy to found "the Order of the Mustard Seed" and commit his life to seeing the gospel go forth to the farthest corners of the world. At 16 when he left for university, he passed on to his mentor the names of seven groups of boys. He had started all seven small groups to mentor younger boys in spiritual accountability, prayer, and Bible study. This young man, Count Nikolaus Ludwig von Zinzendorf (1700–1760), would soon become the father of the evangelical mission movement.[46]

Perhaps no evangelical movement has better displayed the evangelical passion for the glory of the Lamb to shine in every place than the early Moravian church led by Zinzendorf.[47] Zinzendorf's love for Jesus was evident early when his family found love letters to Jesus on the grass outside the window of the 6-year-old's bedroom. He wrote some two thousand hymns to describe his love for the Lord, some of which are still sung today (e.g., "Jesus, Thy Blood and Righteousness"). When at age 27, Zinzendorf drafted the Moravian community's constitution, he stated that "the conversion of souls is the chief object" of concern for its members.[48] This passion for the glory of Christ to increase through all tribes and nations coming to know Jesus can also be seen in the Moravian motto, "Our Lamb has conquered; let us follow Him!" (*Vicit agnus noster; eum sequamur*). That same year, on August 13, an outpouring of the power of the Holy Spirit (the "Moravian Pentecost") resulted in the start of a twenty-four hours a day, seven days a week, prayer meeting. This prayer meeting ran continuously for over one hundred years and gave birth to the first church-wide missionary movement among Protestants.

In 1732, five years after the start of the Moravian prayer movement, an appeal from an Afro-Caribbean slave, Antwon

---

[45]Scott Sunquist, "Asia," in *Global Evangelicalism: Theology, History & Culture in Regional Perspective*, ed. Donald Lewis and Richard Pierard (Downers Grove: IVP Academic, 2014), 199.

[46]Gary Kinkel, "Introduction," *In Christian Life and Witness: Count Zinzendorf's 1738 Berlin Speeches* (Eugene: Pickwick, 2010), xv.

[47]For insightful discussion of Zinzendorf's North American missionary activity see Craig Atwood, *Community of the Cross: Moravian Piety in Colonial Bethlehem* (University Park: Pennsylvania State University Press, 2000).

[48]Nikolaus Zinzendorf, "Brotherly Union and Agreement at Herrnhut," in *The Pietists: Selected Writings*, ed. Peter Erb (New York: Paulist, 1983), 327.

Ulrich, led to the sending of the first Moravian missionary.[49] Leonard
Dober, by trade a potter, was sent to the Caribbean Island of St.
Thomas. Beginning with Ulrich's enslaved sister, the Moravians
planted the first Afro-Caribbean-led churches in the Americas. They
endured intense persecution alongside of their Afro-Caribbean
sisters and brothers for their commitment to interracial worship,
marriage, and church leadership.

In 1736, Rebecca Protten, a freed slave, joined the Moravian
missionary movement on St. Thomas. She was fluent in the Creole
trade language used among the slaves. Despite being beaten,
imprisoned, and threatened with a return to slavery, Protten refused
to stop sharing the good news about Jesus. She married a German
Moravian missionary in 1738 and eventually moved to Europe and
then Ghana to continue sharing the good news about Jesus.[50] Georg
Oldendorp, a Moravian historian, was a personal friend of Protten.
He described her as well as other Afro-Caribbean church leaders,
like Mingo, Andreas, Anna Maria, and Magdalena, as "the stars in
a black book of Acts."[51]

By 1782, more than two hundred missionaries had been sent to
locations as varied as Greenland, West Africa, Estonia, and North
America and there were twenty-six active missionary stations.
The Moravian missionaries also played a significant role in the
"conversion" and evangelistic passion of John Wesley, who would
in turn influence the evangelist George Whitefield. Other important
evangelistic and missionary figures working during the 1700s
include the missionary and pastor-theologian Jonathan Edwards
(d. 1758); the preacher and abolitionist John Wollman (d. 1772);
North America's first overseas missionary, the freed slave George
Liele (d. 1828); and the famous William Carey (d. 1834)—their
stories must remain untold here. Instead, we turn to a woman who
may be the most influential female evangelist and theologian since
the book of Acts.

---

[49]Craig D. Atwood, "German Pietism and the Origin of the Black Church in
America," in *A Companion to German Pietism, 1660-1800*, ed. Douglas H. Shantz,
Brill's Companions to the Christian Tradition (Leiden: Brill, 2015), 527–53.
[50]Jon Sensbach, *Rebecca's Revival: Creating Black Christianity in the Atlantic World*
(Cambridge: Harvard University Press, 2006).
[51]Sensbach, *Rebecca's Revival*, 237.

Evangelism and Missions in the 1800s

Thomas Oden has suggested that Phoebe Palmer (1807–1874) might be "the leading woman theologian of the Protestant church."[52] Justin Davis argues that what Friedrich Schleiermacher is to European Protestantism, Palmer is to North American Protestantism.[53] Given that North American evangelicalism is the dominant version of Protestantism in Asia and Africa today, his thesis carries significant weight.[54] While there were many important developments in evangelicalism and missions during the 1800s, we focus here on Palmer's life and teaching.

Phoebe Palmer personally preached to over one hundred thousand people during her fifty-year ministry. During her lifetime she was involved with revivals that brought well over two and a half million people to Christ and hundreds of millions to him over the next century.[55] Charles White identifies Palmer as the link between early evangelical leaders like John Wesley and the birth of the Pentecostal movement. She has been identified as both the mother of the Holiness movement and as the grandmother of global Pentecostalism.[56] Palmer is discussed further in the chapter on the Holy Spirit; here note three of her more important contributions as they relate to evangelical missions. Palmer taught: (1) a life of holiness opens the door for the Holy Spirit to use believers for mission and ministry; (2) every member of Christ's body, including women, has access to the power of the Holy Spirit to testify to the

---

[52]Thomas Oden, "Introduction," in *Phoebe Palmer: Selected Writings* (New York: Paulist, 1988), 14.

[53]Justin A. Davis, *Schleiermacher and Palmer: The Father and Mother of the Modern Protestant Mindset* (Eugene: Pickwick, 2019).

[54]Donald Lewis and Richard Pierard, eds., *Global Evangelicalism: Theology, History & Culture in Regional Perspective* (Downers Grove: IVP Academic, 2014), 127, 197.

[55]J. Edwin Orr, *The Fervent Prayer: The Worldwide Impact of the Great Awakening of 1858* (Chicago: Moody, 1974), 2, 15, 61–8, 121; J. Edwin Orr, *The Second Evangelical Awakening in Britain* (London: Marshall, Morgan & Scott, 1949), 5, 14–15, 36; Douglas A. Sweeney, *The American Evangelical Story: A History of the Movement* (Grand Rapids: Baker Academic, 2005), 136–42; Charles Edward White, *The Beauty of Holiness: Phoebe Palmer as Theologian, Revivalist, Feminist, and Humanitarian* (Grand Rapids: Zondervan, 1986), 47.

[56]Charles Edward White, "Phoebe Palmer and the Development of Pentecostal Pneumatology," *Wesleyan Theological Journal* 23 (1988): 198, 208.

good news of Jesus Christ and his kingdom; and (3) gospel holiness leads God's people to proclaim the love of God in word and deed.

Palmer's ministry began in her home with the establishment of the "Tuesday Meeting for the Promotion of Holiness." This ministry was birthed after her "Day of Days," July 26, 1837, the day she had a radical consecrating experience with the Holy Spirit following the tragic death of one of her children. Palmer resolved to give herself wholly to God and never to place anything, even her beloved spouse or remaining children, before the Lord. The Tuesday meetings began with only women, but soon included men who wanted to learn. They continued for over fifty years with weekly crowds sometimes reaching three hundred people—often including the most prominent clergy and Christian leaders of her day.

In addition to leading the Tuesday meetings, Palmer was deeply committed to evangelism. She was one of the founders of the urban "prayer-meeting revival," which reverberated across the whole of North America.[57] Palmer pioneered the use of revival-type methods in urban contexts that had previously only been used in rural areas (e.g., by George Whitefield). She also made a transition from organizing evangelistic campaigns that centered around clergy (e.g., Charles Finney) to campaigns that were organized by the laity—a strategy one of her theological grandchildren, D. L. Moody, would develop even further.[58] Palmer often passed out tracts throughout New York and engaged in street ministry.[59] After observing that those she led to Christ from lower social classes sometimes did not feel welcome in her higher-class church, she and her husband helped plant a new Methodist church in a low-income community. In 1850, Palmer served as the founding director of the Five Point Mission, the first inner-city mission in the United States. The mission was in such a dangerous community that when Charles Dickens was invited to the neighborhood he refused to go without a police escort. Through the Five Point Mission, Palmer and her husband (a medical physician) started a jobs program, a low-income housing program, a clothing and food distribution center,

---

[57]Charles Edward White, "Holiness Fire-Starter," *Christian History & Biography* 82 (2004): 16–21.

[58]Klaus Fiedler, *The Story of Faith Missions: From Hudson Taylor to Present Day Africa* (Eugene: Wipf and Stock, 2011), 233, nn. 51, 52.

[59]Nigel Scotland, *Apostles of the Spirit and Fire: American Revivalists and Victorian Britain* (Eugene: Wipf and Stock, 2009), 134.

a medical ministry, and a home for unwanted children.[60] Palmer regularly engaged in ministry in a prison known as "The Tombs."[61] There she would preach to female prisoners and young people. She once took a juvenile offender home with her and worked to adopt him until his situation changed and his family was willing to take him back. Palmer was a firm abolitionist along the lines of Abraham Lincoln. She believed, "If slavery is not wrong, nothing is wrong."[62] She launched New York's first Christian ministry to Jews. Yet while Palmer made a significant impact on New York City, her "Jerusalem," she made an even greater impact on her "Samaria" and the "outermost parts of the earth."

Outside of New York, Palmer was best known for her theological writing and preaching ministry. We will return to her theological writings (eighteen books and hundreds of articles) in the chapter on the Holy Spirit; for now we focus on her three "missionary journeys." Palmer believed that the Holy Spirit had been poured out upon the church to fill the church with power for holiness and mission. Her life exemplified this claim as she began to travel and engage in a transatlantic preaching ministry. What we might call her first missionary journey lasted from 1840 to 1858 during which she held revival services in some eighty towns across the United States and Canada.[63] Often these meetings would last for weeks, and several camp meetings in both the United States and Britain have continued to meet every summer since Palmer's visits. Palmer's second missionary journey (1859–63) took her and her husband on a preaching tour described in her book, *Four Years in the Old World*.[64] The trip resulted in over twenty thousand people recording new commitments to Christ at her evangelistic meetings and over a million people coming to Christ across England, Ireland, Scotland, and Wales during the revival movement that she helped launch.[65] Returning to the United States at the close of the Civil War, Palmer's third missionary journey lasted some ten years, from 1863 until 1873. During this decade, Palmer crisscrossed the nation, holding

---

[60]White, *Beauty of Holiness*, 207–30.

[61]Scotland, *Apostles of the Spirit and Fire*, 134.

[62]Scotland, *Apostles of the Spirit and Fire*, 134.

[63]Scotland, *Apostles of the Spirit and Fire*, 124.

[64]Phoebe Palmer, *Phoebe Palmer: Selected Writings*, ed. Thomas Oden (New York: Paulist, 1988), 258–88.

[65]White, "Holiness Fire-Starter," 19.

extended revival meetings from California to New York (sometimes two meetings a day) in over eighty cities and towns in the United States and Canada.[66]

Despite the importance of her preaching and writing, Palmer's most lasting contribution is found in the women and men she discipled. Like Paul, her Timothies, Lydias, Priscillas, and Aquilas would soon turn the world upside down. Significant church leaders shaped by her or one of her disciples include Benjamin Titus Roberts, founder of the Free Methodist Denomination; William and Catherine Booth, founders of the Salvation Army; A. B. Simpson, founder of the Christian and Missionary Alliance; Aimee Simple McPherson, founder of the Foursquare denomination; Charles Mason, founder of Church of God in Christ (the largest African American denomination in the United States); and many others. Missionaries and church planters shaped by her include regular Tuesday meeting attendees like Amanda Smith, the first African American evangelist to preach and do significant work on four continents (North America, Europe, Asia, and Africa); the missionary bishop William Taylor, whose church planting work on every populated continent pioneered many new evangelistic strategies (the evangelical Christian college Taylor University is named after Bishop Taylor);[67] and the first Methodist missionaries sent to China from North America in 1847 (Moses White, Robert Maclay, and Henry Hickok). Palmer's work in England caused her to be known as "the mother of the Keswick movement." The Keswick movement soon produced a wealth of missionaries including Hudson Taylor (who overlapped with Palmer for four years in London) and Amy Carmichael, the movement's first missionary to India.

Palmer's influence on evangelical thought in North America is illustrated by Tom Oden's list of seventeen presidents, founders, or key leaders of universities who by their own testimony were significantly shaped by her thought.[68] To his list we could add at

---

[66]Scotland, *Apostles of the Spirit and Fire*, 127; for a list of the cities and towns visited on these three missionary journeys, see White, *Beauty of Holiness*, 237–44.

[67]Descriptions of Taylor's creative missional activities can be found in William Taylor, *Lessons of Infinite Advantage: William Taylor's California Experiences*, ed. Robert Lay (Lanham: Scarecrow Press, 2010).

[68]Oden, "Introduction," 4; On the importance of higher education for evangelical mission see Charles Habib Malik, *The Two Tasks* (Wheaton: EMIS, 2000); Hank Voss, "The Priesthood of All Believers and the Public(s) Theologian: Wisdom from

least four more schools, since Taylor University (1846), Wheaton College (1860), Moody Bible Institute (1886), and Biola University (1908) were each influenced by Palmer and the Holiness movement through their founders or influential leaders (William Taylor, Charles Blanchard, D. L. Moody, and R. A. Torrey).[69] Palmer also mentored Frances Willard, a key leader in the women's suffrage movement, and Fanny Crosby, whose vision to see one million souls come to Christ through her song writing was kindled under Palmer's nurture. Social movements like Alcoholics Anonymous and the Oxford Movement can be directly traced to her influence. Palmer's example illustrates that the proclamation of the gospel in word and deed was a central emphasis of evangelical mission in the 1800s.

Evangelism and Missions in the 1900s: The Lausanne Movement

If there is a single biblical passage that motivated evangelical missions in the 1900s, it is Jesus's final words as recorded in Matt 28:19–20: "Go therefore and make disciples of all nations, baptizing them in the name of the Father and of the Son and of the Holy Spirit, teaching them to observe all that I have commanded you. And behold, I am with you always, to the end of the age." The command "go," together with the promise of the presence of Jesus, is a powerful combination for evangelicals. In 1910, evangelicals gathered with other Western Protestants to discuss the task of global mission at the Edinburgh World Missionary Conference. The motto for the conference was "the evangelization of the world in this generation." After much suffering, but also much success in the previous century, there was good cause to celebrate. Yet there were also hints of challenges to come. No African, Latin American, or Pacific Island delegates were invited to the conference. One of the few Asian delegates at the conference, the Anglican Vendanayagam Samuel Azariah (d. 1945) challenged the gathering with these prophetic words:

Rev. Dr. Don Davis, Dr. Paige Cunningham, and Rev. Dr. Robert Romero," *Christian Scholars Review* 49 (2020): 387–98.
[69]Fiedler, *Story of Faith Missions*, 233; Albert Edward Thompson, *The Life of A. B. Simpson* (New York: Christian Alliance, 1920), 110.

The problem of race relations is one of the most serious problems confronting the church today ... Through all ages to come the Indian church will rise up in gratitude to attest the heroism and self-denying labors of the missionary body. You have given your goods to feed the poor. You have given your bodies to be burned. We also ask for love. Give us FRIENDS.[70]

In addition to the problem of race relations, a division over the so-called "social gospel" would soon divide the global Protestant missionary community into two opposed groups. Tension between the head (word) and the hands (deed) would soon tear apart the goal of shared mission, sacrifice, and unity for the glory of the Lamb. One group at Edinburgh began to primarily emphasize the importance of missionary involvement in social action, while the other group reacted by emphasizing missionary preaching. While some individuals were able to stay engaged with both groups (e.g., Lesslie Newbigin, David Bosch), institutions were often forced to choose sides. The group emphasizing social justice eventually founded the World Council of Churches in 1948. The group emphasizing the verbal proclamation of the good news about the love of Jesus led to the founding of the National Evangelical Alliance (United States) in 1942 and the global Lausanne Movement in 1974.[71]

Evangelism and Missions in the 2000s

As evangelicals enter their fifth century of mission, the situation is far different from what John Eliot experienced in the 1600s. In 2010, the Lausanne Third World Congress on World Evangelization was held in Cape Town, South Africa, one hundred years after the historic Edinburgh conference. Evangelical leaders from 198

---

[70]Scott Sunquist, *Understanding Christian Mission: Participation in Suffering and Glory* (Grand Rapids: Baker, 2013), 119 (emphasis original).

[71]The actual story is of course much more complicated. The World Evangelical Alliance (WEA) was founded in 1846 in London and is the mother organization for the US-based National Association of Evangelicals. The WEA is currently headquartered in Deerfield, IL, and its global membership consists of some 129 different national evangelical alliances representing over six hundred million evangelicals. For a short discussion of evangelicalism in relation to North America, see Michael Hammond, "Christian Higher Education in the United States: The Crisis of Evangelical Identity," *Christian Higher Education* 18 (2019): 3–15. For a longer version, see Brian Stanley's *The Global Diffusion of Evangelicalism*.

countries gathered in person while hundreds of thousands more participated in various locations around the world. *The Cape Town Commitment* was the product of this process, and it represents an authoritative window into the beliefs of today's global evangelical community. The integral evangelism for which René Padilla and others called in 1974 was fully embraced at Cape Town.[72] The global evangelical church reaffirmed its commitment to "the whole church taking the whole gospel to the whole world."[73]

This brief taste from the last four hundred years of evangelical missions gives cause for both celebration and lament. We can celebrate the hundreds of millions of people who have met Jesus and come to experience the love of God and the friendship of the Holy Spirit through the sacrifice of countless unnamed missionaries. Thousands of languages have had the Bible translated into the vernacular—most of which had no written language prior to the arrival of Bible translators. Public health, education of the masses, economic growth, literacy, emancipation of women, abolition of slavery, and democracy are all centrally connected to the arrival of evangelical missionaries.[74] Even if relatively unknown today, names like John and Alice Harris (Belgian Congo), John Mackenzie (South Africa), Trevor Huddleston (South Africa), Ida Scudder (India), Guido Verbeck (Japan), Timothy Richard (China), James Long (India), Eliza Bridgman (China) represent thousands of evangelical missionaries whose commitment to sharing God's love in word or deed continues to impact the lives of millions across the globe.[75] While there is much to celebrate, there is also cause for lament. As the *Lausanne Covenant* notes, the fact that there are billions who have never heard the name of Jesus some two thousand years after his birth is a scandal. The church's failure to share the good news about Jesus to the whole world is surely cause for repentance and lament. Many Christians in the West need to lament over the more than ten thousand children who will die today from hunger. Their death, while so many who name the name of Christ are wasting

---

[72]For background on Padilla and integral mission see Robert Romero, *The Brown Church: Five Centuries of Latina/o Social Justice, Theology, and Identity* (Downers Grove: InterVarsity, 2020), 142–62.

[73]Rose Dowsett, *The Cape Town Commitment: Study Edition* (Peabody: Hendrickson, 2012), 3.

[74]Woodberry, "Missionary Roots of Liberal Democracy"; Dilley, "World the Missionaries Made."

[75]For brief biographies of these names see Dilley, "World the Missionaries Made."

TABLE 2.4 *2020 Global Distribution of Evangelicals*

		2020
Global South	Africa	144,814,000
	Asia	67,247,000
	Oceania	5,393,000
	Latin America	59,576,000
	Subtotal	**277,030,000**
		2020
Global North	Northern America	50,324,000
	Europe	22,140,000
	Subtotal	**72,464,000**
Global Total		**349,494,000***

* The total number of evangelicals in Table 2.4 comes from the World Christian Database associated with the Center for the Study of Global Christianity. Other researchers, such as those at Operation World, calculate the total 2020 global evangelical population at 653,682,000. Their statistics place 82 percent of evangelicals in the global South. Note also that the World Evangelical Fellowship reports six hundred million members. For discussion and explanation of how each research team defines "evangelical," see "Christianity in Its Global Context," 17.

resources on "earthly things," serving a god in the belly (Phil 3:17–19), is one sign of the evangelical church's need to repent.

Challenges to Evangelism and Mission

Evangelicals have typically recognized that Christian mission is opposed by the world, the flesh, and the devil. We illustrated one of these challenges earlier with René Padilla's concerns about worldliness and the gospel. Any exploration of the challenges to Christian mission needs to begin with recognizing the reality of personal sin (internal), social structures that oppose the freedom, wholeness and justice of the kingdom of God (external), and supernatural principalities and powers (infernal).[76] Of the many challenges that could be explored, we focus on persecution, secularization, and globalization.

The history of evangelical mission is a history of suffering. This history continues into the present with the data indicating approximately nine hundred thousand Christian martyrs in the decade leading up to 2020.[77] A related index maintained by the Pew Research Center reported in 2015 that 5.5 billion people, or 77 percent of the world's population, live in "countries with high or very high levels of restrictions on religion."[78] Evangelicals in Asia have faced this persecution the most as they are often living as a tiny minority in the larger population.[79] The West's involvement with Middle Eastern countries during the first twenty years of this century has made evangelism and mission activities in places dominated by Islamic fundamentalism—countries like Yemen, Iraq, Afghanistan— even more difficult than in previous centuries. Christian communities that had maintained a witness for more than a thousand years ceased to exist across the Middle East during the last two decades.

A second challenge to Christian mission is the militant secular fundamentalism that has come to dominate much of the West and parts of Asia. Vinoth Ramachandra points out that the

---

[76]Don Davis and Terry Cornett, "Empowering People for Freedom, Wholeness, and Justice," in *Foundations for Christian Mission* (Wichita: Urban Ministry Institute, 2005), 310–39; Tormod Engelsviken and A. Scott Moreau, eds., *Spiritual Conflict in Today's Mission: A Report from the Consultation on "Deliver Us from Evil," August 2000, Nairobi Kenya* (Nairobi; Monrovia: Lausanne Committee for World Evangelization; MARC, 2001).

[77]Johnson and Zurlo, "Status of Global Christianity, 2020." Open Doors also tracks martyrdoms and places the ten-year total closer to forty thousand. Even at this lower rate, Open Doors still claims that Christianity is the "world's most severely persecuted religion" (Jason Casper, "The 50 Countries Where It's Hardest to Follow Jesus," ChristianityToday.com, January 15, 2020, https://www.christianitytoday.com/news/2020/january/top-christian-persecution-open-doors-2020-world-watch-list.html).

[78]Alan Cooperman, Peter Henne, and Katherine Ritchey, "Latest Trends in Religious Restrictions and Hostilities" (Pew Research Center, February 26, 2015), 5.

[79]Sunquist, "Asia," 221.

"self-deception" and "latent paternalism" of this movement, which can be as "intolerant as the Islamist jihadist," needs "to learn how narrow and culture-bound their view of reason actually is."[80] Unless the West can learn how to respect divergent viewpoints (including religious ones) and build true multicultural and pluralistic communities, evangelicals will be among those facing increasing challenges in coming decades. As Ramachandra clearly articulates, "Modern nation-states, including liberal democracies, are suspicious of and feel threatened by well-organized ethnic, religious and other communities lest these become rival centers of loyalty."[81] Let those with ears hear what this prophet is saying to the churches.

A third challenge comes in the form of the rapid globalization of today's world. "Globalization" often means that people are becoming more and more aware of diverse cultures and that the world itself is becoming more of a single place with increased interaction between its political, economic, social, cultural, and religious dimensions. Donald Lewis identifies three of globalization's challenges needing consideration by evangelicals.[82] First, global migrations and immigration are taking place on a massive scale, offering challenges and opportunities for mission. Second, the world is becoming rapidly urban as people flock to global cities. A major historical milestone took place in 2009 when the number of urban dwellers exceeded the number of rural dwellers for the first time since the Tower of Babel.[83] While in 1900 there were 20 cities in the world with a population over one million people, today (in 2020) there are 580 (see Table 2.1). Finally, while globalization brings benefits, there is also a dark side; it includes international sex trafficking, exploitation of indigenous peoples, and abuse of the poor.[84]

---

[80]Vinoth Ramachandra, *Subverting Global Myths: Theology and the Public Issues Shaping Our World* (Downers Grove: InterVarsity, 2009), 154–6.

[81]Ramachandra, *Subverting Global Myths*, 138.

[82]Donald Lewis, "Globalization, Religion, and Evangelicalism," in *Global Evangelicalism: Theology, History & Culture in Regional Perspective*, ed. Donald Lewis and Richard Pierard (Downers Grove: IVP Academic, 2014), 76–9.

[83]Todd Johnson and Peter F. Crossing, "Christianity 2014: Independent Christianity and Slum Dwellers," *IBMR* 38 (2014): 28.

[84]Lewis, "Globalization, Religion, and Evangelicalism," 76–9.

Forward: Prayer, Unreached People Groups, and Urban Poverty

The twenty-first century of evangelical mission promises to be the most culturally diverse of any so far. The mission is now taking place from everywhere to everywhere. Three areas to watch include prayer movements, global cooperation to share the gospel among unreached people groups, and the opportunity to serve the three billion living in urban poverty around the globe. First, evangelicals are committed to pursuing ongoing movements of prayer for the advance of the gospel.[85] After the Lausanne Conference ended in 1974, four ongoing working groups were continued—one of which was a group assigned to coordinating ongoing prayer for evangelism. Since 2000, several evangelical groups around the globe have committed to maintaining 24/7 continuous prayer movements after the example of the early Moravian missionaries. An increasing number of evangelicals remain convinced that unless God arises (Psalm 68), there is no hope that the vast challenges to Christian mission in the twenty-first century will be overcome.[86]

Second, evangelicals are compelled to share the love of Christ with those who have never heard this good news. Ralph Winter laid out the importance of this commitment in his 1974 Lausanne address entitled "The Highest Priority: Cross-Cultural Evangelism." In this address he introduced the E-Scale to explain the difference between evangelism and cross-cultural proclamation. Citing Mathew 24:14, Winter argues that evangelicals must especially work to ensure that a witness to Jesus Christ takes place among every people group (see Table 2.2).[87] One aid to the pursuit of this task has been the recognition of the importance of Church Plant Movements, and much current evangelical missionary strategy

---

[85]Glenda Weldon and Earl Robinson, "Prayer in Evangelism," *Lausanne Occasional Papers* 42 (Pattaya: Lausanne Committee for World Evangelization, 2004), https://www.lausanne.org/content/lop/prayer-evangelism-lop-42.

[86]Don L. Davis, *Let God Arise! A Sober Call to Prevailing Prayer for a Dynamic Spiritual Awakening and the Aggressive Advancement of the Kingdom in America's Inner Cities* (Wichita: Urban Ministry Institute, 2000).

[87]Bruce Koch and Ralph Winter, "Finishing the Task: The Unreached Peoples Challenge," *PWCM*, 511.

focuses on how to develop these movements among unreached peoples.[88]

Finally, one result of globalization is that the number of slum dwellers has grown from around 270 million at the time of the 1974 Lausanne conference to a projected 1.6 billion by 2025.[89] Fewer than one in five hundred foreign missionaries works in slums, and less than one in ten thousand national workers do so.[90] With 166,000 new non-Christians moving into cities every day, there is a vast need for workers to be equipped and sent to share God's love for the lost.[91] If one missionary or pastor was trained for each one hundred of these new urban dwellers, the global evangelical church would need to train over six hundred thousand new Christian leaders each year just to reach the new non-Christians moving into the world's cities. These leaders are above and beyond any new leaders needing to be trained for existing global churches. Looking forward, the number of urban slum dwellers is projected to grow by five hundred million people between mid-2020 and 2050. When Jesus looked at crowds like this, his heart was moved with compassion (Matt 9:38–39). Today the Holy Spirit urges believers to do the same thing Jesus told his first-century disciples to do, "Ask the Lord of the harvest to raise up workers for the harvest fields."

In closing, we return to John Stott who was "*ein Lausanner.*"[92] Stott lived his whole life embracing the disciplines of simplicity, generosity, and contentment as called for by the *Lausanne Covenant*.[93] He consecrated his life to participation in the mission of God and so embraced a "wartime, not a peacetime, lifestyle."[94] May Stott's kind of evangelical, the Lausanne kind, increase.

---

[88]David Garrison, *Church Planting Movements: How God Is Redeeming a Lost World* (Midlothian: WIGTake, 2004).

[89]Johnson and Zurlo, "Status of Global Christianity, 2020."

[90]Johnson and Crossing, "Christianity 2014," 28.

[91]Johnson and Zurlo, "Status of Global Christianity, 2020."

[92]Wright, *John Stott*, 6; emphasis original.

[93]"LOP 20: An Evangelical Commitment to Simple Life-Style" (Hoddesdon: Lausanne Committee for World Evangelization, 1980); John Stott, *Issues Facing Christians Today*, 4th ed. (Grand Rapids: Zondervan, 2006), 295–321.

[94]Ralph Winter, "Reconsecration to a Wartime, Not a Peacetime, Lifestyle," in *PWCM*, 705–7.

Recommended Reading

Paul Borthwick, *Western Christians in Global Mission: What's the Role of the North American Church?* (Downers Grove: InterVarsity, 2012).

David J. Bosch, *Transforming Mission: Paradigm Shifts in Theology of Mission* (Maryknoll: Orbis, 1995).

Julia E. M. Cameron, ed., *The Lausanne Legacy: Landmarks in Global Mission* (Peabody: Hendrickson, 2016).

David Garrison, *Church Planting Movements: How God Is Redeeming a Lost World* (Midlothian: WIGTake, 2004).

Andrew F. Walls, *The Missionary Movement in Christian History: Studies in the Transmission of Faith* (Maryknoll: Orbis, 1996).

Ralph Winter, Steven Hawthorne, Darrell Dorr, D. Bruce Graham, and Bruce Koch, eds. *Perspectives on the World Christian Movement: Reader*, 3rd ed. (Pasadena: William Carey, 1999).

Themes

3

"Christ Died for Our Sins": Atonement

Jesus Christ, being himself the only God-Man, who gave himself as the only ransom for sinners, is the only mediator between God and people.

LAUSANNE COVENANT §3

To evangelize is to spread the good news that Jesus Christ died for our sins and was raised from the dead according to the Scriptures.

LAUSANNE COVENANT §4

Evangelical gospel proclamation is dominated by the announcement that "Jesus died for our sins." Although there are debates among evangelical thinkers about what the content of that statement is (or should be), evangelicals typically understand it as: Jesus paid the penalty for our sins by dying for us. Our songs emotively declare, "Thank you for the cross," "I'll never know how much it cost to see my sin upon that cross," and "And can it be that I should gain an int'rest in the Savior's blood? Died He for me, who caused His pain—for me, who Him to death pursued?" We are a community of the cross, a missional people consumed with the proclamation of Jesus's sacrifice. Evangelicalism in its past or present form cannot be understood apart from its crucicentrism. And while it is true that this understanding of the atonement is formed and propagated largely through preaching, music, and popular literature (typical sources of evangelical spiritual and theological formation), it is by no means merely a populist theology. The sacrificial, penal, and substitutionary understanding of the atonement has substantially characterized evangelicalism in both its populist and scholarly thought. We are not merely a community of the atonement, we are a community of the penal substitutionary death of Christ. Surely this is a contentious claim, since much recent reflection has sought to shift the evangelical focus from this view to a wider range of views (and we will explore those emerging perspectives in due course). Nevertheless, it should be clear from our historical survey that the "founders" of the movement and their progeny, while having a robust understanding of Christ's work, were particularly interested in his substitutionary death. We begin our discussion of evangelicals and the atonement by examining a classic account by J. I. Packer, one of the leading evangelical Anglican theologians of the twentieth century.

Doctrine: What Did the Cross Achieve?

In his 1973 lecture entitled "What Did the Cross Achieve?" Packer sets out to defend the biblical and theological soundness, and not so much the rationality, of the penal substitutionary model of the atonement. This distinction between biblical/theological soundness and rationality is important. According to Packer, the debate over the last few hundred years has been dictated by Socinian objections to penal substitution. Reformed apologists, in response to Socinus, tended to make their arguments for the penal substitution overly rationalistic, instead of treating it as a mystery and confession of faith. The beauty of the doctrine was unintentionally distorted as arguments for the atonement were reduced to logical deductions drawing from then current understandings of kingship and justice. This doctrine is fundamentally a *model* about a *mystery*. It is a biblically rooted model that employs certain images as a way to declare, not explain, the truth of what God has done for us in Christ. It is a mystery in that it tries to relate some of the deepest and unfathomable realities of the Christian faith (e.g., Trinity, incarnation, divine love), matters that are not fully explicable.[1] As Packer quips, "One thing that Christians know by faith is that they only know in part."[2] Nevertheless, whatever it is that we can know is given to us in Scripture. The Bible is our source of knowledge of all divine mysteries, including the atonement.

After these methodological and historical considerations, Packer attempts to construct a model of penal substitution that is biblical and addresses some of the criticisms. The "model building" takes place in two stages. In the first stage, Packer tries to make sense of what we mean by "substitution." He begins by citing the *Oxford English Dictionary*'s definition of three terms: substitution, representation, and vicarious. Substitution is defined as "the putting of one person or thing in the place of another"; representation as "the fact of standing for, or in place of, some other thing or person … substitution of one thing or person for another"; vicarious as something or someone "substituted instead of the proper thing or person." Packer's point in citing these definitions is to show that the contemporary aversion to "substitution" in place of these other terms is rooted in a "distinction without a difference." Whatever it means that "Christ died for us" (Rom 5:8), it must involve the notion of substitution. We cannot evade substitution by calling Christ's death vicarious or representative.

In fact, Packer will go on to argue that subjective models of the atonement (i.e., that Christ died to produce an effect *in us*—of love, confession, obedience to God, etc.) as well as *Christus Victor* models (i.e., that Christ's death was primarily about defeating hostile spiritual powers) all must presuppose a substitutionary model. He writes,

It grounds humanity's plight as victim of sin and Satan in the fact that, for all God's daily goodness to us, as sinners we stand under divine judgement, and our bondage to evil is the start of our sentence, and unless God's rejection of us is turned into acceptance we are lost for ever. On this view, Christ's death had

---

[1] J. I. Packer, "What Did the Cross Achieve? The Logic of Penal Substitution," in *Celebrating the Saving Work of God: Collected Shorter Writings of J. I. Packer* (Carlisle: Paternoster, 1998), 85–90.

[2] Packer, "What Did the Cross Achieve," 90.

its effect first on God, who was hereby *propitiated* (or, better, who hereby propitiated himself), and only because it had this effect did it become an overthrowing of the powers of darkness and a revealing of God's seeking and saving love ... [B]y undergoing the cross Jesus expiated our sins, propitiated our Maker, turned God's "no" to us into a "yes," and so saved us.[3]

Substitution in relation to sin's sentence cannot be avoided, even by the strongest "representative" models (i.e., models that stress our solidarity or identification with Christ who represents us, but does not suffer in place of us). Paul's teaching in Rom 3:21–28 cannot be avoided. Christ is there presented as "a propitiation ... by his blood."

This leads to the second stage of model building: making sense of the *penal* dimension of substitution. The basic affirmation in penal substitution is that Christ, motivated by love, endured and exhausted the divine judgment (penal) we deserved (substitution) and purchased for us all the gifts of salvation, such as the forgiveness of sins, adoption, and more.[4] Penal substitution is a model that accounts for the *meaning* of the atonement, not its mechanics, and its primary concern is the remission of sins before a holy God.[5] It tells us the *what* of Christ's atoning work, without trying to explain the *how*. In presenting a robust account of penal substitution Packer aims to avoid the criticisms of it being crude and immoral, overly rationalistic, and impersonal. His formulation places substitution alongside several different themes: retribution, solidarity, mystery, and divine love.[6]

Retribution

Penal substitution presupposes a penalty due to us from God, the Lawgiver and Judge, for failure to meet his demands. This truth is abundantly clear from Rom 1:18–3:20 and throughout the

---

[3]Packer, "What Did the Cross Achieve," 101.

[4]Packer, "What Did the Cross Achieve," 105.

[5]Packer, "What Did the Cross Achieve," 106.

[6]We are not including his discussion here of limited atonement, as our aim is to present Packer as a representative of broader evangelical thought on the atonement. The issue is an important one, but beside the point for this section.

New Testament.[7] God judges lawbreakers, and his judgment is retribution for the violation of his holy law and character. Moreover, we intuitively sense that we should suffer for wrongdoing. In this context, we learn four things about our situation before God. First, concerning *God*, we learn that retribution is approved by God and expresses his character, which is reflected in his law. Physical and spiritual death is an appropriate sentence, and God himself will impose it on us. Second, concerning *ourselves*, we learn that we are powerless to avoid God's sentence, since we are unable to undo our sins of the past and the present. Third, we learn that *Jesus Christ* took our place under God's judgment and experienced in himself the death that was our sentence. In doing so, he purchased our pardon. Fourth, we learn that by *faith*, as we look to Christ and away from ourselves, we escape God's rightful retribution and receive full pardon because of Christ. *Penal* substitution is meant to proclaim the good news that the Son of God "loved me and gave himself for me" (Gal 2:20).[8]

Solidarity

Substitution is immoral, so the Socinian charge goes, for an innocent man should not be punished for someone else's crime. How might this accusation be addressed? Packer appeals to the Pauline description of Jesus as the last Adam (1 Cor 15:45–49; Rom 5:12–21) who includes believers in his sin-bearing in the way the first Adam involved humanity in his sinning. Penal substitution is rooted in our solidarity (or identification) with Christ. Our solidarity with Christ has four "moments," according to Packer. First, Christ took our humanity, being "born of a woman" (Gal 4:4). Second, on the cross Christ identified with us as sinners and included us in his dying (2 Cor 5:14). In other words, he is our unique sin-bearing substitute, but he mysteriously carries us with him in his death on the cross. Adam brought condemnation to

---

[7]For example, the wrath of God rests upon us (Rom 1:18), those who violate God's ways "deserve to die" (Rom 1:32), the judgment of God "rightly falls on those who practice such things" (Rom 2:2), and Jews and Gentiles are equally condemned for violating their respective laws (Rom 2:6–16), since all have sinned and none are righteous (Rom 3:9–20).

[8]Packer, "What Did the Cross Achieve," 108–10.

all, but Christ—the second Adam—brings life and acceptance to all who believe. Third, by virtue of Christ's substitutionary death, we become "the righteousness of God" (2 Cor 5:21), justified and made rich because of the one who became poor on our behalf (2 Cor 8:9). "In him" we become the righteousness of God. Fourth, we are united to Christ not only in his death; we are one with him also in his resurrection and glory. Christ bears our penalty under God's judgment so that we can experience the fullness of new creation life. Thus, there is mystery here. We are somehow one with Christ in his life, death, resurrection, and glory. He is our representative, our trailblazer. Yet, his representation takes the form of bearing our penalty for sin so that he can take us along with him into glory. Representation and substitution go hand in hand.[9]

Mystery

Penal substitution is not an explanation of the "how" behind the atonement. It is a "pointer" to the various mysteries involved in the work of Christ. Among the most important mysteries presupposed by penal substitution, Packer highlights: (1) God's love for humanity (Rom 5:8); (2) the necessity of sending the Son (Rom 8:32); (3) our solidarity in Christ so that his death is our death, and his life our life (Rom 5:17–19; 2 Cor 5:21). Other mysteries that are implied in the atonement could also be included, such as the Trinity, the incarnation, the predestination of free human acts, and so forth. The main point is that the work of Christ is a mystery that cannot be fully explained.[10] Yet, as Packer observes, "What is *above* reason is not necessarily *against* it."[11] Rationalistic criticisms impose standards on God in which he has to work according to human laws and limitations, rather than allowing for mystery given the subject matter.

---

[9]Packer makes this point to show that we cannot sidestep the notion of penal substitution in favor of "representation." Indeed, representation (or solidarity in Christ) is critical, but it must contain within it the centrality of Christ bearing God's judgment for us.

[10]Packer, "What Did the Cross Achieve," 114.

[11]Packer, "What Did the Cross Achieve," 115.

Divine Love

Penal substitution in recent years has been depicted as divine or cosmic child abuse, the atrocious teaching that a docile and innocent Son was punished to appease an irate Father.[12] This charge is answered straightforwardly. The model of penal substitution presupposes an intra-Trinitarian pact, wherein both the Father and Son covenant to rescue humanity from its plight by the Son's self-sacrifice. Not only is there the love of the Father behind the sending of the Son (John 3:16; Rom 5:8; 1 John 4:8–10), but we also have a picture of the Son venturing to take on humanity's punishment of his own volition (John 15:13). Christ's death as a penalty for sin was motivated by divine love and is the ultimate demonstration of that love. That God would lower himself to receive a criminal's death and experience the fullness of God's reaction against sin is the ultimate revelation of love.[13] The atonement is an expression of who God is in himself. He is love and acts accordingly in offering Christ.

A Summary

Packer summarizes his argument in nine theses regarding penal substitution and its implications:

1. God judges all sins, and our conscience confirms this to be right.
2. Our sins merit ultimate penal suffering and rejection from God's presence, and we are helpless to atone for our sins.
3. The penalty for our sins was paid by Jesus by his death on the cross.
4. Through faith in Christ, we receive justification, acceptance, and adoption.
5. Christ's death for us is the sole ground for hope before God. Christ bearing God's punishment means we will not have to throughout eternity.

---

[12]See, e.g., Steve Chalke and Alan Mann, *The Lost Message of Jesus* (Grand Rapids: Zondervan, 2004), 182.
[13]Packer, "What Did the Cross Achieve," 118–19.

6. Our faith in Christ is itself a gift secured by Christ's death.

7. The cross guarantees our salvation.

8. Christ's death for us is the "measure and pledge" of the love of the triune God for us.

9. Christ's death for us summons and constrains us to love, trust, and worship him.[14]

This, in a nutshell, is what the cross achieved. This belief is shared by the New Testament writers and much of the Christian tradition. In Packer, we see a wonderfully careful and characteristic explication of an evangelical doctrine of the atonement. He ably highlights the biblical rootedness of the model as well as its theological logic. Along the way, he raises issues such as the validity of other potential models, as well as criticisms of penal substitution within the evangelical camp (matters we will touch on later). For now, however, the question he puts before us is simply: "Ought we not to reconsider whether penal substitution is not, after all, the heart of the matter?"[15] It has been for many an evangelical.

History: Variations on a Theme

The line of thinking found in Packer's account is not unique to contemporary evangelicalism. In fact, one can discover similar emphases in various writers of the patristic and medieval periods. Justin Martyr, Eusebius of Caesarea, Hilary, Athanasius, Ambrose, Augustine, and Gregory of Nazianzus, for example, held to a form of penal substitution.[16] Yet, it is the medieval theologian, Anselm, who was most influential in laying the bedrock for future iterations of the doctrine of the atonement in the Reformation, in the early

---

[14]Packer, "What Did the Cross Achieve," 121. He lists them using the first person to show that this model of atonement is deeply personal and not merely transactional.
[15]Packer, "What Did the Cross Achieve," 123.
[16]See Steve Jeffery, Michael Ovey, and Andrew Sach, *Pierced for our Transgressions: Rediscovering the Glory of Penal Substitution* (Wheaton: Crossway, 2007), 161–83; and Garry J. Williams, "Penal Substitutionary Atonement in the Church Fathers," *Evangelical Quarterly* 83 (2011): 195–216. These essays present a counter to the often-cited account of patristic and medieval atonement theories in Gustav Aulén, *Christus Victor: An Historical Study of the Three Main Types of the Idea of the Atonement* (New York: Macmillan, 1969).

evangelical period, and up to the twentieth century. Thus, it is fitting that we begin our historical survey with the formidable archbishop of Canterbury.

A Medieval Precedent

The "satisfaction model" of atonement is normally ascribed to Anselm as articulated in his *Cur Deus Homo*.[17] His treatment is an exercise in faith-seeking understanding, in which he assumes Scripture's teaching while trying to defend and articulate the rationality of the atonement using arguments from reason alone. The main question he seeks to answer is the title of the work: Why did God become human in order to redeem us rather than employing some other way? In other words, why was this form of atonement necessary? His response (and argument) can be summarized in six points.[18] First, sin is defined as not giving to God what is owed him. What is owed God is having the whole will of a rational creature subject to the will of God. To honor God is to fully subject our wills to his. Thus, to dishonor God is to not render to God this honor, namely our wills. This takes away the honor due him. This is the essence of sin (I.11). Second, this dishonor must not only be repaid or restored, but the sinner "must pay back more than he took, in proportion to the insult which he has inflicted" (I.11). Repayment and compensation are required for the dishonor done to God. Third, since (1) the payment must be in proportion to the size of the sin and (2) the size of the sin is incalculable, it is impossible for humanity to repay and compensate for the sins committed (I.19–23). Fourth, since God cannot violate the moral order of the universe, he must either punish humanity or accept satisfaction on their behalf (I.24–25). Fifth, satisfaction for sin must be made by a human being, since it is humanity—Adam's descendants—that owes the debt to God (II.8). However, no human

---

[17]The satisfaction theory is found in earlier writers like Tertullian (second century), Hilary of Poitiers (fourth century), and Athanasius (fourth century). See, e.g., Tertullian, *On Modesty*, ANF 4, 203. Cf. Robert D. Culver, "The Doctrine of Atonement before Anselm," *Global Journal of Classical Theology* 4 (2004), accessed October 7, 2020, https://www.globaljournalct.com/the-doctrine-of-atonement-before-anselm/. References in parentheses are from Anselm's *Why God Became Man*.
[18]We are drawing from the helpful summary given by James Beilby and Paul R. Eddy, "The Atonement: An Introduction," in *The Nature of the Atonement*, ed. James Beilby and Paul R. Eddy (Downers Grove: InterVarsity Press, 2006), 15–16.

being is able to repay and compensate for the debt. Finally, the only one able to make satisfaction for the debt owed is one who is both God and man. Only one who is God can give a payment worthy of God (i.e., greater than everything but God himself). Yet, it is humanity that is under obligation to make this payment. Thus, in Jesus the God-man, full satisfaction is made the only way it could have been made (II.6–7).[19] This is a model of the work of Christ that integrates incarnation with atonement, seeking to make sense of some of the most profound mysteries of the faith. It is a view that would hold significant sway in the West and over evangelical thought surrounding the atonement.

Reformation Restatements

John Calvin provides one of the most distinctive and robust treatments of the work of Christ during the Reformation.[20] His account weaves together the person and work of Christ, beginning with a question similar to Anselm's: why did the Mediator have to both true God and true man? In a subtle departure from Anselm's argument, he responds that it was not an absolute necessity that this be the case. Rather, God saw it as best and decreed this course of action (II.12.1). So, *cur Deus homo*, why did God become a man? First, in order to impart to us what is naturally his, namely sonship. More importantly, Calvin notes,

> It was [the Redeemer's] task to swallow up death. Who but the Life could do this? It was his task to conquer sin. Who but very Righteousness could do this? It was his task to rout the powers of world and air. Who but a power higher than world and air could do this? Now where does life or righteousness or lordship and authority of heaven lie but with God alone? (II.12.2)

---

[19]Anselm also points out that if a human or angel made atonement for humanity, then we would be in debt slavery to that creature. But it is not proper for human beings to be slaves to anyone except God (see I.5).

[20]We use Calvin's account because of its richness, clear resonances with Anselm (and the tradition), and its influence over subsequent treatments. Other Reformation-era statements could be cited, such as the Augsburg Confession and Thirty-Nine Articles, which view Christ's death as a sacrifice that reconciles the Father to us and takes away our original sin and actual sins (Article 3). Cf. The Formula of Concord (Section 3 on "The Righteousness of Faith") and The Book of Common Prayer (Litany) References in parentheses are from Calvin, *Inst.*

Therefore, the Mediator had to be God himself.

Why did the Mediator have to be a man? Since it was humanity that became lost through its disobedience, it must be a human who "counters" with obedience, satisfies God's judgment, and pays the penalty for sins. Thus, the Son becomes one with sinful humanity to take its place. Calvin concludes, "Since neither as God alone could he feel death, nor as man alone could he overcome it, he coupled human nature with divine that to atone for sin he might submit the weakness of the one to death; and that, wrestling with death by the power of the other nature, he might win victory for us" (II.12.3). While for Anselm, divinity was necessary for the value of the sacrifice, for Calvin it was necessary for the defeat of death, sin, and Satan. Notice, while satisfaction is a central motif, Calvin also includes other key motifs in his doctrine of atonement.

He returns again to the atonement in his discussion of the threefold office of the Mediator—prophet, king, and priest (II.15). It is under the office of priest that Calvin specifically delves into the atonement proper, and his discussion extends into the next two full chapters of the *Institutes*. Christ's priestly office primarily consists in his offering a sacrifice that obtains God's favor and appeases God's wrath toward sinners. Christ's death is an "expiation" (II.15.6). Commenting on the book of Hebrews' depiction of Christ's ministry, Calvin writes, "The priestly office belongs to Christ alone because by the sacrifice of his death he blotted out our own guilt and made satisfaction for our sins" (II.15.6). Notice he, like Anselm (and others) before him, uses the language of satisfaction to describe the meaning of Christ's death. His focus, however, is not on the restoration of divine honor or debt, but on guilt and the need for a sacrifice to satisfy God's just judgment on sinners.

The atonement is an act of divine love: "In a marvelous and divine way he loved us even when he hated us" (II.16.4). God loves those he created, and thus seeks to rescue them. How, specifically, has Christ accomplished this? "By the whole course of his obedience" (II.16.5). In other words, Christ's whole life was atoning, from birth to death to resurrection and ascension. Calvin illustrates this point, for example, by showing that even Jesus's trial before Pilate and his conviction in a human court was part of the act of atoning. Nonetheless, it is Christ's death that takes center stage since it is the culmination of the obedient life and, according to Scripture, the chief means by which satisfaction is made. Christ's death on the cross means that he bore the curse of the law for us (Deut 21:23;

Gal 3:13–14). The cross also spells Christ's victory over the powers (Col 2:14–15). Christ is our redemption, ransom, and propitiation—but only as he is a sacrificial victim. His blood is a satisfaction as well as a "laver"—it appeases God's wrath and also cleanses us (II.16.6). It destroys the power of death and mortifies the power of the flesh (II.16.7). In the cross, Christ experiences the torments of God-forsakenness—his "descent into hell"—so that we do not have to (II.16.10). We can see that Calvin has a robust vision of the atoning work of Christ. While his focus is on the substitutionary death of Christ as sin-bearer, he wants us to see that the whole person (or history) of the God-man is atoning and this atonement has a number of dimensions.

Early Evangelical Preaching on the Atonement

One of the most important influences on evangelicals, John Wesley, did not have a systematic theory of the atonement.[21] However, he was clearly an advocate of penal substitution. He writes, "The voluntary passion of our Lord appeased the Father's wrath, obtained pardon and acceptance for us, and, consequently, dissolved the dominion and power which Satan had over us through our sins."[22] While there are Christus Victor themes present, Wesley's emphasis is on the removal of guilt and wrath, which thus frees us from the power of Satan. Elsewhere he claims that Christ's death is "a full, perfect and sufficient sacrifice, oblation and satisfaction for the sins of the whole world."[23] Wesley avoided debates between Calvinists and Socinians and the accompanying atonement theories like those of Hugo Grotius and John Owen, preferring rather to keep his treatment rooted to Scripture and the Anglican Prayer Book.[24] According to passages like Rom 3:25, the atonement is an act of retributive justice meant "to appease an offended God."[25] Christ

---

[21]See Darren Cushman Wood, "John Wesley's Use of the Atonement," *The Asbury Journal* 62, no. 2 (2007): 55–70.

[22]John Wesley, *Explanatory Notes on the New Testament*, Col 1:14, accessed October 7, 2020, http://wesley.nnu.edu/john-wesley/john-wesleys-notes-on-the-bible/notes-on-st-pauls-epistle-to-the-colossians/#Chapter+I.

[23]John Wesley, *The Works of John Wesley: Sermons 71–111*, ed. Albert C. Outler, Works of John Wesley 3 (Nashville: Abingdon, 1986), 93.

[24]Alan C. Clifford, *Atonement and Justification: English Evangelical Theology 1640–1790: An Evaluation* (Oxford: Oxford University Press, 1990), 133–4.

[25]Wesley, *Explanatory Notes* on Rom 3:25.

satisfied God's judgment by being a propitiation for our sins through his blood. Justice, which reflects God's character, demands that sin be punished. The punishment we deserve is enacted on Christ. Yet, the cross is also the supreme act of God's love toward us. Thus, in the cross God's "attributes harmonize; every attribute is glorified, and not one superseded no, nor so much as clouded."[26] Wesley, however, is hesitant to make Christ's active obedience a key feature in his understanding of the atonement.[27] One of his concerns, as always, is practical. Certainly, Christ's atoning work is the only grounds and starting point for holy living. Full pardon for sin is the foundation for a pious life. Yet, if Christ fulfilled the law for us, what is left for us to do? Motivation for holy living is undermined.[28] Nevertheless, one writer places Wesley squarely in the tradition of John Calvin, even claiming that he is more Calvinist than puritans like John Owen.[29]

Jonathan Edwards's reflections on the atonement are found scattered throughout his sermons and theological notebooks (his "Miscellanies").[30] In an important entry in his notebook entitled "The Necessity of Satisfaction" (Miscellanies 779), he outlines to some degree the logic of the atonement. First, justice requires that sin be punished and punished in proportion to the heinousness of the crime. Thus, "God should punish all sin with infinite punishment; because all sin, as it is against God, is infinitely heinous, and has infinite demerit, is justly infinitely hateful to him, and so stirs up infinite abhorrence and indignation in him." God must punish sin in this way unless there can be "some answerable repentance and sorrow" or "other compensation" made. Since there is no amount of repentance answerable to the crime, there is the need for satisfaction.

---

[26]Wesley, *Explanatory Notes* on Rom 3:26.

[27]Harald Lindstrom, *Wesley and Sanctification: A Study in the Doctrine of Salvation* (Nappanee: Francis Asbury Press, 1998), 73. Wesley also observes that Christ's obedience for us is not "expressly asserted" in Scripture (Wesley, "Letter to James Hervey—Oct 15, 1756," *Letters*, vol. 3). See Wood, "Wesley's Use of the Atonement," 61.

[28]We may even see this practical concern in his preference for sacrificial rather than forensic imagery, believing that the former stimulates piety better than the latter. See Wood, "Wesley's Use of the Atonement," 59–61.

[29]Clifford, *Atonement and Justification*, 134.

[30]George Whitefield, as another major shaper of evangelical thought, might also be mentioned here. His treatment of the atonement, though less rigorous, is largely in line with Edwards and the Reformed tradition.

Second, the holiness of God disposes him to punish sin. He must of necessity abhor sin. Third, he must punish sin as a vindication of his majesty, which has been maligned by sin. Fourth, as the Lawgiver, he must assign and enact punishment for the violation of his law. For to violate the law is to violate the Lawgiver.[31] The basic point from this entry is that sin is infinitely heinous and odious to God and must be punished in a manner fitting the crime, unless this other compensation can be made.

Christ is the punishment and compensation needed. Christ offered himself on the cross as an act of love to the elect.[32] "Christ indeed suffered the full punishment of the sin that was imputed to him, or offered that to God that was fully and completely equivalent to what we owed to divine justice for our sins."[33] This is Anselmian and Reformation theology. Divine honor *and* justice must be restored and satisfied, and only Christ could do this. In contrast to Old Testament sacrifices, the sacrifice of Christ is the only sacrifice that is in itself and on its own account acceptable to God.[34] The sacrifices under the law were types that did not really make atonement or procure forgiveness. Christ's sacrifice, by contrast, was holy, propitiatory, and meritorious. It was holy in terms of the thing offered (Christ himself), the "altar" upon which the sacrifice was made (Christ's divine nature), and the act of sacrificing it (giving his life for the sake of God's holiness and justice). The sacrifice of Christ was an act of propitiation; it made satisfaction for "the injury done to God." Christ, of his own accord, offered what justice demanded. He was our substitute and representative, whose sacrifice becomes accepted as our own—as the payment for what the law demands. On the cross he bore the wrath of God for human sin.[35] Finally, his act was meritorious in that it not only satisfied justice, but it also merited God's favor, blessing, and eternal life.[36] Moreover, while Edwards's emphasis was squarely on the death of Christ, he also

---

[31] *WJE* 18:434–49.

[32] *WJE* 20:331.

[33] *WJE* 20:375.

[34] *WJE* 14:443.

[35] He bore wrath in at least two ways. First, he saw more clearly than anyone the extent of God's hatred for sin and the punishment required. This would have caused great anguish of soul to Christ. Second, he endured the effects of God's wrath, especially the Father's anger and forsaking (*WJE* 20:329–34).

[36] *WJE* 14:449–54.

made room for the life of Christ to have atoning significance. He writes:

> I would observe that both Christ's satisfaction for sin and also his meriting happiness by his righteousness were carried on through the whole time of his humiliation. Christ's satisfaction for sin was not only by his last sufferings, though it was principally by them. But all his sufferings, and all the humiliation that he was subject to, from the first moment of his incarnation to his resurrection, were propitiatory or satisfactory.[37]

The sufferings of Christ, as the substitute and representative of humanity, were propitiatory and meritorious. His obedience to God's law and obedience to the Father's will (that he act as Mediator) were all atoning in Edwards's view.[38]

The main line of Edwards's thinking on the atonement is consistent with Anselm, Calvin, and other early evangelical preachers like Wesley and Whitefield. However, Edwards has been charged with holding to a governmental view of the atonement because of a few statements within his corpus.[39] Some of his heirs, claiming him as their father, propounded this view—that God punishes Christ to demonstrate the heinousness of sin and uphold the moral order, rather than as a penal substitute.[40] This was reflective of an

---

[37] WJE 9:306. Edwards may have expressed some dissatisfaction with the traditional Reformed distinction between active and passive obedience, if that meant that the latter brought satisfaction while the former was meritorious. He sees active and passive as both propitiatory *and* meritorious. See discussion in Michael J. McClymond and Gerald R. McDermott, *The Theology of Jonathan Edwards* (New York: Oxford University Press, 2011), 251.

[38] "All his sufferings from the beginning were propitiatory, as every act of obedience was meritorious" (Misc 497, WJE 13:539–40); "Though the redemption of Christ does consist in his positive righteousness as much as his propitiation, he entered into the holiest of all with his whole ransom, or price of redemption; but half of this consisted in his obedience" (Misc 845, WJE 20:66).

[39] For example, Edwards writes, "The justice of God obliges him to punish sin: for it belongs to God as the supreme Rector of the universality of things, to maintain order and decorum in his kingdom, and to see to it that decency and right takes place at all times, and in all cases ... [T]herefore, his justice naturally disposes him to punish sin as it deserves" (WJE 18:437).

[40] B. B. Warfield lists Joseph Bellamy, Samuel Hopkins, John Smalley, Stephen West, Jonathan Edwards Jr., and Nathanael Emmons among these heirs. He further claims that the Grotian theory was not only a popular view among Calvinist churches but was also prevalent in Wesleyan Methodist churches in the UK and the United

already-present impulse among the heirs of evangelicalism to shift the focus from substitution, sacrifice, and wrath to other mediating models for the atonement. In fact, the late eighteenth and the entirety of the nineteenth century saw numerous attempts to find alternatives to the popular evangelical conception of the atonement, particularly coming from the outskirts of evangelicalism. Apart from governmental theories, other alternatives included the related theory of moral influence advocated by Horace Bushnell (1802–1876), the representative flesh model of Edward Irving (1792–1834), and the vicarious repentance model of John McLeod Campbell (1800–1872).[41] These were attempts to account for the atonement without the need for penal or retributive justice inflicted upon Jesus as our substitute. Nevertheless, the quest for alternatives to penal substitution notwithstanding, B. B. Warfield, in a 1902 lecture, sums up the place of this model within the evangelical world at the turn of the twentieth century:

> It has not been lost from the hearts of the Christian community. It is in its terms that the humble Christian everywhere still expresses the grounds of his hope of salvation. It is in its terms that the earnest evangelist everywhere still presses the claims of Christ upon the awakened hearer. It has not even been lost from the forum of theological discussion. It still commands powerful advocates wherever vital Christianity enters academic circles.[42]

Mainstream evangelicalism (if we can call it that) remained committed to penal substitution as the model that best captures the work of Christ. Yet, as Warfield would also note, this search for

---

States ("Atonement," in *The Works of Benjamin B. Warfield*, vol. 9, *Studies in Theology* (Grand Rapids: Baker, 2003), 275). See also Oliver D. Crisp, "The Moral Government of God: Jonathan Edwards and Joseph Bellamy on the Atonement," in *After Jonathan Edwards: The Courses of the New England Theology*, ed. Oliver D. Crisp and Douglas A. Sweeney (New York: Oxford University Press, 2012), 82–90.

[41] Horace Bushnell, *The Vicarious Sacrifice: Grounded in Principles of Universal Obligation* (New York: C. Scribner, 1866); Edward Irving, *The Doctrine of the Incarnation Opened in Six Sermons* in *The Collected Writings of Edward Irving*, vol. 5 (London: Alexander Strahan, 1865), 3–446; John McLeod Campbell, *The Nature of the Atonement* (London: Macmillan, 1873).

[42] B. B. Warfield, "Modern Theories of the Atonement," in *Works* 9:287. One such academic defender is Charles Hodge (1797–1878). See, e.g., Charles Hodge, *Systematic Theology* (Peabody: Hendrickson, 1999), 2:464–543.

nonpenal models would continue in full force into the next century (and beyond).[43]

Current Challenges: Mixed Metaphors and a Nonviolent Cross

It is not an overstatement to say that the history of evangelical atonement talk in the twentieth and twenty-first centuries is a history of relativizing and rejecting penal substitution. Certainly, there have been able defenders of penal substitution in almost every decade of this period, but much of the scholarly energy has been directed toward rethinking atonement.[44] Kevin Vanhoozer helpfully outlines three "waves" of debate in these centuries.[45] The first saw penal substitution as somewhat of a dividing line between evangelicals and liberals. The second, concentrated in the middle of the twentieth century, was focused on exegetical issues and involved debates between biblical scholars like C. H. Dodd, on one side, and Leon Morris and Roger Nicole, on the other. The key issue at hand was what to make of the theme of wrath and the term "propitiation," with Dodd concluding that the key term *hilaskesthai* (normally translated as "propitiate") does not mean "propitiate," but rather "to forgive," "expiate," or "cleanse from defilement."[46] One might

---

[43]Warfield, "Modern Theories of the Atonement," 286–7.

[44]For example, in the 1900s–1920s, defenders included Denney, Warfield, and Bavinck; 1930s and 1940s—Berkhof and Machen; 1950s and 1960s—Morris, Nicole, Murray, and Berkouwer; 1970s—Packer; 1980s—Stott; 1990s—Letham and Blocher; 2000s—Carson and Gaffin, as well as several edited volumes; 2010s—Macleod and Gathercole.

[45]Kevin Vanhoozer, "Atonement," in *Mapping Modern Theology: A Thematic and Historical Introduction*, ed. Kelly M. Kapic and Bruce L. McCormack (Grand Rapids: Baker Academic, 2012), 197. The first wave was a carryover of the previous century and concerned the rationality and necessity of penal substitution. What divided evangelicals and nonevangelicals on the issue was what they did with penal substitution. James Denney, in his able defense of a form of penal substitution, noted that seeing love and justice meet at the death of Christ for sinners is what "divides interpreters of Christianity into evangelical and non-evangelical." This was indeed the case early in the twentieth century. See James Denney, *The Atonement and the Modern Mind* (New York: A. C. Armstrong, 1903); and *Studies in Theology*, 3rd ed. (London: Hodder and Stoughton, 1895), 100–51.

[46]C. H. Dodd, "*Hilaskesthai*, Its Cognates, Derivatives, and Synonyms, in the Septuagint," *JTS* 32 (1931): 356. This conclusion was already reached in his earlier

say that this second wave of debate strengthened the exegetical grounds for alternative evangelical perspectives, while also helping to refine the exegetical foundations of the traditional view. The third wave, our chief concern, involved an uneasiness *among evangelicals* over penal substitution, whether it is biblical and whether it should be the central and defining view of the atonement.[47] The concerns, to a large extent, mirrored those of the broader Christian world in decades past and can be grouped into two categories.[48]

The first is *methodological* and has to do with the Bible's use of metaphor to describe the atonement. The charge against proponents of the penal substitutionary view is as follows: (1) they read metaphors too literally; (2) they do not account for the time-conditioned nature of metaphor—leading us to limit possible metaphors or import our cultural understandings into biblical metaphors; and (3) they do not sufficiently acknowledge the significance of the plurality and divergence of metaphors used in Scripture.[49] These charges lead to at least two conclusions among critics. First, given the symbolic and time-/culture-conditioned nature of atonement language, it is unwise to take judicial and legal imagery too seriously. Second, one cannot make the legal metaphor a totalizing account of the atonement, since there are other (and even contradictory) metaphors, one not more important than the others.[50] Vanhoozer sums up the matter well: "The formal challenge for atonement theory in postmodernity consists in justifying the

work, *The Meaning of Paul Today* (1920). Among the most forceful and definitive responses came in Leon Morris, *The Apostolic Preaching of the Cross*, 3rd ed. (Grand Rapids: Eerdmans, 1965), especially chapters 5 and 6, where he defends penal substitution and propitiation.

[47]See, e.g., D. Tidball, D. Hilborn, and J. Thacker, eds., *The Atonement Debate: Papers from the London Symposium on the Theology of Atonement* (Grand Rapids: Zondervan Academic, 2009); Mark Baker and Joel Green, *Recovering the Scandal of the Cross: Atonement in New Testament and Contemporary Contexts*, 2nd ed. (Downers Grove: InterVarsity, 2006).

[48]For an outline of postmodern concerns, see Kevin J. Vanhoozer, "The Atonement in Postmodernity: Guilt, Goats and Gifts," in *The Glory of the Atonement: Biblical, Theological and Practical Perspectives*, ed. Charles E. Hill and Frank A. James III (Downers Grove: InterVarsity, 2004), 369–73.

[49]See, e.g., Green and Baker, *Recovering the Scandal of the Cross*, 190.

[50]On the issue of metaphor among critics, see Henri Blocher, "The Sacrifice of Jesus Christ: The Current Theological Situation," *European Journal of Theology* 8 (1999): 27; and especially, Henri Blocher, "Biblical Metaphors and the Doctrine of the Atonement," *Journal of the Evangelical Theological Society* 47 (2004): 632–4.

move from many metaphors to one, and from the one metaphor to a single concept."[51] Indeed, in questioning penal substitution, Henri Blocher quips, "Metaphors are used as missiles."[52]

The second concern—closely related to the first—is *theological*. What are we saying about God when we speak of his wrath having to be appeased by the suffering of an innocent? Penal substitution, as mentioned earlier, is seen by some as a form of "cosmic child abuse." The Father comes off as petty and unloving, and demonstrates this by exacting "an eye for an eye."[53] Furthermore, the divine violence that occurs at the cross of Christ becomes a sanctioning of violence in human society.[54]

It is in light of these concerns that several alternative proposals have been put forward by evangelicals, especially in the late twentieth and into the twenty-first centuries. Gregory Boyd, for example, argues that the Christus Victor model—that in the life, death, and resurrection of Jesus God defeated Satan and the powers of evil— is the most fundamental and is able to integrate the others best.[55] This model holds that in the wisdom of God, demonic powers were outsmarted by God by putting Christ to death. Satan and his legions did not realize that Christ's death would be their demise.[56] This view, moreover, is able to make sense of the whole of Christ's life—not just his death—as a victory over the powers. Finally, this Christus Victor view is able to affirm "the essential truth of substitutionary models" without succumbing to the problems of divine retributive justice and wrath. Rather, "Jesus died as our substitute and bore our sin and guilt by voluntarily experiencing the full force of the rebel kingdom we have allowed to reign on earth."[57] God was not inflicting wrath. Rather, the Son freely surrendered himself to evil agents to do with him as they may. In this way, Jesus bears the

---

[51]Vanhoozer, "Atonement in Postmodernity," 371.

[52]Blocher, "Biblical Metaphors," 630.

[53]Vanhoozer, "Atonement in Postmodernity," 372.

[54]See, e.g., J. Denny Weaver, *The Nonviolent Atonement*, 2nd ed. (Grand Rapids: Eerdmans, 2011), 1–12.

[55]Gregory A. Boyd, "Christus Victor View," in *Nature of the Atonement*, 24. He develops this view in his other works, including *God at War* (1997) and *The Crucifixion of the Warrior God* (2017). Robert Webber advocates for a retrieval of the Christus Victor model among evangelicals. See *Ancient-Future Faith: Rethinking Evangelicalism for a Postmodern World* (Grand Rapids: Baker, 1999), 43–67.

[56]Boyd, "Christus Victor View," 36–8.

[57]Boyd, "Christus Victor View," 43.

full consequences of our sin. J. Denny Weaver's *The Nonviolent Atonement* presents a variation of this model called the "narrative Christus Victor" view, which argues that the demonic realities that Christ overcomes (and we overcome as imitators) are societal structures rather than personal beings.[58]

An increasing trend, especially in the twenty-first century, is to give attention to non-Western accounts of the atonement. For example, in some Asian contexts, where the atonement is framed in terms of "honor and shame," Christ's work may be seen as (1) restoring God's honor and remove our shame by (2) Christ supremely honoring God and paying the honor-debt, bearing the shame and alienation we rightly bear so that (3) we might receive the honor of being sons of God. The chief focus of the atonement, then, is social and communal—on God's honor and our shame, with less focus on God's law. The atonement is about repairing the familial and covenantal dishonor and shame caused by humanity's sins. Christ's suffering and death are about saving God's "face," which is a Chinese way of speaking about honor and shame.[59] Other examples speak of the atonement as expressing the "pain of God," as healing our body and souls, as "vicarious service to the family," as cleansing from sin, among other things.[60] Some of these approaches focus on sacrifice and substitution, while others do not. Yet, they all present alternatives to penal substitution, and part of their value is in pointing out that other viable models can and will emerge out of non-Western environments in the way that the penal view emerged from the West.

Perhaps the dominant perspective (or mood) among critics is what can be called a "kaleidoscopic" view. According to this view, the Scriptures present many different images of the atonement and all are vital to capturing the significance of Christ's work. The variety of images derives from the fact that you have different authors

---

[58]Weaver, *Nonviolent Atonement*, 306–13. Cf. Chalke and Mann, *Lost Message of Jesus*.

[59]See Jackson Wu, *Saving God's Face: A Chinese Contextualization of Salvation through Honor and Shame* (Pasadena: WCIU Press, 2012), chapters 4 and 5. Baker and Green present a Japanese version that resembles this account (*Recovering the Scandal of the Cross*, 192–209).

[60]See Simon Chan, *Grassroots Asian Theology: Thinking the Faith from the Ground Up* (Downers Grove: InterVarsity, 2014), 91–128; and Mark D. Baker, ed., *Proclaiming the Scandal of the Cross: Contemporary Images of the Atonement* (Grand Rapids: Baker Academic, 2006), for examples.

addressing different cultural contexts, and trying to show how the atonement addresses different aspects of the human situation. For example, Paul speaks of Christ's work as substitution, sacrifice, reconciliation, redemption, and more, while John speaks of it as illumination and revelation.[61] The New Testament displays an array of voices, none more significant than the other.[62] Joel Green and Mark Baker, in an important volume, raise questions about the penal substitution model, while arguing that the diversity of biblical models (and historical models) signals that there is not and has never been a foundational atonement model.[63] The church's speech about the atonement must be part of a "living tradition," which seeks to articulate the meaning of Christ's work in ever new contexts.[64] Manifold models of the atonement are legitimate as long as they are attentive to Scripture's way of speaking of the atonement and how and why certain terms are used in context.[65] This is why Baker and Green devote a chapter to giving voice to various "contextual" models of atonement, and why a companion volume was produced to further explore the variety of contemporary images.[66] Variety, plurality, diversity—indeed, these are the key words, as they capture the present state and future trajectories of evangelical thought on the atonement.

Ways Forward: Resituating Penal Substitution

The question that continues to hang in the air is: what is the future of penal substitution among evangelicals? On the one hand, this is

---

[61]Joel B. Green, "Kaleidoscopic View," in *Nature of the Atonement*, 167.

[62]Baker and Green, *Recovering the Scandal of the Cross*, chapters 2 and 3. Colin Gunton may be grouped in this category. See his *Actuality of Atonement: A Study of Metaphor, Rationality and the Christian Tradition* (Edinburgh: T&T Clark, 1988). See also Scot McKnight, *A Community Called Atonement* (Nashville: Abingdon, 2007). A recent "conservative" treatment is Donald Macleod, *Christ Crucified: Understanding the Atonement* (Downers Grove: IVP Academic, 2014). Macleod maintains the importance of penal substitution but places it alongside several other interdependent images.

[63]Baker and Green, *Recovering the Scandal of the Cross*, 72–83.

[64]Baker and Green, *Recovering the Scandal of the Cross*, 257.

[65]Baker and Green, *Recovering the Scandal of the Cross*, 259.

[66]Baker, *Proclaiming the Scandal of the Cross*.

an easy question to answer given the proliferation of recent defenses of it.[67] Evangelicalism will continue to be defined in some way by the belief that Jesus paid a penalty for our sins. However, is penal substitution able to integrate some of the concerns of critics and be presented in a more robust way? How might we relate a "legal" account of the atonement to other biblically valid and valuable models?

One recent proposal by Jeremy Treat seeks to integrate penal substitution with a Christus Victor view. Rather than merely asserting a both/and, which is quite common, he argues for "Christus Victor *through* penal substitution."[68] He argues that sin—as hostility toward God—is the main problem facing humanity. Satan, the false king and ruler of this world, "rules through his tempting, deceiving, accusing, death-bringing word."[69] Christ liberates people from Satan by removing the ground of Satan's accusation, namely the problem of sin. Thus, a Christus Victor model requires the penal substitution model (cf. Heb 2:5–18, Col 2:13–15, and 1 Jn 3:4–9).[70] Moreover, God defeats Satan through "Jesus the servant-king who rules through obedience, truth, and suffering—resulting in life."[71] While the whole history of Jesus is redemptive, the decisive point of his kingly victory is at the cross, for that is where sin is atoned for, propitiation occurs, and thus Satan—the false king—is defeated.[72] Kingdom and cross go hand in hand. That which militated against God's kingdom advance—sin and Satan—is dealt with by Christ's death.

What Treat is doing is not merely reconciling falsely dichotomous views (which he does do), but he is placing the (penal

---

[67]For example, Hill and James, eds., *Glory of the Atonement* (several essays); Jeffery, Ovey, and Sach, *Pierced for Our Transgressions*; J. I. Packer and Mark Dever, *In My Place Condemned He Stood: Celebrating the Glory of the Atonement* (Wheaton: Crossway, 2008).

[68]Jeremy R. Treat, *The Crucified King: Atonement and Kingdom in Biblical and Systematic Theology* (Grand Rapids: Zondervan, 2014), 193–226.

[69]Treat, *Crucified King*, 204.

[70]Treat recognizes that he is not alone in making this connection (Treat, *Crucified King*, 193). For example, see Henri Blocher, "*Agnus Victor*: The Atonement as Victory and Vicarious Punishment," in *What Does It Mean to Be Saved? Broadening Evangelical Horizons of Salvation*, ed. John Stackhouse (Grand Rapids: Baker Academic, 2002), 67–91.

[71]Treat, *Crucified King*, 209.

[72]Treat, *Crucified King*, 214–20.

substitutionary) atonement in a broader context—the kingdom story. He is not alone in this. Kevin Vanhoozer, N. T. Wright, and Hans Boersma, for example, attempt to put the atonement in a covenantal context: Jesus bears the covenant curse and fulfills covenantal demands for us to bring us the gifts of God—a new covenant, the promised land, release from exile, the Holy Spirit, and so forth.[73] The penalty for covenant disobedience was exile, a separation from God. Vanhoozer writes, "The shed blood is a sign that God has proved [his] covenantal faithfulness precisely by undergoing the sanctions, legal and relational, for covenant disobedience."[74] Boersma places the atonement in the context of the entire history of humanity and Israel. Adopting Irenaeus's recapitulation view, he presents Jesus as the new Adam and new Israel who relives and redoes humanity's history for the purpose of fulfilling our calling and covenantal obligations. The violence done to Christ on the cross is "penal representation" since Christ is the one person that stands in for all of us, with the emphasis that Christ represents us but does not replace us. The cross comes after a long history of God's patience and is a form of "restorative justice" that leads to shalom; it is God's decisive "No" to evil that makes way for "the eschatology reality of pure hospitality."[75] Other treatments call for greater attention to the Trinitarian context of the atonement.[76] Context, context, context—a cardinal rule of interpretation—applies in our formulations of the atonement. These recent works still point to the fact that penal substitution is key to understanding Christ's work, but it cannot be abstracted or extracted from its broader contexts—biblical or theological.[77]

---

[73]Vanhoozer, "Atonement in Postmodernity," 396–401; N. T. Wright, *Jesus and the Victory of God* (Minneapolis: Fortress, 1992); Hans Boersma, *Violence, Hospitality, and the Cross: Reappropriating the Atonement Tradition* (Grand Rapids: Baker Academic, 2006).

[74]Vanhoozer, "Atonement in Postmodernity," 398.

[75]Boersma, *Violence, Hospitality, and the Cross*, 177–8. He calls his account a "modified Reformed" position (p. 10). It is admittedly difficult to not see substitution in this account.

[76]See, e.g., Adam J. Johnson, *Atonement: A Guide for the Perplexed* (London: Bloomsbury, 2015); Robert J. Sherman, *King, Priest, and Prophet: A Trinitarian Theology of Atonement* (London: T&T Clark, 2004).

[77]Daniel Treier helpfully exhorts evangelicals to frame penal substitution historically, biblically, ethically, theologically, and relationally (*Introducing Evangelical Theology* (Grand Rapids: Baker Academic, 2019), 211–14).

Recommended Reading

Mark Baker and Joel Green, *Recovering the Scandal of the Cross: Atonement in New Testament and Contemporary Contexts*, 2nd ed. (Downers Grove: InterVarsity, 2006).

James Beilby and Paul R. Eddy, ed., *The Nature of the Atonement* (Downers Grove: InterVarsity Press, 2006).

Charles E. Hill and Frank A. James III, eds., *The Glory of the Atonement: Biblical, Theological and Practical Perspectives* (Downers Grove: InterVarsity, 2004).

Leon Morris, *The Apostolic Preaching of the Cross* (Grand Rapids: Eerdmans, 1955).

John R. W. Stott, *The Cross of Christ*, 2nd ed. (Downers Grove: InterVarsity, 2006).

Jeremy R. Treat, *The Crucified King: Atonement and Kingdom in Biblical and Systematic Theology* (Grand Rapids: Zondervan, 2014).

4

"You Must Be Born Again": Conversion

To proclaim Jesus as "the Saviour of the world" is ...
to invite everyone to respond to him as Saviour and
Lord in the wholehearted personal commitment of
repentance and faith.

LAUSANNE COVENANT §3

When people receive Christ they are born again
into his kingdom.

LAUSANNE COVENANT §5

Evangelicalism is characterized, as we saw, by a drive to reach all peoples with the gospel. The chief aim of this drive is conversion to Jesus Christ. To the evangelical mind, there is little more important than that a person walk through the gateway from death to life. For what does it profit a man to gain the world and yet lose his soul? For evangelicals, notes one observer of nineteenth-century evangelicalism, "the vital difference which divided the whole human family into two groups" was whether one was converted or not.[1]

---

[1] George W. E. Russell, *The Household of Faith: Portraits and Essays* (London: Hodder and Stoughton, 1902), 240.

Reflecting on the "uppermost concerns" of evangelicals, Martyn Lloyd-Jones writes, "The evangelical is a man who emphasizes the rebirth: a new beginning, born of the Spirit, new life in Christ."[2] It is not that evangelicals are the only group concerned about conversion. Rather, it is that the concern for conversion so shapes their view of the world, mission, the Christian life, church ministry, theology, and even how one narrates one's own life, that conversionism (as Bebbington calls it) must be identified as a distinguishing mark of the movement. This chapter traces evangelical *thinking* about conversion and how we theologize about it. We begin with a characteristic account of the nature and necessity of conversion from one of evangelicalism's "founders": John Wesley. From there we situate evangelical theologies of conversion historically, before confronting some of the ongoing challenges and suggesting some ways forward.

John Wesley on the Nature and Need for Conversion

In a private encounter between Jesus and Nicodemus, the religious leader, the Lord, tells him that entry into the kingdom is only for those who have been "born again." Nicodemus marvels, and Jesus responds, "You should not be surprised at my saying, 'You must be born again' " (Jn 3:7). This nighttime conversation recorded in John's Gospel served as the basis for significant evangelical preaching and teaching on conversion. In fact, it is said that John Wesley preached on John 3:7 over sixty times between 1740 and 1760.[3] One such sermon, entitled "The New Birth," captures the essence of Wesley's views on conversion, and also encapsulates a broader evangelical consensus on the reality and necessity of conversion. Through this sermon, we will examine how evangelicals theologize about the new birth.

---

[2]D. M. Lloyd-Jones, *What Is an Evangelical?* (Carlisle: Banner of Truth, 1992), 56.
[3]Albert C. Outler, "The New Birth: An Introductory Comment," in *The Works of John Wesley*, vol. 2, ed. Albert C. Outler (Nashville: Abingdon, 1985), 186.

"The New Birth"

Wesley begins his sermon by declaring that there are two fundamental doctrines in the Christian faith: justification and the new birth. He describes the former as "that great work which God does *for us*, in forgiving our sins," and the latter—new birth—as "the great work which God does *in us*, in renewing our fallen nature."[4] While many had written clearly and thoroughly on justification, Wesley saw the need to provide a "full" and "clear" account of the new birth. Thus, he provides an account framed by three questions: (1) what is the foundation, (2) nature, and (3) purpose of the new birth?[5]

Foundation

The foundation of the doctrine of the new birth is the creation of humanity in the image of God. According to Wesley, the *imago Dei* consists chiefly in his "moral image," that is, that we were made reflecting God's attributes of love, justice, mercy, truth, holiness, and righteousness. However, because human beings were not created immutable, they were "able to stand, and yet liable to fall."[6] Hence, humanity fell by a willful act of disobedience, not wanting to be governed by God's will but by their own. As a result, we lost both the love and knowledge of God and became "unholy as well as unhappy." In short, the image of God (i.e., the moral image) was lost and we died spiritually. "In Adam all died" (1 Cor 15:22). Everyone born into the world bears the image of the devil, rather than of God, being devoid of righteousness, holiness, and life. This corruption of our nature, Wesley says, is the foundation of the new birth: "Everyone that is born of a woman must be born of the Spirit of God."[7]

---

[4]John Wesley, "The New Birth," in *The Works of John Wesley*, vol. 2, ed. Albert C. Outler (Nashville: Abingdon, 1985), 187. While these truths may be experienced simultaneously, Wesley, like Calvin and others, believes justification must precede conversion or new birth in our "order of thinking." Cf. John Calvin, *Institutes of the Christian Religion*, III.11.1.

[5]Wesley, "New Birth," 187–8.

[6]Wesley, "New Birth," 189.

[7]Wesley, "New Birth," 190.

Nature

We should not expect to be able to give an exact account of how the new birth occurs. Jesus himself guards against speculation in this matter by pointing Nicodemus to the fact that, although we do not know how the wind "begins and ends, rises and falls," we do know that it does blow. In the same way, the new birth does occur, but precisely how the Spirit works in one's heart is impossible to explain.[8] Nevertheless, we can describe what the new birth is.

To do so, Wesley expands on Jesus's image of natural birth. He notes that before a child is born, he has eyes and ears, but is unable to see or hear. Yet, when he is born, he can see light, hear distinct sounds, and breathe in a new way. In the same way, until a person is born of God, his spiritual senses remain "locked up": he is unable to see and delight in Christ, incapable of truly hearing God's voice, shut out from the knowledge of God.[9] The new birth awakens our spiritual senses; it makes us alive to God. Wesley's summary definition of the new birth is worth quoting in full:

> It is that great change which God works in the soul when he brings it into life: when he raises it from the death of sin to the life of righteousness. It is the change wrought in the whole soul by the almighty Spirit of God when it is "created anew in Christ Jesus," when it is "renewed after the image of God," "in righteousness and true holiness," when the love of the world is changed into the love of God, pride into humility, passion into meekness; hatred, envy, malice, into a sincere, tender, disinterested love for all mankind. In a word, it is that change whereby the "earthly, sensual, devilish" mind is turned into "the mind which was in Christ."[10]

In short, the new birth is the Spirit's work of changing a heart that is dead, corrupt, and opposed to God, and bringing it to life, making it conform (at least in its basic constitution) to the likeness of Christ.

---

[8]Wesley, "New Birth," 191.

[9]Wesley, "New Birth," 192–3.

[10]Wesley, "New Birth," 193–4. Throughout the sermon Wesley quotes or alludes to dozens of Scripture texts, as can be seen even within this definition of the new birth.

Purpose

Wesley lists three main purposes or ends of the new birth. First, without the new birth there could be no holiness. He defines holiness vividly as "the image of God stamped upon the heart"; it consists in having "a continual, thankful love" to God that motivates love for neighbor, fills us with kindness, gentleness, and long-suffering, teaches us to be blameless in the way we speak and conduct ourselves. Holiness is the offering of our whole self as a sacrifice to God. Yet, without the new birth this holiness could not take place, since the new birth is the inauguration of that process of sanctification.[11]

Second, the new birth is necessary for attaining eternal life since, according to Hebrews 12:14, "without holiness no man shall see the Lord." For Wesley, this passage of Scripture is self-explanatory. Unless one is holy—not merely in externals, like attending church, or being generally moral—one cannot inherit eternal life. Holiness is fundamentally love for God and neighbor. Therefore, external acts unaccompanied by such love contribute nothing to salvation. Since the new birth is the foundation of true holiness, it is absolutely necessary for eternal life.[12]

Third, the new birth is required if one wants to be happy in this world, because happiness is bound up with holiness. Wesley quotes the Roman poet Juvenal: *Nemo malus felix*—no bad man can be happy. The reason is that unholy characteristics like envy, malice, and hatred actually make us miserable. Yet our nature is bent toward these traits until we are born again. Therefore, being born of God is essential not only to our eternal happiness but also our present joy.[13]

Some Clarifications

Wesley closes his sermon with three qualifications and one implication of his teaching on the new birth. First, the new birth is distinct from water baptism. Drawing upon the *Westminster Larger Catechism*, which describes a sacrament as containing two parts— an "outward and sensible sign" and an "inward and spiritual

---

[11]Wesley, "New Birth," 194–5.
[12]Wesley, "New Birth," 195.
[13]Wesley, "New Birth," 195–6.

grace"—he argues that the waters of baptism are the visible sign of
the inward work of new birth.[14] Baptism is a human act performed
on the body, whereas regeneration is change effected in the soul by
God alone. Related to this is Wesley's second clarification, namely
that baptism is not always accompanied by new birth. He allows
that the two are always connected in the case of infants, but not so
with those of "riper years."[15]

A third clarification involves the relationship between the new
birth and sanctification. Here Wesley responds to a recent work that
conflated regeneration and sanctification, speaking of the former
as a lifelong process of conforming to Christ's image. For Wesley,
there *is* a lifelong process, but that process is called sanctification.
Regeneration, the new birth, is the entryway to that ongoing
and progressive work of sanctification. Just as a natural birth is
an instantaneous (or occurring over a short time) beginning to
a lifetime of growth, so the new birth happens in a moment and
launches us into the spiritual life.[16]

Finally, Wesley observes that the most caring thing one can do is
relay the message of the new birth to those on a path to damnation.
Thus, he closes his sermon with the straightforward exhortation
to the unregenerate: "You must be born again!" Even if one is
baptized, living an outwardly moral life, attending church regularly,
partaking of the Lord's Supper, praying much, and reading the best
Christian books, the need still remains: you must be born again.
None of these things profit us if we are not born again. It is all
or nothing. So, how should someone respond to this exhortation?
They are to plead to the Lord for the new birth: "Deny whatever
thou pleasest, but deny not this: let me be 'born from above'. Take
away whatsoever seemeth thee good, reputation, fortune, friends,
health. Only give me this: to be 'born of the Spirit'!"[17] Only the
Lord can bring about that necessary change that opens the door to
happiness, holiness, and eternal life.

---

[14]Wesley, "New Birth," 196. See *Westminster Larger Catechism*, questions 163
and 165.

[15]He sees infant baptismal regeneration as in line with Anglican teaching: "It is
certain our Church supposes that all who are baptized in their infancy are at the
same time born again" (Wesley, "New Birth," 197).

[16]Wesley, "New Birth," 198.

[17]Wesley, "New Birth," 199–201.

Significant Evangelical Themes

As a way of summarizing Wesley's account of conversion, we can draw out some themes from his sermon that still characterize evangelical doctrines of conversion, as well as some that will become less common among later evangelicals. Wesley, first, views new birth as among the most important teachings for Christians to embrace, alongside justification by grace. Already in the eighteenth century, Wesley was contending for a form of "born again Christianity." Second, the fall of humanity and the consequent corruption of our natures forms the basis for conversion. A popular twentieth-century gospel tract echoes this sentiment when it says, "Man is sinful and separated from God. Therefore, he cannot know and experience God's love and plan for his life."[18] Original sin—at least in terms of inherited corruption—is the foundational reason we need to be converted. Third, for Wesley the central aim of the new birth is holiness, out of which flows both eternal life and temporal happiness. Holiness is the lynchpin for Wesley, but this will not always be the case for later evangelicals, who tended to focus more heavily on eternal life as the main goal. The question of how baptism relates to new birth was front and center for Wesley in a way that would become less common to future evangelicals. He was writing within an environment where significant Christian traditions held baptism to be regenerative in some sense (e.g., Roman Catholics, Lutherans). The question that lies beneath the surface is whether regeneration or conversion is something we effect, or something entirely reliant upon God when and where he wills. Finally, in the final climactic moments of Wesley's sermon we see the classic evangelical call: be born again! If you want to be saved, you must be born again. The concern here is the salvation of souls. However, it is not so much a call to "make a decision" for Christ, but rather an appeal to seek the Lord who is the only source of the new birth. A sermon on conversion was technically a sermon on regeneration, which represents one aspect of conversion—the divine side of the equation. While we have only looked at a single sermon (not even a treatise), this sermon captures the heart of past

---

[18]"Have You Heard of the Four Spiritual Laws?" Cru, accessed Aug 9, 2020, https://crustore.org/media/Four_Spiritual_Laws_English_.pdf.

and present evangelical thinking on conversion, even if more themes will eventually emerge.

History: The Emergence of an Evangelical View

Evangelicalism, as a distinct tradition within other traditions, has a particular set of emphases as it thinks about the nature, means, and ends of conversion. To better understand what makes its emphases distinct, we will try to situate it within the stream of shifting views on conversion from the early centuries of the church to the mid-twentieth century. Evangelical understandings of conversion did not drop down from heaven; they were hammered out in conversation with past and present articulations of conversion. Thus, we will survey preceding views of conversion, explore the formative periods of evangelical belief—the Puritan and Revival eras—and identify how these early evangelical views were taken up by the heirs of the movement.

The Reformation

When thinking about conversion at the time of the Reformation, our minds might go to Luther's dramatic discovery of the gospel of justification by faith. While this was probably not Luther's conversion, we can learn something of his theology of conversion from it. Unlike the patristic period where conversion was a multistage process culminating in baptism, or the medieval emphasis on renouncing the world and submitting oneself to a monastic rule of life, Luther stressed the unilateral work of God.[19] Conversion was not an ongoing process that required deliberate labors toward becoming righteous.[20] For Luther, the converted life is a life of walking by faith in the justifying God.

---

[19]See, e.g., Anonymous, *The Apostolic Tradition of Hippolytus*, trans. Burton Scott Easton (Cambridge: Cambridge University Press, 1934), §16–23; Leonard P. Hindsley, "Monastic Conversion: The Case of Margaret Ebner," in *Varieties of Religious Conversion in the Middle Ages*, ed. James Muldoon (Gainesville: University of Florida Press, 1997), 31; Saint Benedict, *The Rule of Saint Benedict*, trans. Leonard Doyle (Collegeville: Liturgical Press, 2001), 19–20.

[20]Gordon T. Smith, *Transforming Conversion: Rethinking the Language and Contours of Christian Initiation* (Grand Rapids: Baker Academic, 2010), 64–5.

Calvin also did not leave us much by way of an account of his own conversion. In the preface to his commentary on the Psalms, he writes, "Since I was too obstinately devoted to the superstitions of Popery to be easily extricated from so profound an abyss of mire, God by a sudden conversion subdued and brought my mind to a teachable frame." Calvin from that point received "some taste and knowledge of true godliness."[21] Whether or not this is a portrait of Calvin's own conversion, he does speak extensively about the reality of conversion. He uses three words somewhat interchangeably to describe this reality: repentance, regeneration, and conversion. How he defines these terms gives insight into how he views conversion. To begin, he writes, "I am aware of the fact that the whole of conversion is understood under the term 'repentance,' and faith is not the least part of conversion."[22] Repentance is defined as a turning of one's life to God that arises from fear of him. It is comprised of both the mortification of the flesh (dying to sin) and the vivification of the spirit (being raised to live a holy life in Christ). Both of these—mortification and vivification—happen to us "by participation in Christ." Calvin concludes, "Therefore, in a word, I interpret repentance as regeneration, whose sole end is to restore in us the image of God that had been disfigured and all but obliterated through Adam's transgression."[23] Repentance is regeneration. This repentance is an ongoing "race" that only begins when one is "subdued" by God, but is meant to be carried out throughout life.[24]

What of faith, then? Conversion begins when the Holy Spirit enables faith, which is a "firm and certain knowledge of God's benevolence toward us ... revealed to our minds and sealed upon our hearts."[25] This faith unites us to Christ—enables us to participate in him—resulting in the "double grace" of justification and regeneration.[26] Thus, to sum up: faith brings us into union with Christ, from which repentance (i.e., mortification and vivification) arises. Repentance is synonymous with regeneration and conversion,

---

[21]John Calvin, *Calvin's Commentaries—Volume 4: Joshua/Psalms 1–35*, trans. Henry Beveridge and James Anderson (Grand Rapids: Baker, 2003), xlii.
[22]Calvin, *Institutes*, III.3.5, 597.
[23]Calvin, *Institutes*, III.3.9, 601.
[24]Calvin, *Institutes*, III.3.9, 601–2.
[25]Calvin, *Institutes*, III.2.7.
[26]Calvin, *Institutes*, III.11.1, 725.

which result in the gradual restoration of the full image of God to humanity. In Calvin, conversion is a process not a point, even though the process must obviously begin at some point.

Anabaptist thinking on conversion focused chiefly on the transformation of one's life that springs from faith. Their teaching was often formulated in conversation with their (and others') theology of baptism. The following from Menno Simons's *The New Birth* captures the heart of their concerns:

> You imagine, moreover, that you were born again in your baptism, and that you received the Holy Ghost. Faithful reader, reflect that if it had so happened to you as you say, you would have to acknowledge that your regeneration took place without the hearing of the Word, without the faith and knowledge of Christ, and without all ordinary knowledge and understanding. You would have to acknowledge besides that the afore-mentioned birth and the received Spirit are altogether without effect, wisdom, power, and fruit in you: yes, vain and dead … Those who have the Spirit of the Lord, bring forth the fruits of the Spirit.[27]

Three central themes emerge from this statement. First, baptism and conversion are not synonymous. In fact, conversion precedes and takes precedence over baptism.[28] Second, conversion takes place only as someone understands and responds to God's word. Third, conversion involves the transformation of the whole person so that they die to sin, are regenerated by the Spirit, and bear fruit to God. Thus, conversion, regeneration, and "amendment of life" were all "a single transaction essential for all true believers."[29] The subtle emphasis in Anabaptism was that conversion was *the conscious decision to follow Christ in a new way of life.*

---

[27]Menno Simons, "The New Birth," in *The Complete Writings of Menno Simons*, ed. J. C. Wenger, trans. Leonard Verduin (Scottdale: Herald, 1956), accessed 9 April 2020, https://www.bluffton.edu/courses/tlc/NislyL/hum2/MennoSimons.htm.

[28]See Schleitheim Confession, article 1 on baptism, in John H. Leith, ed., *Creeds of the Churches: A Reader in Christian Doctrine from the Bible to the Present*, 3rd ed. (Philadelphia: Westminster John Knox, 1982), 284.

[29]George R. Brunk, III and S. F. Pannabecker, "Conversion," in *Global Anabaptist Mennonite Encyclopedia Online* (Scottdale: Herald, 1989), accessed 9 April 2020, https://gameo.org/index.php?title=Conversion.

Of Puritans and Pietists

While many streams, including those outlined above, fed into evangelical conceptions of conversion, the two most significant were Puritanism and Pietism. J. I. Packer observes that Protestants of the seventeenth century regarded the Puritans' careful handling of the doctrine of conversion as one of their unique gifts to Protestantism.[30] A key early work was Joseph Alleine's *An Alarm to the Unconverted* (1672), in which he describes what conversion is not, what it is, why it is necessary, the marks and miseries of the unconverted, directions for conversion, and the right motives for conversion. Conversion is not, according to Alleine, a profession of faith, baptism, moral righteousness, outward piety, or any other form of superficial change.[31] Conversion, rather, is "the thorough change both of the heart and life."[32] He elaborates on the various aspects of conversion as follows:

- The *author* of conversion is the Holy Spirit.
- Free grace and the work of Christ are the "internal" and "external" *moving causes* of conversion.
- The *instrument* of conversion is the word of God.
- The *goal* of conversion is twofold: human salvation and God's glory.
- The *subject* of conversion is the whole life—mind, will, affections, and conduct.
- In conversion, we turn *from* sin, Satan, the world, and our own righteousness, and turn *to* the triune God and the ways of Christ.[33]

After delineating why conversion is necessary and what marks the unconverted, Alleine offers fourteen "directions" or counsel for those seeking conversion. These directions involve acts like meditating on the depth of one's sinfulness and miserable plight, renouncing one's

---

[30]J. I. Packer, *A Quest for Godliness: The Puritan Vision of the Christian Life* (Wheaton: Crossway, 1994), 292.

[31]Joseph Alleine and Richard Baxter, *Alleine's Alarm and Baxter's Call* (New York: Eaton & Mains, 1915), 11–14.

[32]Alleine and Baxter, *Alarm*, 18.

[33]Alleine and Baxter, *Alarm*, 18–48.

sins, treasuring God above all things, "accepting" the offer of Christ for the forgiveness of sins, resolving to follow God's law without turning back, being fervent in prayer for conversion, and forsaking all forms of temptation.[34] "Thus have I told thee what thou must do to be saved," concludes Alleine. "Be doing, and the Lord will be with thee."[35] In many ways, while predating evangelicalism proper, Alleine's tract is the classic evangelical treatise on conversion. Wesley's sermon, with which we opened, follows a quite similar pattern, although it is more succinct.[36]

In one influential strand of Pietist thought—the Moravians— we can trace another line of thinking on conversion. In Moravian thought, the climax of the conversion experience is when a person comes to rest on God's grace alone and no longer lean on his or her own power.[37] Conversion is not the beginning of a process in which one grows in holiness. Rather, it is initiation into a life in which one grows in greater awareness and appreciation of the gracious benefits of the cross of Christ. We never overcome sin in any meaningful sense.[38] But the truly converted rest in the fact of Christ's overcoming on our behalf and meditate on the truth of our justification by his blood.

The Revival Generation

Reformation, Puritan, and Pietist streams converged in the eighteenth century to form what we recognize as the evangelical tradition. The conversion theologies of these antecedent traditions would exert a great influence on how evangelicals envisaged conversion. The three towering figures at the "founding" of

---

[34]Alleine and Baxter, *Alarm*, 117–37. We see similar directions in Richard Baxter's *A Call to the Unconverted*, where he provides ten directions for conversion.

[35]Alleine and Baxter, *Alarm*, 137–8.

[36]What does not come out in Alleine's treatment is the issue of assurance of salvation. According to much Puritan thinking, assurance is not the common experience of every Christian, and thus not part of the conversion process, as some later evangelical writers and practitioners will propound. See Packer, *Quest for Godliness*, 182. One writer argues that premature assurance was a sign that one was in fact *not* a true convert. See Edmund S. Morgan, *Visible Saints: The History of a Puritan Idea* (New York: New York University Press, 1963), 69–71.

[37]Gisela Mettele, "Constructions of the Religious Self: Moravian Conversion and Transatlantic Communication," *Journal of Moravian History* 2 (2007): 24–31.

[38]Mettele, "Constructions of the Religious Self," 10.

evangelicalism—John Wesley, George Whitefield, and Jonathan Edwards—helped shape evangelical thought on conversion through their analysis of the experiences of those to whom they brought the message of salvation. Now, while the contributions of Whitefield and Wesley are worthy of exploration, Jonathan Edwards was likely the most influential and careful thinker on the nature of conversion in the eighteenth century.[39] In 1737, he published a wildly popular account of the mini-revivals he experienced in Northampton (between 1734 and 1735), entitled *A Faithful Narrative of the Surprising Work of God in the Conversion of Many Hundred Souls in Northampton, and the Neighbouring Towns and Villages of Hampshire in New-England*. In this work, he carefully describes the beginnings, nature, dangers, and effects of the revivals in his area. Of particular note, however, are the descriptions he gives of the way people experienced conversion. Taking account of about three hundred recent conversions, he attempts to give an accurate picture of what preceded, accompanied, and resulted from these conversions. Toward the end of the work, he highlights two particular examples in order to give a clearer idea of how God had been working—a young woman named Abigail Hutchinson and a 4-year-old named Phebe Bartlet. Though differing in some details, the pattern of their conversions is remarkably similar. Even in the 4-year-old, we see the pattern of first hearing the word of God, an awakening to the things of God, a recognition of her own sinfulness, a despairing of God's wrath, and the breakthrough of salvation, which is evidenced by rapturous joy in God, confidence in God's saving grace, love for God, and a deep concern for others' souls.[40]

Conversions, as Edwards described them, followed a general threefold pattern: (1) a conviction of sin that is experienced as either a fear of judgment or misery; (2) a sense of despair induced by this fear of damnation; (3) feelings of joy due to having one's sins forgiven.[41] Yet, while there was certainly a pattern to the work of God in conversion, Edwards was resistant to fixing any pattern in stone. He writes, "There is a vast difference, as has been observed, in the degree, and also in the particular manner of persons'

---

[39]C. C. Goen, "Editor's Introduction," *WJE* 4:27.
[40]See *WJE* 4:191–9 (Hutchinson) and 4:199–205 (Bartlet).
[41]Goen, "Editor's Introduction," 28–9.

experiences, both at and after conversion." He goes on, "There is an endless variety in the particular manner and circumstances in which persons are wrought on, and an opportunity of seeing so much of such a work of God will shew that God is further from confining himself to certain steps, and a particular method, in his work on souls, than it may be some do imagine."[42] These remarks are critical because later evangelists would ignore these and other cautions from Edwards and make his "morphology" of conversion and the experiences of Hutchinson and Bartlet, in particular, the "templates for how many others would picture the normative spiritual journey."[43] Indeed, for some, the inability to express one's conversion according to the pattern found in *Faithful Narrative* would be a sign that they are not converted.[44]

An additional characteristic of Edwards's and early evangelical thinking on conversion was what some have called "preparationism," that is, the idea that certain steps can be taken to make someone ready for conversion. The belief was that, while we cannot effect or anticipate the regenerating work of the Spirit, we should prepare our hearts for salvation through introspective meditation.[45] The notion is drawn from Old Testament texts that call Israel to "prepare" their hearts, typically in the case of readying oneself for worship. In the New Testament, Paul speaks of the law as a schoolmaster preparing us for Christ (Gal 3:24) and as that which awakens him to the reality of his sin and need for the Christ (Rom 7:7–12). The story of the Prodigal Son also provides a paradigm for conversion: the son becomes conscious of sin, grows in his awareness of his lost estate, and resolves to seek his father. His desperation in light of his plight drives him to submit to his father's will.[46] There is a delicate balance here between the belief that only the Spirit changes hearts when and where he wills, and yet that there is a human role in conversion.

---

[42]He adds, "The work of God has been glorious in its variety, it has more displayed the manifoldness and unsearchableness of the wisdom of God" (*WJE* 4:185).

[43]Mark A. Noll, *The Rise of Evangelicalism: The Age of Edwards, Whitefield and the Wesleys* (Downers Grove: InterVarsity, 2003), 92.

[44]Goen, "Editor's Introduction," 29.

[45]Norman Pettit, *The Heart Prepared: Grace and Conversion in Puritan Spiritual Life*, 2nd ed. (Middletown: Wesleyan University Press, 1989), 2.

[46]Charles Lloyd Cohen, *God's Caress: The Psychology of Puritan Religious Experience* (Oxford: Oxford University Press, 1986), 77–9.

While we are called to prepare our hearts, and "turn or burn," we also must wait upon God to change us.[47]

In the summer of 1740, Edwards preached a sermon that aimed to establish that "there is such a thing as conversion."[48] The sermon entitled "The Reality of Conversion" was a reflection on Jesus's conversation with Nicodemus in John 3:10–11, where Jesus affirms in the strongest terms the reality and necessity of conversion. In the first part of the sermon, Edwards establishes through reason, Scripture, tradition, and experience that there is such a thing as conversion. His most extensive appeal is to the lives of notoriously wicked people and the martyrs. He argues that the change that occurred in them must have been supernatural, so much so that (in the latter case) people were willing to die for a God they had never seen. What else but the miracle of conversion could account for such devotion?[49] As interesting as that line of argument may be, what is most striking is Edwards's "Application" section, where he offers no less than seventeen "directions" to prepare for conversion and three exhortations on how to use the directions. He advises against "halting between two opinions" and self-flattery, encourages moral reform, and calls people to make the most of every opportunity and means.[50] Edwards concludes the sermon saying, "If you follow these directions, in all probability, you will be converted."[51] No method or procedure can guarantee conversion, but they can put you in the "way of God" and make conversion highly likely. In offering directions for conversion, Edwards was following a practice common among New England Puritans. Yet, this aspect of Edwards's theology of conversion will be transmuted and altogether abandoned by later generations of evangelicals.

---

[47]"There is no remedy, but thou must either turn or burn" (Alleine and Baxter, *Alarm*, 69).

[48]Jonathan Edwards, "The Reality of Conversion," in *The Sermons of Jonathan Edwards: A Reader*, ed. Wilson H. Kimnach, Kenneth P. Minkema, and Douglas A. Sweeney (New Haven: Yale University Press, 1999), 83.

[49]Edwards, "Reality of Conversion," 84–90.

[50]Edwards, "Reality of Conversion," 92–103.

[51]Edwards, "Reality of Conversion," 104.

Nineteenth-Century Developments

Toward the end of the eighteenth century and into the nineteenth century there would be an increasing move away from aspects of the religion of Wesley, and especially of Whitefield and Edwards. There was a particular distaste for traditional Calvinism and its (apparent) overemphasis on divine agency in conversion, to the neglect of the human agent. During this period of widespread religious fervor known as the Second Great Awakening, ministers adopted "new measures" to help facilitate conversions. These new measures involved revival or camp meetings that lasted days, which involved dramatic preaching for conversion, sustained prayer, and, most notoriously, the anxious bench. The meetings tended to be emotionally charged and pressure filled, which would increase the likelihood of decisions to follow Christ. The anxious bench, in particular, was typically a pew (or set of pews) situated at the front of the meeting. Those moved by the preacher's sermon were urged at the end of the sermon to make an immediate response by coming to the anxious bench in full view of the congregation, where they would receive more exhortation, counsel, and prayer. It was thought that this technique (along with the others) would reduce procrastination and facilitate quicker decisions, and increase revival momentum as more and more people witnessed conversions happening right before their eyes.[52] Following eighteenth-century preachers like Edwards, they gave "directions" for conversion, but sought to increase the effectiveness of these directions by carefully managing the setting, ethos, and timing in which these directions would be followed to their proper conclusion—instantaneous conversion.

A figure that well represents these theological and practical shifts is the nineteenth-century revivalist, Charles Grandison Finney (1792–1875).[53] Finney believed that, by prescribing certain directions and establishing a particular pattern for conversion, preachers

---

[52]John Wolffe, *The Expansion of Evangelicalism: The Age of Wilberforce, More, Chalmers and Finney* (Downers Grove: InterVarsity, 2007), 73–6.

[53]Admittedly, Finney is an extreme form of these new tendencies, but because his influence was/is so pervasive he deserves our attention. It is worth noting that Finney was not alone in employing these methods. Even his more conservative and Calvinist opponents were shifting away from traditional Calvinism and using these devices in their contexts. See Wolffe, *Expansion of Evangelicalism*, 74.

like Edwards unwittingly inculcated a passivity in anxious sinners toward their own conversion. Rather than immediately responding to God, potential converts delayed as they waited to experience the prescribed pattern for conversion.[54] Instead, for Finney, conversion is sudden, immediate, instantaneous. The anxious bench was a place where one publicly expresses their determination to follow Christ, and sincere prayer would be the means of effecting the immediate conversion. In this way, the bench and prayer functioned like baptism—the means of initiating one into the faith.[55]

Another important nineteenth-century shift, already hinted at in Finney, was toward the centrality of the "sinner's prayer" to evangelical notions of conversion. What is the sinner's prayer? It is a short heartfelt prayer expressing penitence, faith in God's promise of salvation, and a plea for saving mercy. Once prayed sincerely, the anxious sinner could be assured of his salvation.[56] What is important is that prayer shifted from being a preparation for saving faith to becoming the act of faith itself.[57] Conversion came to be seen as a decision, not a process, brought about instantly in an act of prayer. As one expert puts it, "The sinner's prayer thus made conversion more punctual; that is, it tended to collapse the process to one point."[58] The prominence of the sinner's prayer among evangelicals was a gradual development. Nevertheless, it would become the predominant mode of expressing and effecting conversion in the next century and even into the twenty-first century.

Challenges: Lingering Tension Points

The revivalism (i.e., the stress on individual response to the gospel call) in the nineteenth century that became concretized in institutions, churches, and parachurches exerted a heavy influence on twentieth- and twenty-first-century evangelical thought on conversion. Revivalism's emphasis on personal ownership of the

---

[54]Lincoln A. Mullen, *The Chance of Salvation: A History of Conversion in America* (Cambridge: Harvard University Press, 2017), 29–30.
[55]Mullen, *Chance of Salvation*, 31. See Charles G. Finney, *Lectures on Revivals of Religion*, 2nd ed. (New York: Leavitt, Lord, 1835), 248.
[56]Mullen, *Chance of Salvation*, 32–44.
[57]Mullen, *Chance of Salvation*, 42.
[58]Mullen, *Chance of Salvation*, 35.

faith, on not unnecessarily delaying a decision to follow Jesus, its attempt to remove barriers to conversion, and its general optimism that conversion was possible were indeed positive contributions. However, many of the current challenges within evangelical thought concerning conversion are responses to problematic features of nineteenth-century revivalistic doctrines of conversion. We will highlight four ongoing challenges that spring from our evangelical forbears.

Conversion as a One-Time Decision

The crusade evangelism of the twentieth century, characterized by Billy Sunday, Billy Graham, and others, followed much of the philosophy and modes of its predecessors. The point of a great deal of evangelism was to get people to receive or "accept" Christ, ideally right there and then, after hearing and being moved by a powerful gospel presentation. Conversion is a decision that is traceable to a point in time. At least two issues emerge. First, conversion is seen as punctiliar, rather than as a process. Almost entirely lost is the Reformation, Puritan, and early evangelical emphasis on the various processes involved in conversion. Certainly, the process of conversion must begin at some point, but is the beginning the conversion itself? Rather, as J. I. Packer observes,

> Conversion itself is a process. It can be spoken of as a single act of turning in the same way that consuming several dishes and drinks can be spoken of as a single act of dining, and revivalism encourages us to think of a simple, all-embracing, momentary crisis as its standard form. But conversion ... is better understood if viewed as a complex process that for adults ordinarily involves the following: thinking and re-thinking; doubting and overcoming doubts; soul-searching and self-admonition; struggle against feelings of guilt and shame; and concern as to what realistic following of Christ might mean. It may culminate in a personal crisis that will afterwards be remembered as "the hour I first believed."[59]

---

[59]J. I. Packer, "The Means of Conversion," *Crux* 25, no. 4 (1989): 18.

The conversions of the Apostle Paul, or of figures like Augustine, are seen as paradigmatic. Conversion is sudden and dateable. However, this is often not the case for many in the faith, especially those growing up in Christian families (an issue to be discussed later).

Second, and related, conversion and salvation have become conflated. The point at which one gets converted, he or she is "saved." Typically, conversion (and thus salvation) is brought about by praying the sinner's prayer, accepting Christ as your Savior, or inviting Jesus into your heart. Since salvation and conversion are synonymous, and conversion is a one-time past-tense reality, then salvation is something one receives at one time for all time.[60] This thinking has sometimes expressed itself in what some call an "easy believism," the notion that all one needs to do is accept Christ as Savior without any corresponding demand to regularly submit to him as Lord. Once saved (read: "converted"), you are always saved.[61]

Conversion as a Human Act

Within evangelicalism, the notion of a "decision" has become overblown and now dominates the imagination regarding the nature of conversion. To be sure, conversion involves a personal decision: will I follow Christ or not? However, the human action of deciding is not the decisive word concerning conversion. As stated earlier, the evangelical emphasis on choosing to follow Jesus is a gift to the church. Entry into the kingdom is not "of blood" (Jn 1:12). Nevertheless, the stress on human volition can betray an overconfidence in the ability of human beings to respond positively to God. Calls to decision often lack a corresponding emphasis on the need for the Spirit—something characteristic of Reformation, Puritan, and early evangelical preaching on conversion. For example, according to the *Four Spiritual Laws*, probably the most widely used tract in the twentieth century, from the moment the

---

[60]Smith, *Transforming Conversion*, 3–7.
[61]An example of a recent corrective attempt is Matthew W. Bates, *Salvation by Allegiance Alone: Rethinking Faith, Works, and the Gospel of Jesus the King* (Grand Rapids: Baker Academic, 2017). Also see his *Gospel Allegiance: What Faith in Jesus Misses for Salvation in Christ* (Grand Rapids: Brazos, 2019).

person receives Christ "as an act of the will" Christ comes into his life, his sins are forgiven, he became a child of God, and now begins the "adventure" for which he was created. What is noteworthy is that conversion, or faith, is described merely as an act of the will rather than as a work of the Spirit. Hear the facts, believe the facts, and you are converted. Yet, for our forebears, God's work is the main work in conversion, not ours (even Wesley and Whitefield, for example, would agree on this point).[62]

Conversion, Baptism, and Community

A lingering effect of the revivalist tradition on evangelicalism is the disconnection of conversion from baptism. If conversion is seen as an individual decision, a personal and interior act, then a communal and external event like baptism becomes incidental to conversion.[63] To its credit, at the end of the *Four Spiritual Laws*, there is encouragement to attend a Christ-honoring and Bible-preaching church. However, there is no mention of the place of baptism. Perhaps this neglect reflects modern evangelicalism's allergy to seeing anything other than personal faith as being salvific. Baptism can be nothing more than a symbol or sign of a conversion that has already taken place. To say anything more than that would be to attach too much significance to a human work or would approach something like baptismal regeneration. However, it is difficult to avoid the New Testament's close association of baptism, conversion, and discipleship to Jesus. The Great Commission of Matthew 28 calls believers to make disciples by "baptizing them in the name of the Father and of the Son and of the Holy Spirit." When asked how to be saved and experience the gift of the Spirit, Peter proclaims, "Repent and be baptized every one of you in the name of Jesus Christ for the forgiveness of your sins" (Acts 2:38). David Wells points out that in all the conversion narratives in the book of Acts, baptism is explicitly mentioned and performed immediately

---

[62]Related to this is the perennial issue of the *ordo salutis*: does regeneration precede or follow faith and conversion? While there may be disagreement on this issue—roughly along Reformed and Arminian lines—there is agreement among thoughtful evangelicals that the ongoing converted life requires a new birth wrought by the Spirit.

[63]Smith, *Transforming Conversion*, 10.

upon believing in Christ.[64] Moreover, Paul speaks of baptism as that which unites us to Christ in his death and resurrection (Rom 6:3–4). In fact, he is using the term "baptism" to capture the whole of the conversion experience.[65] Thus, while salvation is by God's grace through faith, it is not disconnected from baptism. Rather than speaking of baptism as an expression of conversion, perhaps it is better to speak of it as part of conversion, as a necessary part. We see in the third-century document the *Apostolic Tradition* that baptism was the climax of the conversion experience.[66] A (perhaps) typical evangelical response to framing the matter this way is to ask: is baptism absolutely necessary for salvation? If not, then how is it necessary? The tension—especially for those evangelicals who desire to be more attuned to the sacramental dimensions of the faith—is trying to maintain how something can be necessary while not being *absolutely* (i.e., without exception) necessary.

Baptism not only unites us with Christ, it also incorporates us into the body of Christ. This raises the issue of the community's role in conversion. In the early centuries, the readiness of someone for conversion (i.e., baptism) was established (or confirmed) by the church. Among the Puritans, the truth of one's conversion narrative was affirmed by the community. In fact, among all those groups who hold to some form of first communion or confirmation, the community plays the vital role in completing the initiation of the convert. However, the revivalist strand within modern evangelicalism has loosened the connection between church and conversion. We can become a Christian at a camp meeting, in a football stadium, or on our own, without the mediation of the church, since conversion is a transaction between the individual and God. An unfortunate outcome of this thinking is an overly individualistic approach to Christian growth. Gordon Smith writes, "If the genesis of the spiritual life is largely an individual transaction, then it follows that the rest of the spiritual life is transacted on one's own, in one's own space, on one's own terms."[67] Since the church is superfluous to

---

[64]David F. Wells, *Turning to God: Biblical Conversion in the Modern World* (Grand Rapids: Baker, 1989), 44.

[65]Gordon T. Smith, *Beginning Well: Christian Conversion & Authentic Transformation* (Downers Grove: InterVarsity, 2001), 186–7. See also Douglas J. Moo, *Encountering the Book of Romans: A Theological Survey* (Grand Rapids: Baker Academic, 2002), 113.

[66]Anonymous, *Apostolic Tradition*, §21–2.

[67]Smith, *Transforming Conversion*, 9.

conversion, it then becomes "the dispenser of religious experiences and opportunities that I can take or leave."[68] Perhaps as an extreme reaction to the Roman Catholic dictum that there is no salvation outside of the church—*extra ecclesiam nulla salus*—evangelicals have largely divorced salvation from church. The church cannot be *the* mediator of salvation, therefore it cannot be *a* mediator at all. However, Robert Webber points out encouraging signs that there is a growing shift among evangelicals who want to view conversion not only as *to Christ* but also *into a community*. Conversion is about having one's outlook and lifestyle reshaped by participation in an alternative community.[69]

Conversion of Second-Generation Christians

The notion that conversion is a sudden, one-time decision does not work well when we consider the children of believers. The popular conversion narrative of someone making a sudden and radical decision to follow Jesus out of their old sin-laden life tends to alienate what we might call second-generation Christians or children of believers. As a consequence, these are often led to say things like "I don't have a testimony." Every tradition acknowledges some age of accountability when a child most own the faith. So, are Christian parents to catechize or evangelize their children? Those who hold the former may tend to assume too much of the child's faith and not take seriously enough the child's need to choose to follow Christ. On the other hand, those who hold the latter may too strongly emphasize conversion as punctiliar and thus wait for an event that is atypical for children of believers. Evangelicals must develop ways to speak of the distinctive process of children of believers coming to faith. Both Wells and Smith advocate patience with children's conversions, as these often come with the child's own development into adulthood.[70]

---

[68]Smith, *Transforming Conversion*, 10.

[69]Robert E. Webber, *Ancient-Future Faith: Rethinking Evangelicalism for a Postmodern World* (Grand Rapids: Baker Academic, 1999), 143.

[70]Wells, *Turning to God*, 60–1; and Smith, *Transforming Conversion*, 13–14, and *Beginning Well*, 213. A somewhat related concern is how to understand the conversion of Jews and Muslims, who share some significant categories of thought with Christianity and whose conversions might be viewed as the fulfillment of their own religion. See Wells, *Turning to God*, 97–109.

Ways Forward: Broadening Conversion

We have looked at four challenges and tension points regarding current evangelical reflection on conversion, and more could certainly be mentioned. And while there are challenges, there are also several paths forward for evangelicals, three of which seem especially pertinent.

Conversion in All Its Dimensions

First, we must be more attentive to the multidimensional nature of conversion. Scot McKnight, for example, argues that there are at least six dynamics to conversion from both a biblical and sociological perspective.[71] Gordon Smith describes seven elements of Christian conversion, the first four of which are "internal," while the last three are "external":

Internal:

- Belief: the intellectual component
- Repentance: the penitential component
- Trust and assurance of forgiveness: the affective component
- Commitment, allegiance, and devotion: the volitional component

External:

- Water baptism: the sacramental component
- Reception of the Spirit: the charismatic component
- Incorporation into Christian community: the corporate component[72]

---

[71]Scot McKnight, *Turning to Jesus: The Sociology of Conversion in the Gospels* (Louisville: Westminster John Knox, 2002). He speaks of context, crisis, quest, encounter, commitment, and consequences—all of which occur within a social matrix and are not sequential steps to conversion.

[72]Smith, *Beginning Well*, 138–53.

This is a remarkably helpful and biblical way to frame conversion since the Bible tends to sum up conversion using one or two of these components at a time, but never citing all seven simultaneously. For instance, in Acts 2:38, repentance and baptism are described by Peter as the means to conversion. In Rom 10:10–11, belief, trust, and allegiance are highlighted, while in 1 Cor 12:3, the baptism of the Spirit and incorporation into the body are Paul's emphases. Thus, conversion should not be limited to one kind of action, but should include elements that involve both internal heart and mind changes, as well as external enactments. A tension point for evangelicals will continue to arise from our aversion to "mere externals" having any spiritual value. Baptism does not save, nor does being part of a church. However, these are indispensable elements of what it means to be converted. Again, conversion is not merely an internal change or a decision, even if faith, repentance, and trust are central. Scripture does not divorce the external from the internal: those who are to be Christians must be baptized into the church.

The Telos of Conversion

Along similar lines, what needs to be recovered is an expansive sense of the goal of conversion. In popular preaching, conversion can sometimes be too narrowly focused on getting to heaven and escaping divine punishment. While we never want to minimize those goals, they are insufficient and can breed deformities in our preaching and understanding of conversion. What does the gospel invite us to do? It calls us to believe (Jn 3:16), receive (Jn 1:12), follow (Mk 1:17), become a disciple of (Lk 14:27), and express allegiance to (Rom 10:9–10) Jesus. This range of images for being and becoming a Christian suggests that conversion is quite self-involving and has more than the goal of getting to heaven. What we saw in the preaching of Wesley, for example, was an understanding that the new birth had a variety of aims: holiness, eternal life, and temporal happiness. The notion that we are being called to something like holiness is foreign in many gospel presentations. If the goal of the Christian life is conformity to Christ (Rom 8:29; Eph 1:4), then the goal of conversion can be nothing less than full transformation. According to Jonathan Edwards, love for God is root and fruit of the converted life. What Wesley describes as holiness, Edwards speaks of as love: "The essence of all true religion lies in holy love."[73] While the eschatological orientation of much conversion preaching is welcome (we are, according to 1 Peter 1, born again to hope), this eschatological frame can be bolstered by speaking of the perfecting of human persons and not just of their being rescued from hell.

Clarity on "Process" Language

As we saw, throughout the various eras of the church people have conceived of conversion as some sort of *process*. It is noteworthy, however, that the meaning of the "process" of conversion varies. Is conversion a largely public process of catechesis, scrutiny, and external conformity that culminates in baptism (as we see in a document like the *Apostolic Tradition*)? Is conversion the lifelong process of life change, as we saw in Calvin and even the monastics? Or is it a stage-by-stage process of coming to grips with our depravity and then discovering the goodness of the gospel (as in Puritan and Moravian thought)? Or when we say conversion is a process, do we simply mean that it typically takes someone a good amount of time and a variety of experiences before they decisively become Christians? While from the perspective of one's experience, conversion is a process—requiring walking through certain stages like belief and baptism—from a theological perspective it seems less than helpful to speak of conversion *itself* as a process—especially a lifelong process. If conversion is a new birth, like natural birth it must have a real beginning and culminating point. While we may speak of a "birth process," the birth itself happens over the span of a very short time. The hope of parents is that this newly birthed child will grow into mature adulthood. Yet, that growth process is not a continual birth or rebirth; it is simply growth. Conversion contains several elements, as noted above, yet the event itself is the *beginning* of the Christian life. So, while we do not want to overdo the punctiliar dimension of conversion, it is difficult to see it as anything other than the initiation of a process that began at a certain point in time.

---

[73]*WJE* 2:107.

Conclusion

Evangelicals—past and present—have much to offer the church regarding conversion. The past evangelical emphasis on the need for conversion and the centrality of the Spirit in bringing new birth are major contributions. The call to decision common in modern evangelical preaching is also commendable. In pointing to ways forward, we are not negating these vital contributions, but rather seeking to augment and strengthen the tradition most characterized by the call to conversion.

Recommended Reading

Matthew W. Bates, *Salvation by Allegiance Alone: Rethinking Faith, Works, and the Gospel of Jesus the King* (Grand Rapids: Baker Academic, 2017).

Gordon T. Smith, *Beginning Well: Christian Conversion & Authentic Transformation* (Downers Grove: InterVarsity, 2001).

Gordon T. Smith, *Transforming Conversion: Rethinking the Language and Contours of Christian Initiation* (Grand Rapids: Baker Academic, 2010)

David F. Wells, *Turning to God: Reclaiming Christian Conversion as Unique, Necessary, and Supernatural* (1989; repr., Grand Rapids: Baker, 2012).

5

"You Have Been Saved by Grace": Justification

Jesus Christ ... now offers the forgiveness of sins and the liberating gifts of the Spirit to all who repent and believe.

LAUSANNE COVENANT §4

Salvation is a gift. Accomplished by God at staggering cost, salvation is nevertheless given to us freely. Salvation is the kind of gift that changes us. But first comes the gift, and then comes the change. The gift of salvation comes to God's enemies and changes them into friends. It comes to those who are not God's people and changes them into sons and daughters. This sequence is not reversible. We cannot first work ourselves into God's friendship or family, hoping to gain salvation as a result. Such a salvation would not be a gift. If salvation is to be a gift, it must come first, by faith, and not as a result of works. The doctrine of justification by faith secures and celebrates the wonder that salvation is a gift.

Evangelicals rejoice in the doctrine of justification. It is at the heart of the evangelical experience of conversion. In Bunyan's great allegory, justification is the three Shining Ones stripping the newly unburdened Christian of his rags and clothing him instead with change of raiment—the imputation of the righteousness of Christ. Justification names the receiving of forgiveness, the enjoyment of God's favor, and the hope of glory. Justification is also at the heart of the evangelical story. Martin Luther said, "Here I stand!" And evangelicals have continued to stand with him.

This chapter draws particularly on the work of American pastor-theologian John Piper. John Piper is serious about joy. His 1986 book *Desiring God* taught a generation of American evangelicals that knowing the Bible and serving our neighbor are but means to the all-encompassing end of enjoying God himself. For many years Piper's annual pastors' conferences introduced evangelicals to great figures in the history of Christianity. And his model of preaching as "expository exultation" has captured the hearts of pastors across the English-speaking world. Over the decades Piper has also emerged as one of evangelicalism's most influential exponents of the doctrine of justification by faith. In books and blogs, articles and conferences and sermons, Piper has proclaimed this centerpiece of Paul's gospel and defended it against both criticism and misrepresentation.

Doctrine: Righteousness from God

God considers sinners righteous. That is justification. God does not consider all sinners righteous, but only those who trust Jesus for salvation. That is justification by faith. "God, be merciful to me, a sinner!" says the tax collector. "This man went down to his house justified," says Jesus (Lk 18:13–14). Justification is God's outrageously counterintuitive way of seeing the unjust as just by trust. To trust Jesus for salvation is not to earn salvation, but simply to receive it as a gift.

This section begins by explaining justification by faith as taught in Galatians, including the role of law and good works. We then explore the concept of imputation as well as the relation between justification and three other major elements of a broader theology of salvation: union with Christ, adoption, and sanctification.

Justification by Faith in Galatians 2–3

Paul's Letter to the Galatians is his most spirited declaration of the doctrine of justification by faith. Paul writes this letter because some leaders in Galatia were teaching a doctrine of justification by works, that we somehow obey our way into God's favor. Paul is outraged. He says these teachers have perverted the gospel so badly that it is no longer good news (Gal 1:6–7). Twice Paul threatens them with a solemn "anathema" (Gal 1:8–9)—essentially, "Go to hell!"[1] And for good measure, Paul suggests that these teachers would do well to castrate themselves (Gal 5:12).

The reason Paul is so upset is that this bad-news no-gospel changes the very character of salvation. Salvation as a gift given becomes salvation as a debt paid. As Paul uses the term, "works" are the things that God commands. So, justification "by works" means justification by doing the things God commands. If justification is by works, then sinners first change themselves—they sculpt themselves morally by a program of obedience—and the result is a well-deserved "salvation." This is salvation by achieving not receiving. If the shocking claim of justification by faith is that God considers *sinners* righteous, the sensible claim of justification by works is that God considers the *obedient* righteous. But no matter how sensible, such a salvation is no good news for sinners, and it is no gift. Piper rightly warns us, "If we would have the gift of justification, we dare not work."[2]

In order to counter this no-gospel of justification by obedience, Paul sets his teaching of justification by faith at the center of a salvation graciously given and gratefully received. The gift of salvation begins in the generosity of the triune God. The Father "sent forth his Son" to us (Gal 4:4). Christ "gave himself" for us (Gal 1:4; 2:20). The Father also "sent the Spirit of his Son into our hearts" (Gal 4:6) and now "supplies the Spirit" to us (Gal 3:5, 2, 14). And this abundance of divine self-giving is "so that we might receive adoption as sons" (Gal 4:5). How does one receive this gift of salvation? Again and again Paul insists that the gift of salvation cannot be earned by obedience, but only received "by faith in Christ" (Gal 2:16; 3:2, 5, 8, 11, 22, 24). Faith brings justification and with it all the riches of salvation.

In order to counter the credibility of the false teachers in Galatia, Paul also sets forth the impeccable credentials of the gospel of justification by faith. To begin with, it was not men but Jesus Christ and God the Father who appointed Paul an apostle and preacher of the gospel (Gal 1:1). Moreover, it was not men but Jesus Christ

---

[1]John Piper, "Galatians 1: No Other Gospel: The Formal and Material Principles of the Reformation," in *Christ Has Set Us Free: Preaching and Teaching Galatians* (Wheaton: Crossway, 2019), 36.
[2]John Piper, *Desiring God*, 2003 edition (Sisters: Multnomah, 2003), 171.

who revealed the gospel message to Paul (Gal 1:11–12). (This happened when Paul was persecuting Jesus, murdering Christians, not when he was some hero of righteousness in God's sight![3]) And James, Peter, and John, the leading apostles in Jerusalem, had both acknowledged Paul's apostleship and affirmed Paul's message as the common gospel of the entire Christian church (Gal 2:1–10). The gospel of justification by faith, in other words, is apostolic, dominical, and universal. There are no exceptions.

To prove this point, Paul relates an incident that happened in Antioch (Gal 2:11–14). Peter himself, though he affirmed the doctrine justification by faith, had begun to deny it in practice. He once shared table fellowship with gentile Christians who did not follow the ceremonial commands of the Old Testament. This was practical acknowledgment that God considers us righteous by faith, not because we obey the law. But under pressure from Jewish traditionalists, Peter had stopped eating with gentile Christians. This implied that God considers righteous only those who obey Old Testament law. Could an exception to the universal doctrine of justification by faith be made for Peter? Paul writes, "I opposed him to his face." Paul publicly rebuked Peter and summoned him back to his former practice.

Paul's rebuke of Peter now becomes his rebuke of those in Galatia who are tempted to do like Peter. Justification, Paul insists, is not by obeying, but by believing. "We know that a person is not justified by works of the law but through faith in Jesus Christ" (Gal 2:16). Paul repeats himself for emphasis, "So we also have believed in Christ Jesus, in order to be justified by faith in Christ and not by works of the law." And to make matters perfectly clear, he explains that justification not only *is not* by obedience, but it *cannot* be by obedience: "By works of the law no one will be justified." The principle stands. This climactic, threefold declaration of justification by faith is Paul's public rebuke of those who want to impose obedience to Old Testament law on the churches in Galatia.

Revolutionaries are regularly surprised at how hard it is to run a country. So Paul asks the theological revolutionaries in Galatia to imagine what it would actually be like to run justification on obedience to the law. How "sensible" would it be? In fact, it would be madness. It would be, says Paul, "to nullify the grace of God,"

---

[3]John M. G. Barclay, *Paul and the Gift* (Grand Rapids: Eerdmans, 2015), 356–60.

to refuse God's gift. Why? If justification is by obedience—if we could simply obey our way into God's favor—then "Christ died for no purpose" (Gal 2:21)! If a little obedience could do the trick, the horror of crucifixion is not the right tool for the job. It would be like using a battle axe to slice tomatoes. A paring knife would work better, and an axe-wielding cook we would consider unstable. Even the Galatians' own experience should have taught them that God considers us righteous not when we obey, but when we believe. "Did you receive the Spirit by works of the law or by hearing with faith?" (Gal 3:2). Receiving the gift of the Spirit by faith is proof that God considers us righteous by faith. A little reflection should make clear that the implications of justification by obedience are theologically impossible—a pointless crucifixion?!—and contradicted by experience.

Abraham is Paul's case in point. According to Genesis, Abraham was justified by faith. He "believed God, and it was counted to him as righteousness" (Gal 3:6; Gen 15:6). God made a covenant with Abraham and promised him land, descendants, and blessing (Gal 3:8; Gen 12:3). Abraham believed God's promise, and God considered Abraham righteous. There was no law involved in this transaction. The law did not even exist in Abraham's day (Gal 3:17).

Paul's simple observations about Abraham raise complex questions about the law. If the law did not make the Israelites righteous, why did God give it to them (Gal 3:19)? Paul explains, "The law was our guardian until Christ came, in order that we might be justified by faith" (Gal 3:23). That is, for over a thousand years, the law served to "guard" God's people. Strangely, it did so precisely by condemning them. This happens in three ways. To begin with, the law identifies as sin what we might not otherwise recognize as sin. "Through the law comes knowledge of sin" (Rom 3:20). Again, "I would not have known what it is to covet if the law had not said, 'You shall not covet'" (Rom 7:7; Exod 20:17; Deut 5:21). Moreover, the law actually provokes sin from our rebellious hearts by the mere prohibition of it. "Sin, seizing an opportunity through the commandment, produced in me all kinds of covetousness" (Rom 7:8). In other words, by identifying and provoking sin, "the law came in to increase the trespass" (Rom 5:20; Gal 3:19). Finally, the law pronounces a universal curse on sinners. We may occasionally obey certain laws, but never "all things written in the Book of the Law" (Gal 3:10). The law demands perfect obedience in all things for all our lives. But "no one living is righteous before you" (Ps

143:2; Gal 2:16; 5:4). Even those who want to impose the law on the Galatians "do not themselves keep the law" (Gal 6:13). How then could Christians look to the law for God's acceptance when the law pronounces God's curse? Such a backwardly repurposed law would be a prison and slavery (Gal 3:23; 4:8–11; 4:21–5:1) and leave the Galatians "severed from Christ" (5:4). As Paul explains it, then, the purpose of the law is to identify, provoke, and curse sin! But precisely in doing so, the law also mercifully protects us from the delusion of self-righteousness. It keeps us humble. As a result of the law's guarding, we desperately await "the Deliverer [who] will come from Zion" (Rom 11:26; Isa 59:20), Christ, who "redeemed us from the curse of the law by becoming a curse for us" (Gal 3:13).[4]

If the law's role is to guard us in this sense, what is the role of obedience to the law? What is the role of "good works" in the Christian life? If one purpose of the law is to condemn us for our disobedience, another purpose of the law is to bless us for our obedience. The law is "the embodiment of knowledge and truth" (Rom 2:20). It is "holy and righteous and good" (Rom 7:12). Obedience to God's perfect law is "life and peace" (Rom 8:6; Ps 19:7–8). A major aim of the law is to promote love: "The whole law is fulfilled in one word: 'You shall love your neighbor as yourself' " (Gal 5:14; Lev 19:18). The God of love "has sent the Spirit of his Son into our hearts" (Gal 4:6) to bear the rich fruits of love (Gal 5:16–25). For Christians to live in loving community is to "fulfill the law of Christ" (Gal 6:1–2). Though obedience does not justify us, it is the means to a blessed and well-lived life that reflects our relationship with Jesus.

Justification by Faith in Theological Context

Paul's proclamation of justification by faith in Galatians 2–3 is so triumphant that it can sound like the comprehensive account of the Christian gospel. It is not. Justification is only one element—however vital!—among others in the Bible's teaching about salvation. It is but the signature ingredient in the complex recipe of salvation as gift. To understand justification by faith, we need to survey several more aspects of biblical teaching. We will look first at the means

---

[4]John Piper, *The Future of Justification: A Response to N. T. Wright* (Wheaton: Crossway, 2007), 197–201.

by which righteousness comes to us in justification. This is what is known as imputation. Second, we will trace the connection between justification and the closely related doctrines of union with Christ, adoption, and sanctification.

Imputation explains how it is that God "considers" sinners righteous. Genesis says that Abraham's faith was "counted" or "credited" or "reckoned" to him—that is, imputed to him—as righteousness (Gen 15:6; Gal 3:6; Rom 4:3–9, 22–24).[5] Faith was the occasion for God to impute righteousness to Abraham. The reason is that faith obtains God's forgiveness. When Abraham believed God's promise, God both forgave Abraham's sins and started considering him righteous. This is the crucial, twofold transaction of justification: the nonimputation of sins and the imputation of righteousness. It is both pardon and acceptance.[6] Paul makes a direct identification of this twofold exchange in Romans 4. The person "against whom the Lord will not count his sin" (Rom 4:8; Ps 32:2) is the very same "to whom God counts righteousness apart from works" (Rom 4:6). The "not counting" of a person's sins goes hand in hand with counting that person righteous.[7] "Whenever sins are *not* counted, a positive righteousness *is* counted."[8] In the language of Isaiah, the Lord's servant "shall bear their iniquities" and "make many to be accounted righteous" (53:11).

Our union with Christ explains how God can justly make the twofold imputation of justification. Explanation is certainly required! The Old Testament does not treat sinners lightly. "I will not acquit the wicked" (Ex 23:7). "Woe to those … who acquit the guilty" (Isa 5:22–23). "He who justifies the wicked … [is] an abomination to the LORD" (Prov 17:15). Clearly God cannot simply set aside the law and ignore our sins and pretend that we are righteous. So he

---

[5]John Piper, *Counted Righteous in Christ: Should We Abandon the Imputation of Christ's Righteousness* (Wheaton: Crossway, 2002), 54–7.

[6]J. I. Packer and R. M. Allen, "Justification," in *Evangelical Dictionary of Theology*, 3rd ed., ed. Daniel J. Treier and Walter A. Elwell (Grand Rapids: Baker Academic, 2017), 455–8 (456).

[7]Piper, *Counted Righteous*, 116–18.

[8]Piper, *Future of Justification*, 75, 68–9, 81–3. Cf. Robert H. Gundry, "The Nonimputation of Christ's Righteousness," in *Justification: What's at Stake in the Current Debates*, ed. Mark Husbands and Daniel J. Treier (Downers Grove: IVP, 2004), 17–45; D. A. Carson, "The Vindication of Imputation: On Fields of Discourse and Semantic Fields," in *Justification: What's at Stake in the Current Debates* ed. Mark Husbands and Daniel J. Treier (Downers Grove: IVP, 2004), 46–78.

sends his Son both to render wholehearted obedience to the law and to suffer strict punishment for every violation of the law. Once the law has been perfectly fulfilled by Christ, and sinners are united by faith to Christ, God can justly consider these sinners righteous. As Piper explains, this is how God "acquits the guilty, but is not guilty in doing so."[9] In Paul's terms, this is how God can be "just and the justifier" (Rom 3:26). United with Christ, what is ours (sin!) becomes his, and what is his (righteousness!) becomes ours. "For our sake" God made Christ "to be sin ... so that in him we might become the righteousness of God" (2 Cor 5:21; cf. Jer 23:5–6; 1 Cor 1:30).

Adoption further explains the role of obedience in the life of the justified. The highest privilege of our union with Christ is adoption by God. To be united to the Son is to become a son. It is to be born again as a son. And a true son obeys his father. Obedience does not make us sons and daughters. But it does display the family resemblance to Christ, the perfectly obedient Son, and it conforms us to the likeness of our glorious Heavenly Father (Gal 4:1–7; Mt 5:48; 2 Cor 3:18; Eph 4:24; 1 John 3:2). The Son says to the Father, "I delight to do your will, O my God; your law is within my heart" (Ps 40:8; Heb 10:5–10). And as sons and daughters we too exclaim to our Father, "Oh how I love your law!" (Ps 119:97; 1:1). We plead, "Give me understanding, that I may keep your law and observe it with my whole heart" (Ps 119:34). We pray, "Your will be done" (Mt 6:10). Our adoption is a gift, and our obedience declares and perfects our sonship.

Sanctification, finally, follows necessarily from justification. Sanctification is becoming holy, and Scripture speaks of it both as status and as process. "We have been sanctified" and we "are being sanctified" (Heb 10:10, 14). Sanctification as status, as a past, completed event, is designation for holy purposes. Jesus himself speaks of those who are "sanctified by faith in me" (Acts 26:18; cf. 1 Cor 1:2; Acts 20:32). Paul assures the "saints," that is, the holy ones in Corinth, "you were washed, you were sanctified, you were justified in the name of the Lord Jesus Christ and by the Spirit of our God" (1 Cor 6:11). Sanctification as process, on the other hand, is discipleship, leaving our sins, becoming more like Jesus (Rom 6:10–11). It is the lifelong transformation of sinner to saint. It is

---

[9]Piper, *Desiring God*, 61.

the restoration of the image of God. "Let us cleanse ourselves from every defilement of body and spirit, bringing holiness to completion in the fear of God" (2 Cor 7:1; cf. Rom 6:19–22; 12:2; Col 1:10–11). Union with Christ explains why sanctification always accompanies justification. By faith the Spirit "not only unites us to Christ for justification, but also empowers us for sanctification."[10] Union with Christ includes sanctification as status and initiates sanctification as process.

In theological context, justification highlights the nature of salvation as a gift. The one great gift of salvation includes the gift of forgiveness, the nonimputation of sins. It includes the gift of the righteousness and holiness of Christ. It includes the gift of union with Christ and adoption by God. And it launches us into the life of grateful obedience and spiritual transformation. None of this is earned. All of it is grace. The joyful task of faith is simply to receive.

History: Reformation and Revision

There is a reason why we are not Roman Catholic. That reason is justification by faith, the doctrine at the epicenter of the Protestant Reformation. To tell the story of justification by faith, we begin by surveying the teaching of Luther and Calvin and the Roman response at the Council of Trent. We then note two developments that represent common and opposite misconceptions of justification. Some extreme Pietists argued that justification is to some extent based on our sanctification. Some extreme Lutherans and Puritans argued that, for those who are justified, the law plays no further role in sanctification. We conclude by examining the thought of John Wesley, one of the guiding lights of the evangelical movement, who emphasizes both the priority of justification by faith and the necessity of law and good works in sanctification.

Justification in the Protestant Reformation

Martin Luther is the great champion of justification by faith. He describes it as "the true meaning of Christianity."[11] The reason

---

[10]Piper, *Desiring God*, 70.
[11]Luther, *Lectures on Galatians* 2:16, in *LW* 26:136.

Luther so esteems justification by faith is because he had been taught a false meaning of Christianity: that we are justified by faith *and obedience*. Luther was not sure he had either. In his intense moral seriousness, all he could sense was the enslavement and condemnation of the law. He lived in fear of damnation. But then God opened Luther's eyes to behold wondrous things in Scripture, namely that salvation is a gift, not an achievement. Luther realized that God imputes righteousness to us. When Luther finally saw in Romans that righteousness is "a gift of God," he was euphoric. As he later described his experience, "Here I felt that I was altogether born again and had entered paradise itself through open gates."[12] For the next three decades, Luther dedicated his life to proclaiming this good news. And the Protestant Reformation was begun.

Luther's treatise, *The Freedom of a Christian* (1520), is one of his most exuberant and memorable accounts of the doctrine of justification. Luther follows Scripture closely in identifying the major aspects of justification. It is by faith, based on union with Christ, resulting in a twofold imputation, and flowing out into a life of good works. In Luther's vivid description, it is "the wedding ring of faith" that "unites the soul with Christ as a bride is united with her bridegroom."[13] This union, in which "everything they have they hold in common," brings about a remarkable, twofold exchange. "Christ is full of grace, life, and salvation. The soul is full of sins, death, and damnation. Now let faith come between them and sins, death, and damnation will be Christ's, while grace, life, and salvation will be the soul's." As an overflow of these riches in Christ, Christians do "all kinds of works" in service to the neighbor and in this way "become as it were a Christ to the other."[14] It is vital to note that, for Luther, while justification is not in any way by obedience, justification by faith always results in obedience.[15] As he writes in his *Preface to Romans*,

---

[12]Luther, "Preface to the Complete Edition of Luther's Latin Writings, Wittenberg, 1545," in *LW* 34:337.

[13]Luther, *The Freedom of a Christian*, in *LW* 31:351–2.

[14]Luther, *Freedom*, 358, 365–8; Robert Kolb and Charles P. Arand, *The Genius of Luther's Theology: A Wittenberg Way of Thinking for the Contemporary Church* (Grand Rapids: Baker Academic, 2008), 155–7.

[15]Mark Mattes, "Luther on Justification as Forensic and Effective," in *The Oxford Handbook of Martin Luther's Theology*, ed. Robert Kolb, Irene Dingel, and L'ubomír Batka (Oxford: Oxford University Press, 2016), 264–73.

Faith ... is a divine work in us which changes us and makes us to be born anew of God ... It kills the old Adam and makes us altogether different men, in heart and spirit and mind and powers; and it brings with it the Holy Spirit. O it is a living, busy, active, mighty thing, this faith. It is impossible for it not to be doing good works incessantly. ... It is impossible to separate works from faith.[16]

In other words, faith works![17]

Calvin closely followed Luther's account of justification by faith and set it in a broad, theological framework. Like Luther, Calvin was convinced of the strategic importance of the doctrine of justification. It is, he says, "the main hinge on which religion turns."[18] Calvin places justification as the centerpiece of his account of redemption in Book 3 of the *Institutes*. With breathtaking mastery and comprehensive vision, Calvin traces out how we are united to Christ (*Institutes* 3.1) by faith (3.2), resulting in sanctification (3.3–10) and justification (3.11–19).[19] Calvin conspicuously addresses sanctification first before turning to justification. Sanctification is not an afterthought. Like Luther—and like Paul (Rom 6:1–4)—Calvin, too, wants to make perfectly clear that the Christian life is a striving after holiness.

Christ was given to us by God's generosity, to be grasped and possessed by us in faith. By partaking of him, we principally receive a double grace: namely, that being reconciled to God through Christ's blamelessness, we may have in heaven instead of a Judge a gracious Father; and secondly, that sanctified by Christ's spirit we may cultivate blamelessness and purity of life.[20]

---

[16]Luther, "Preface to the Epistle of St. Paul to the Romans 1546 (1522)," in *LW* 35:370–1.

[17]See also Luther, *Lectures on Galatians* 2:16–17, in *LW* 26:133, 145; *Augsburg Confession* VI; *Smalcald Articles* 3:13.

[18]John Calvin, *The Institutes of the Christian Religion*, trans. Ford Lewis Battles, ed. John T. McNeill (Philadelphia: Westminster, 1960), 3.11.1 (726).

[19]François Wendel, *Calvin: Origins and Development of his Religious Thought*, trans. Philip Mairet (1963; repr., Grand Rapids: Baker, 2002), 256.

[20]Calvin, *Institutes* 3.11.1 (725).

Christ is a gift ("given ... by God's generosity"). And our union with Christ (Christ "grasped and possessed by us") results in the double grace of adoption ("a gracious Father") and sanctification ("blamelessness and purity of life").[21] But all of this comes to us by justification. "Therefore, we explain justification simply as the acceptance with which God receives us into his favor as righteous men. And we say that it consists in the remission of sins and the imputation of Christ's righteousness."[22] Justification, once again, consists of the remission or nonimputation of sins, along with the imputation of Christ's righteousness.[23] It is based on our union with Christ and flows out into a life of joyful obedience.[24]

The Roman Catholic Council of Trent saw things differently.[25] Its language is explicitly formulated against Protestant teaching. "If any one says that the sinner is justified by faith alone, meaning that nothing else is required to co-operate in order to obtain the grace of justification ... let him be anathema."[26] "If any one says that justifying faith is nothing else than confidence in divine mercy, which remits sins for Christ's sake ... let him be anathema."[27] In other words, more than faith is required for justification. "Faith, unless hope and charity be added to it, neither unites man perfectly with Christ nor makes him a living member of His body."[28] Faith requires these additions because justification is understood not as the event that begins the Christian life, but as the entire Christian life. "Justification itself ... is not only a remission of sins but also the sanctification and renewal of the inward man ... whereby an unjust man becomes just."[29] Justification, in other words, is not merely the

---

[21]Barbara Pitkin, "Faith and Justification," in *The Calvin Handbook*, ed. Herman J. Selderhuis (Grand Rapids: Eerdmans, 2009), 294–7.

[22]Calvin, *Institutes* 3.11.2 (727).

[23]Calvin, *Commentary on 2 Corinthians* 5:21, in *The Second Epistle of Paul the Apostle to the Corinthians and the Epistles to Timothy, Titus and Philemon*, Calvin's New Testament Commentaries, vol. 10 (Grand Rapids: Eerdmans, 1996), 81–2.

[24]J. Todd Billings, *Union with Christ: Reframing Theology and Ministry for the Church* (Grand Rapids: Baker Academic, 2011), 26–9.

[25]John W. O'Malley, *Trent: What Happened at the Council* (Cambridge: Harvard University Press, 2013), 107–16.

[26]The Council of Trent, Decree on Justification, Canon 9, in John H. Leith, ed., *Creeds of the Churches: A Reader in Christian Doctrine from the Bible to the Present*, 3rd ed. (Philadelphia: Westminster John Knox, 1982), 421.

[27]Decree on Justification, Canon 12 (421).

[28]Decree on Justification VII (412).

[29]Decree on Justification VII (411).

event of God considering sinners righteous because of Christ but also the process of God making sinners righteous in themselves. Protestants held that union with Christ necessarily involves both the initial event of justification and the ongoing process of sanctification. Rome identifies justification with sanctification, making justification also an ongoing process.[30] And justification (as a process) is also by obedience. Christians, "through the observance of the commandments of God … increase in that justice received through the grace of Christ and are further justified."[31] At the end of this process, Christians merit eternal life. "Those justified … have, by those very works which have been done in God, … truly merited eternal life."[32] In other words, justification is both by faith and by obedience. Salvation is therefore both gift and accomplishment. With the lines of disagreement so starkly drawn, it is small wonder that four centuries would pass before Protestants and Catholics would see any significant progress toward a common understanding of the nature of justification.

Misunderstandings of Justification

In those centuries, while Protestants remained broadly committed to the doctrine of justification, two tendencies emerged that challenged some of its basic commitments. They did so, moreover, in ways that have set the pattern for subsequent misunderstandings of the doctrine of justification.

On the one hand, some extreme Pietists taught that justification is by both faith and a transformed life, a position ironically near to that of Trent.[33] Pietism itself was a remarkable movement of renewal of the seventeenth and eighteenth centuries that emphasized practical Christianity and heartfelt devotion to the Lord. Since Luther's day, generations of Christians had grown up confident that God graciously pardons and accepts sinners who trust Christ for forgiveness. They asked different questions about

---

[30]Ludwig Ott, *Fundamentals of Catholic Dogma* (Fort Collins: Roman Catholic Books, 1954), 250–7.

[31]Decree on Justification X (414), Canon 24 (423).

[32]Decree on Justification XVI (419).

[33]Jaroslav Pelikan, *Christian Doctrine and Modern Culture (since 1700)*, vol. 5 of *The Christian Tradition: A History of the Development of Doctrine* (Chicago: University of Chicago Press, 1991), 142–3.

the gospel than Luther had. "Now the question was what graces God gives to persons after He forgives their sins."[34] The major Pietist leaders remained just as convinced of the vital truth of justification by faith as they were passionate about the sanctified life of God's adopted children. But if justification is necessarily connected to sanctification, how much sanctification should we expect to see in those who are justified?[35] At what point does a lack of sanctification call into question someone's justification? And if we deny that someone is justified because they have not reached a certain degree of sanctification, have we not effectively claimed that justification is both by faith and by sanctification? Some taught that being born again is not a single event, but rather a process that is accompanied by a struggle for conversion.[36] If being born again is the result of long labor pains of strenuous moral effort, then we are indeed justified in part by sanctification. Salvation becomes partly gift and partly accomplishment. A contemporary example would be the more extreme Pentecostal claim that one must speak in tongues to be considered a Christian.[37]

On the other hand, some extreme Lutherans and Puritans taught that justified Christians should have nothing more to do with obeying the law. Christians should certainly still strive to imitate the beautiful example of Jesus out of gratitude for God's mercy. But obeying rules out of a sense of duty would be positively harmful. Pastors should neither exhort their congregations to obey the law nor use the Ten Commandments for moral guidance. Luther's own friend and colleague, Johann Agricola, sparked what came to be called the "Antinomian Controversy."[38] An anti-nomian is anti-law,

---

[34]Johannes Wallmann, "Johann Arndt (1555–1621)," in *The Pietist Theologians: An Introduction to Theology in the Seventeenth and Eighteenth Centuries*, ed. Carter Lindberg (Malden: Blackwell, 2005), 28.

[35]K. James Stein, "Philip Jacob Spener (1635–1705)," in *The Pietist Theologians*, 89–93.

[36]Richard F. Lovelace, "Cotton Mather (1663–1728)," in *The Pietist Theologians*, 119–21. J. V. Fesko, "The Ground of Religion: Justification in the Reformed Tradition," in *The Doctrine on Which the Church Stands or Falls: Justification in Biblical, Theological, Historical, and Pastoral Perspective*, ed. Matthew Barrett (Wheaton: Crossway, 2019), 721–4.

[37]Addressed in J. I. Packer, *Keep in Step with the Spirit: Finding Fullness in Our Walk with God*, rev. ed. (Grand Rapids: Baker, 2005), 161–71.

[38]Martin Brecht, *Martin Luther*, vol. 3, *The Preservation of the Church 1532–1546*, trans. James L. Schaaf (Minneapolis: Fortress, 1993), 156–72; Luther, *Against the*

and Agricola believed that, if the law is irrelevant for justification, then it is also irrelevant for the whole Christian life. Through no fault of Luther, this suspicion of law and ethics has continued to haunt several rooms in the Lutheran house.[39] A century after Agricola, Anne Hutchinson came to similar conclusions and set off another antinomian controversy in Puritan Massachusetts.[40] In more recent years, the "Lordship Salvation" controversy flared over the claim that justifying faith can merely trust Christ as Savior, without also obeying Christ as Lord.[41]

Faithful proclamation of justification by faith must avoid these two, typical misunderstandings. Justification is not sanctification, nor is it without sanctification. They are distinct and inseparable. The gospel involves both the grateful receiving of righteousness and the vigorous pursuit of holiness. It is to the enduring honor of John Wesley that he understood this so clearly and proclaimed it so powerfully.

Wesley on Justification

John Wesley loved the doctrine of justification by faith. This love began with a kind of conversion experience not unlike Luther's and as one of Luther's writings was being read aloud.[42] Wesley describes this experience, which came during a season of deep spiritual turmoil:

Antinomians 1539, in *LW* 47:99–119; Formula of Concord, Epitome IV, in Robert Kolb and Timothy J. Wengert, eds., *The Book of Concord: The Confessions of the Evangelical Lutheran Church* (Minneapolis: Fortress, 2000), 497–500.

[39]Michael Banner, *Christian Ethics: A Brief History* (Malden: Wiley-Blackwell, 2009), 56–70.

[40]Emery Battis, *Saints and Sectaries: Anne Hutchinson and the Antinomian Controversy in the Massachusetts Bay Colony* (Chapel Hill: University of North Carolina Press, 1962); David D. Hall, ed., *The Antinomian Controversy, 1636–1638: A Documentary History*, 2nd ed. (Durham: Duke University Press, 1990).

[41]John R. Stott and Everett F. Harrison, "Must Christ Be Lord to be Savior?" *Eternity* 10, no. 9 (September 1959): 13–18, 36–7, 48; Zane Clark Hodges, *Absolutely Free: A Biblical Reply to Lordship Salvation* (Grand Rapids: Zondervan, 1989); Michael S. Horton, ed., *Christ the Lord: The Reformation and Lordship Salvation* (Grand Rapids: Baker, 1992).

[42]Fred Sanders, *Wesley on the Christian Life: The Heart Renewed in Love* (Wheaton: Crossway, 2013), 52–9.

In the evening I went very unwillingly to a society in Aldersgate-Street, where one was reading Luther's preface to the Epistle to the Romans. About a quarter before nine, while he was describing the change which God works in the heart through faith in Christ, I felt my heart strangely warmed. I felt I did trust in Christ, Christ alone, for salvation: and an assurance was given me that He had taken away *my* sins, even *mine*, and saved *me* from the law of sin and death.[43]

Wesley's change of heart has understandably been labeled one of the great turning points in the history of Christianity.[44] Over the next five decades of relentless ministry, any friend of justification by faith was a friend of Wesley—even John Calvin! Years later Wesley could look back on his experience of justification and write, "I think on justification just as I have done any time these seven-and-twenty years; and just as Mr. Calvin does. In this respect I do not differ from him an hair's breadth."[45]

Wesley's *Standard Sermons* are a masterpiece of gospel proclamation and the clearest account of his teaching. In Sermon 5, "Justification by Faith," Wesley explains, "The plain scriptural notion of justification is pardon—the forgiveness of sins," whereby all past sins "are blotted out" so that God treats us "as if we had never sinned."[46] The two elements here are "pardon and acceptance,"[47] the washing away of sins and the imputation of Christ's righteousness. "To all believers the righteousness of Christ is imputed ... in that very hour" when they believe.[48] This justification comes to sinners by faith and flows out into a life of born-again renewal.

This then is the salvation which is through faith: ... a salvation from sin, and the consequences of sin, both often expressed in

---

[43]John Wesley, "Journal for May 24, 1738," in *The Works of John Wesley* (1872; reprint Grand Rapids: Zondervan, 1958–9), 1.103.

[44]Mark Noll, *Turning Points: Decisive Moments in the History of Christianity*, 3rd ed. (Grand Rapids: Baker, 2012), 215–37.

[45]Wesley, "Journal for May 14, 1765," in *Works* 3.212.

[46]Wesley, Sermon 5.2.5, "Justification by Faith," in *Works* 5.57. Sanders, *Wesley on the Christian Life*, 131–4.

[47]Wesley, Sermon 5.4.7 (63); cf. *Westminster Confession of Faith* 11.1.

[48]Wesley, Sermon 20.2.1, "The Lord our Righteousness," in *Works* 5.237. Cf. William Burt Pope, *A Compendium of Christian Theology*, 2nd ed. (New York: Hunt & Eaton, 1889), 2.446–8.

the word *justification*; which, taken in the largest sense, implies a deliverance from guilt and punishment, by the atonement of Christ actually applied to the soul of the sinner believing on him, and a deliverance from the power of sin, through Christ formed in his heart. So that he who is thus justified, or saved by faith, is indeed born again. He is born again of the Spirit unto a new life, which "is hid with Christ in God" [Col 3:3].[49]

It is through union with Christ ("Christ formed in his heart") that we are "born again of the Spirit unto a new life."

Wesley thus shares the classic Protestant understanding of justification and its intimate connection to sanctification. Justification, he explains,

is not the being made actually just and righteous. This is *sanctification*, which is, indeed, in some degree, the immediate *fruit* of justification, but, nevertheless, is a distinct gift of God, and of a totally different nature. The one [justification] implies what God *does for* us through his Son; the other [sanctification], what he *works in* us by his Spirit.[50]

Against the extreme Pietists, Wesley insists that justification must come first. The teaching that "a man must be sanctified (that is, holy) before he can be justified," Wesley finds "flatly impossible ... For it is not a *saint* but a *sinner* that is forgiven."[51] Once we are justified by faith, however, the striving after holy obedience begins. Against the extreme Lutherans and Puritans, Wesley asserts that Christians zealously pursue obedience to "the moral law, ... the great, unchangeable law of love, the holy love of God and of our neighbor."[52] Wesley's aim was "to preach [the law] in its whole extent, to explain and enforce every part of it," so that Christians would "do good, in every possible kind, and in every possible degree, to all men."[53]

---

[49]Wesley, Sermon 1.2.7, "Salvation by Faith," in *Works* 5.11–12. Sanders, *Wesley on the Christian Life*, 200–5.

[50]Wesley, Sermon 5.2.1 (56).

[51]Wesley, Sermon 5.3.2 (58). See also Sermon 43.3.2, "The Scripture Way of Salvation," in *Works* 6.48.

[52]Wesley, Sermon 5.4.1 (60).

[53]Wesley, Sermon 36, "The Law Established Through Faith: Discourse II," 1.1, 3.3, in *Works* 5:459, 465. Sanders, *Wesley on the Christian Life*, 151.

Challenges from Scholars and Churchmen

In evangelical circles today, the doctrine of justification faces challenges from two quarters. On the one hand, certain biblical scholars have proposed a radically different understanding of the context in which Paul wrote about justification. On the other, ecumenically minded leaders, both evangelical and Roman Catholic, have asked whether our sixteenth-century split over the doctrine of justification need still divide us.

The New Perspective on Paul

Within the world of biblical studies, scholars have offered what has come to be called the New Perspective on Paul. The movement was initiated by E. P. Sanders's *Paul and Palestinian Judaism* (1977) and was transmitted to evangelical circles largely through the work of James Dunn and N. T. Wright.[54] The main idea of the New Perspective is that Paul's talk of justification is not about how we are right with God, but rather about who can be part of the Christian community. Justification is not about God's pardon and acceptance of sinners, but about the church's inclusion of outsiders within its social and ritual boundaries. Such a view of justification is not merely a challenge to Protestants, but to Roman Catholics and Eastern Orthodox as well.[55] If the New Perspective is right, then for most of two thousand years Christianity has been wrong.

Though proponents of the New Perspective vary widely in their views,[56] they are largely agreed on two main points. First, Sanders's work showed that there was a variety of approaches to the law in the Judaism of Paul's day.[57] Not all were self-righteous Pharisees. Some saw in the law of Moses a religion of grace, with its own provision for the forgiveness of sins. For them, "doing the law was a means

---

[54]Barclay, *Paul and the Gift*, 159–65.
[55]Piper, *Future of Justification*, 60–1.
[56]Timo Laato, "The New Quest for Paul: A Critique of the New Perspective on Paul," in Matthew Barrett, ed., *The Doctrine on Which the Church Stands or Falls: Justification in Biblical, Theological, Historical, and Pastoral Perspective* (Wheaton: Crossway, 2019), 295.
[57]Barclay, *Paul and the Gift*, 151–8.

of staying in the covenant, not of getting into it in the first place."[58] If we see Paul's opponents in Galatia as having emerged from a different kind of Judaism, then Paul's response to these opponents must be seen in a different light. If Paul's opponents had never believed in salvation by circumcision (cf. Acts 15:1), would they really have been preaching this to the Galatians? Instead—so the reasoning goes—Paul's opponents must have been telling believers in Galatia that, in order to stay in the church, they needed to follow the law of Moses. And then Paul's own talk about justification by faith would likewise be a matter of staying in the church, not getting right with God.[59]

Second, scholars of the New Perspective have pointed out that, when Paul is talking about justification, the specific laws he deals with are largely ritual. Paul speaks of circumcision (Rom 2:25–29; Gal 2:1–14; 5:2–3), observance of the Sabbath and Old Testament festivals (Gal 4:10), whether to eat with gentiles (Gal 2:12), and whether ritually unclean food may be eaten (Rom 14:13–23). These are the practices that set Jew apart from gentile.[60] So when Paul says we are not justified by works of the law, he means that our membership in God's covenant people no longer depends on these rituals.[61]

While the New Perspective itself has yielded valuable insights and helped drive decades of intense research into the letters of Paul, there are many who still find much to prefer in the old Paul. First, those who favor the classic perspective are grateful for an immeasurably enriched understanding of Paul's first-century world.[62] Nevertheless, our understanding of Paul's world can neither simply overrule Paul's own representation of this world nor force us to understand Paul's teaching in, say, Galatians in a way that contradicts what he says in Romans. Piper identifies the dubious assumption among adherents of the New Perspective "that we can

---

[58]James D. G. Dunn, *The Theology of Paul the Apostle* (Grand Rapids: Eerdmans, 1998), 338.

[59]Dunn, *Theology of Paul*, 340; N. T. Wright, *What Saint Paul Really Said: Was Paul of Tarsus the Real Founder of Christianity?* (Grand Rapids: Eerdmans, 1997), 113–33.

[60]Dunn, *Theology of Paul*, 356.

[61]Dunn, *Theology of Paul*, 359–66.

[62]D. A. Carson, Peter T. O'Brien, and Mark A. Seifrid, *Justification and Variegated Nomism*, vol. 1, *The Complexities of Second Temple Judaism*, vol. 2, *The Paradoxes of Paul* (Grand Rapids: Baker Academic, 2001, 2004).

be more confident about how we interpret secondary first-century sources than we are of how we interpret the New Testament writers themselves."[63] Second, while ritual observance is certainly part of the issue in Romans and Galatians, it is not the only issue. Paul's claim is not merely that the rituals of the law cannot justify, but that the whole law, especially the moral commands, is powerless to do so.[64] Finally, the New Perspective proposes subtle or technical meanings for Paul's use of words like "justify" and "righteous" and "works" and "law." Those of the old perspective point out that, while Paul's gospel is indeed astonishing, he mostly uses normal words in normal ways to communicate it. By the same token, Paul's audiences are unlikely to have caught esoteric connotations in Paul's standard biblical vocabulary.[65] As Stephen Westerholm puts it, "No Galatian would have heard 'justified' and thought 'entitled to sit at the family table'."[66] The classic doctrine of justification by faith has thus actually emerged stronger—more clearly understood, more confidently held—as the result of the challenge of the New Perspective.

Evangelicals and Catholics Together

With the publication of "Evangelicals and Catholics Together: The Christian Mission in the Third Millennium" (1994), the evangelical world was all astir once again over the doctrine of justification.[67] Much of the stir came from the range and prominence of evangelical leaders whose endorsement was published with the statement— among others, Bill Bright, Os Guinness, Richard Mouw, Mark Noll, Thomas Oden, J. I. Packer, Pat Robertson, and representatives from the Southern Baptist Convention, the Assemblies of God, the World Evangelical Fellowship, and the National Association

[63]Piper, *Future of Justification*, 34.
[64]Luther, *Lectures on Galatians* 2:15–16, in *LW* 26:120–3; Calvin, *Institutes* 3.11.19 (749); Wesley, Sermon 35.3, in *Works* 1.448; Stephen Westerholm, *Justification Reconsidered: Rethinking a Pauline Theme* (Grand Rapids: Eerdmans, 2013), 75–85.
[65]Piper, *Future of Justification*, 24, 57–8.
[66]Westerholm, *Justification Reconsidered*, 68.
[67]"Evangelicals and Catholics Together," *First Things* 43 (May 1994), 15–22. See Timothy George, "Unity," in *Evangelicals and Catholics Together at Twenty: Vital Statements on Contested Topics*, ed. Timothy George and Thomas G. Guarino (Grand Rapids: Brazos, 2015) 1–5.

of Evangelicals. What "Evangelicals and Catholics Together" (ECT) proposed is that evangelicals and Catholics should come together not in doctrine, nor in worship, but in mission, that is, in our engagement with the non-Christian world. Because the doctrine of justification has been at the heart of Protestant-Catholic noncooperation, ECT claims that there is enough basic agreement about justification to warrant cooperation.

What ECT says about justification is this: "We affirm together that we are justified by grace through faith because of Christ."[68] That is all. Protestants have often looked on Roman Catholics as believing in works righteousness, in earning salvation by good works. And so we might hesitate to team up with them on public issues. But what would we think of a group of Roman Catholics who could affirm this ECT statement about justification? Would that ease our suspicions enough for us to join them in working for things like religious freedom, parental rights in education, the dignity of human life, a just economy, and "a renewed spirit of acceptance, understanding, and cooperation across lines of religion, race, ethnicity, sex, and class"? Evangelical critics charged that ECT's least-common-denominator approach to justification obscures disagreements too deep to ignore.[69]

As a result, ECT participants drafted a second statement, "The Gift of Salvation" (1998), to clarify the extent of both agreement and disagreement over the doctrine of justification. The crucial lines about justification are as follows: "We agree that justification is not earned by any good works or merits of our own; it is entirely God's gift. ... We understand that what we here affirm is in agreement with what the Reformation traditions have meant by justification by faith alone (sola fide)."[70] Evangelicals were stunned to hear this, coming as it did from a host of Roman Catholic luminaries as formidable as their evangelical counterparts. As the ECT participants acknowledged, however, individual churchmen cannot speak officially for the Roman Catholic Church. Would Rome herself affirm a Protestant understanding of justification by faith? No, as can be seen from the official, Vatican-approved *Catechism*

---

[68]"Evangelicals and Catholics Together," 16.
[69]J. I. Packer, "Crosscurrents among Evangelicals," in *Evangelicals and Catholics Together: Toward a Common Mission*, ed. Charles Colson and Richard John Neuhaus (Dallas: Word, 1995), 149–56.
[70]"The Gift of Salvation," *First Things* 79 (Jan 1998): 20–3 (21).

of the Catholic Church (1994), which affirms decisive statements of the Council of Trent, as well as from the official (and tantalizingly ambiguous) *Joint Declaration on the Doctrine of Justification* (1999), signed with the Lutheran World Federation.[71] For evangelicals, the question remains, what are the negotiable and the nonnegotiable elements of the doctrine of justification?[72]

Forward: Justification by Faith after Reformation 500

One nonnegotiable element of the doctrine of justification is surely clear. Any formulation of justification must celebrate and safeguard the character of salvation as a gift. We receive it "without payment" (Rev 21:6; Isa 55:1). "It is not sixteenth-century or twenty-first-century anachronistic psychologizing to say that *the good news* for Paul was, *first*, that a persecutor of Jesus could be given a right standing before God through faith."[73] When it comes to justification, there can be no earning or deserving or meriting. It is sinners whom God justifies. If only the worthy have a claim on justification, the unworthy are excluded. An elitist gospel cannot make disciples of all nations. On the contrary, "it is because grace belongs to no one that it goes to everyone."[74]

It will remain the task of evangelical churches to offer this gift of salvation to everyone. Justification, the wondrous, free exchange of pardon instead of condemnation, righteousness instead of sin, and acceptance instead of rejection—this is good news indeed! Justification by faith must be a prominent theme in our preaching and teaching, our catechizing and evangelizing. It must also be a regular theme. Sometimes good news is hard to believe. Sometimes believing God's justification of the ungodly is almost impossible.

---

[71]*Catechism of the Catholic Church* (San Francisco: Ignatius, 1994), §§1989, 1995, 2019; *Joint Declaration on the Doctrine of Justification* (Grand Rapids: Eerdmans, 2000); A. N. S. Lane, *Justification by Faith in Catholic-Protestant Dialogue: An Evangelical Assessment* (London: T&T Clark, 2002), 119–26.
[72]Gavin Ortlund, *Finding the Right Hills to Die On* (Wheaton: Crossway, 2020), 87–93.
[73]Piper, *Future of Justification*, 87.
[74]Barclay, *Paul and the Gift*, 572.

Luther called such belief "the highest art among Christians."[75] As often as I struggle with sin, I need to be told that my Heavenly Father still looks on me "as if I had never sinned or been a sinner, as if I had been as perfectly obedient as Christ was obedient for me."[76]

Justification by faith offers especially timely comfort for a culture preoccupied with questions of identity.[77] Western culture is full of people who are weighed down by the burden of self-realization and frustrated by the incoherence of conferring worth upon themselves.[78] To those who are trapped in this particular cultural narrative, justification by faith announces that both our identity and our dignity come to us from outside. They do so not as personal accomplishment, but as the gift of God. The good news of justification by faith, joined as it is with our union with Christ and adoption by God, is that God himself confers upon us the identity and dignity of children of God. "And if children, then heirs—heirs of God and fellow heirs with Christ, provided we suffer with him in order that we may also be glorified with him" (Rom 8:17). The cost of such justification is humility. "Only if we repent and admit we are far worse than we ever imagined can we become justified, adopted, and united with Christ, and therefore far more loved and accepted than ever we hoped."[79] And the result is a boundless love, gratitude, and generosity. Only the justified Christian can say,

> Why should I not therefore freely, joyfully, with all my heart, and with an eager will do all things which I know are pleasing and acceptable to such a Father who has overwhelmed me with his inestimable riches? I will therefore give myself as a Christ to my

---

[75]Luther, *Lectures on Galatians* 2:20, in *LW* 26:178; Luther, "Sermon on the Sum of the Christian Life 1532," in *LW* 51:284–5.

[76]Heidelberg Catechism, Q. 60; John Piper, "Gutsy Guilt," *Christianity Today* 51, no. 10 (October 2007): 72–6.

[77]Tim Keller, *Preaching: Communicating Faith in an Age of Skepticism* (New York: Penguin, 2015), 133–9.

[78]For lucid explanations of how the message of justification by faith impacts those of Hindu and Islamic cultures, both of which teach an equivalent of justification by works, see Sunand Sumithra, "Justification by Faith: Its Relevance in Hindu Context," in *Right With God: Justification in the Bible and the World*, ed. D. A. Carson (Grand Rapids: Baker, 1992), 216–27; and Chris Marantika, "Justification by Faith: Its Relevance in Islamic Context," in *Right with God: Justification in the Bible and the World*, ed. D. A. Carson (Grand Rapids: Baker, 1992), 228–42.

[79]Keller, *Preaching*, 138.

neighbor, just as Christ offered himself to me; I will do nothing in this life except what I see is necessary, profitable, and salutary to my neighbor, since through faith I have an abundance of all good things in Christ.[80]

The gospel of justification remains as urgent a message as ever.

At the same time, we must acknowledge that justification is not the whole gospel. It would be sadly self-defeating if, in our zeal to proclaim God's justification of sinners, we reduced the gospel to justification. Justification by faith can only be rightly preached within the broader context of union with Christ, adoption, and sanctification.

Recommended Reading

R. Michael Allen, *Justification and the Gospel* (Grand Rapids: Baker Academic, 2013).

John M. G. Barclay, *Paul and the Gift* (Grand Rapids: Eerdmans, 2015).

Matthew Barrett, ed., *The Doctrine on Which the Church Stands or Falls: Justification in Biblical, Theological, Historical, and Pastoral Perspective* (Wheaton: Crossway, 2019).

John Piper, *The Future of Justification: A Response to N. T. Wright* (Wheaton: Crossway, 2007).

Stephen Westerholm, *Justification Reconsidered: Rethinking a Pauline Theme* (Grand Rapids: Eerdmans, 2013).

---

[80]Luther, *The Freedom of a Christian*, in *LW* 31.367.

6

"Be Holy as I Am Holy": Sanctification

We affirm that we who proclaim the gospel must exemplify it in a life of holiness and love; otherwise our testimony loses its credibility.

MANILLA MANIFESTO, LAUSANNE MOVEMENT

Without holiness no one will see God (Heb 12:14); for it is "the pure in heart" who see God (Matt 5:8). So what is holiness? What does it mean to be "pure in heart"? Do I desire holiness? Am I already holy, or should I be waiting for *something* (a burning in my heart?) or *someone* (the Holy Spirit) to make me holy? For serious readers of Scripture, these questions demand answers. One thing is clear; there is amazing beauty in holiness. Have you met a man or woman afire with the beauty of holiness? Perhaps your mom or a mentor comes to mind?[1]

Evangelical doctrines of sanctification begin in Christ, continue in Christ, and find their end in Christ (1 Cor 1:30). If justification speaks to redemption *accomplished*—that which was achieved during Christ's earthly life—then sanctification is a common Protestant way of speaking about redemption *applied*—the work the ascended Christ is currently doing through the Holy Spirit.

---

[1]For twenty stories of saints made beautiful by holiness see V. Raymond Edman, *They Found the Secret: 20 Transformed Lives That Reveal a Touch of Eternity* (1960; repr., Grand Rapids: Zondervan, 1984).

Justification makes us free from sin's guilt, and sanctification makes us free from sin's power. The cross made both possible. Sanctification and justification are two sides of the same coin. However, sanctification is more than a coin; it is the believer's life breath. Sanctification occurs as the Spirit conforms believers to the image of Christ for the glory of God (2 Cor 3:18). Like all work of the triune God, Father, Son, and Spirit always work together even if it is appropriate to see one person as the lead actor (e.g., creation, redemption). The Spirit presently applies and completes (or perfects) the work of sanctification in God's people.[2]

Like salvation, there are past (1 Cor 1:2, 30; 1 Pet 1:1-2; Heb 10:10, 29), present (Rom 12:1-2; 1 Thess 5:23; 2 Cor 7:1), and future aspects to sanctification (2 Thess 1:10). Within God's saving work, justification's emphasis is on the past, sanctification's emphasis is on the present, and glorification's on the future.[3] The Holy Spirit works continually in believers—teaching, counseling, convicting, and comforting us—all toward the end (*telos*) of becoming like Christ—the goal of spiritual maturity. This maturity includes fruits like love, joy, peace, patience, kindness, goodness, faithfulness, gentleness, and self-control (Gal 5:22-25), but its chief characteristic is Christ being formed in us (Gal 4:19).

The doctrine of sanctification addresses how saints draw near to Jesus and find powerful transformation through the Holy Spirit's power (Jas 4:8). The chapter's first section situates sanctification in its biblical context before exploring John Owen's spiritual classic, *The Mortification of Sin*. The second section surveys the development of the doctrine of sanctification, especially noting its relationship to spirituality (a believer's growing love relationship with Father, Son, and Holy Spirit) and mysticism (a believer's increasing awareness and dependence upon the presence of God). The third section explores places where "dragons lie"—challenges facing evangelicals today. Finally, the conclusion describes Dallas Willard's vision for developing an evangelical theology of discipleship.

---

[2]John Webster, *Holiness* (Grand Rapids: Eerdmans, 2003), 51-2; John Murray, *Redemption Accomplished and Applied* (Grand Rapids: Eerdmans, 1955), 146.
[3]For sanctification's emphasis on the past, see Don J. Payne, *Already Sanctified* (Grand Rapids: Baker Academic, 2020).

Doctrine: John Owen (1616–1683), "Be Killing Sin, or It Will Be Killing You"

Holiness, according to the Nicene Creed, is one of the four marks of the church. Evangelicals agree, confessing the church as both holy and human. To be human is to be born into brokenness, sinful from the time our mothers conceived us (Ps 51:5; Rom 3:23). How can the church be both holy and human, broken and beautiful? One of the first Christian theologians, the Apostle Paul, observed, "Great indeed is the *mystery* of godliness" (1 Tim 3:16). Glorious mystery is at the heart of the doctrine of sanctification (Col 1:27; 2:9; Eph 3:14–19). Just as the presence of God once led Israel as a pillar of cloud (Ps 99:5–9) or filled Solomon's grand temple, so the Holy Spirit now guides and fills believers—the new temple (1 Cor 3:26; 6:19)! Indeed, the same Spirit that caused Jesus to rise from the dead is living and active within us (Rom 8:9–11). The mystery at the heart of sanctification is why Roman Catholics have historically discussed the concept of sanctification as a component of mystical theology.[4]

Sanctification's Vocabulary

There are at least two aspects to the mystery of sanctification. First, how can an unholy human be holy while continuing to do unholy things? Second, if the Holy Spirit sanctifies (Rom 15:16; 1 Cor 6:11; Eph 4:30; 1 Thess 4:7–8; 2 Thess 2:13; 1 Pet 1:2), then why are believers commanded to also participate in sanctification? For example, Hebrews commands believers to "strive for... the holiness without which no one will see the Lord" (Heb 12:14). The English word "strive" calls readers to pursue intense and purposeful holiness. Table 6.1 lists ways the New Testament calls believers to participate in the Holy Spirit's work of sanctification.

Paul describes the believer's cooperative participation with God in Philippians:

---

[4]On mystical theology see Evan B. Howard, *The Brazos Introduction to Christian Spirituality* (Grand Rapids: Brazos, 2008), 18–19.

TABLE 6.1 *Human Participation in Sanctification*

Action Believers Are Called to Do	Author/s	Text
Pursue holiness, righteousness and godliness.	Paul, Author of Hebrews	1 Tim 6:11; Phil 3:12; 2 Tim 2:22; Heb 12:14
Train yourself to be godly.	Paul, Author of Hebrews	1 Tim 4:7–8; Tit 2:12; Heb 5:14
Learn how to show godliness and be like Christ.	Paul	Eph 4:20; 1 Tim 5:4
Press on to become more like Christ.	Paul	Phil 3:12–16
Cleanse yourself ... and bring holiness to completion.	Paul	2 Cor 7:1 cf. Ps 15
Put to death sinful actions.	Paul	Rom 8:13; Col 3:5
Put on or clothe yourself with Christ/new self.	Paul	Rom 13:14; Gal 3:27; Eph 4:24; Col 3:5–17
Walk in the good works God prepared for us to do.	Paul	Eph 2:10; 4:1
Draw near to God.	James	Jas 4:8
Make every effort to increase godliness.	Peter	2 Pet 1:5–6
Be(come) Holy!	Peter Paul	1 Pet 1:15–16 Rom 12:1 (Lev 11:44–45)

Source: Table created by Hank Voss.

Therefore, my beloved, as you have always obeyed, so now, not only as in my presence but much more in my absence, work out your own salvation with fear and trembling, for it is God who works in you, both to will and to work for his good pleasure. (Phil 2:12–13; cf. Lev 20:7–8)

The Holy Spirit provides the power in believers' sanctifying actions, but the believer still has a role to play. Elsewhere Paul uses the analogy of a gardener planting seeds. The gardener may be the one who plants, waters, and weeds, but God causes the seed to grow (1 Cor 3:6–9). We work, but only because God's work makes our work possible. Two principles are at work here.[5] First, sanctification (or spiritual growth) involves both God's work and our work. Second, our work is always dependent upon the prior work of the Father, the Son, and the Holy Spirit (Eph 2:10).

Theologians wrestle with this tension as the *concursus Dei*— divine "concurrence," the exploration of how God is *with* us, or *accompanies* us in all things (Rom 11:36; 1 Cor 12:6; Phil 2:13).[6] Reformed theologians tend to emphasize monergistic versions of divine concurrence and sanctification, while Wesleyan theologians emphasize synergistic ones.[7] Evangelicals have not accepted a single explanation for how the Holy Spirit and humans work together in sanctification. Part of the problem relates to different traditions using different language or conceptual terms to discuss the same "theological judgment."[8] For example, *The Oxford Handbook of Evangelical Theology* does not include a chapter on "sanctification" but instead includes one entitled "Discipleship," while Alister McGrath's *Christian Theology* uses "personal holiness" and "spirituality" instead of "discipleship" or "sanctification."[9] The

---

[5]Robert L. Saucy, *Minding the Heart: The Way of Spiritual Transformation* (Grand Rapids: Kregel, 2013), 118–21.

[6]Karl Barth, *CD* 3.3.102–7.

[7]Compare the following: Michael Scott Horton, *The Christian Faith: A Systematic Theology for Pilgrims on the Way* (Grand Rapids: Zondervan, 2011), 314–15, 670, 684–6; Diane Leclerc, *Discovering Christian Holiness: The Heart of Wesleyan-Holiness Theology* (Kansas City: Beacon Hill, 2010), chap. 7.

[8]Treier, "Concept," *DTIB*, 129–30.

[9]In evangelical communities, we also read about sanctification using conceptual terms like "piety," "holiness," "godliness," "Christian perfection," "perfect love," "discipleship," "the imitation of Christ," "the Christian life," "spiritual maturity," "Christian maturity," "Christian spiritual formation," "evangelical spirituality,"

diverse vocabulary reminds us that there is mystery, an antinomy, in sanctification—God works, but we work too.[10]

If we understand sanctification as "the process of becoming holy, conforming to the pattern of Jesus Christ," then the definition of "holy" is of central importance.[11] Believers are made holy as we draw near to Christ, leaving behind sin and experiencing growing relational intimacy with the Father, the Son, and the Holy Spirit. As Peterson notes,

> Love and holiness are two related aspects of the Christian life. Holiness will be preeminently expressed in love and love will be the essential means by which holiness is maintained. In effect, holiness abounds when love abounds.[12]

This connection between love and holiness helps explain why sanctification and spirituality go together like "Holy" and "Spirit."[13] They are near synonyms. Christian *Spirit*-uality and sanctification are both about the Holy Spirit's walk *with* the believer (relationship), work *in* the believer (transformation), and witness *through* the believer (vocation).[14] Four conceptual terms that can help order the overlapping concepts between spirituality and sanctification are: (1) Christian spirituality, (2) Christian mysticism or mystical theology, (3) spiritual theology, and (4) spiritual formation. These four terms are defined in Table 6.2 and will be used in the discussion below.[15]

If we include non-Protestant Christian traditions, sanctification's terminology grows. In Orthodox and Roman Catholic traditions, concepts related to sanctification are usually discussed

---

the "victorious Christian life," "the exchanged life," "the deeper Christian life," "the Spirit-filled life," and still others. Alister E. McGrath, *Christian Theology: An Introduction*, 6th ed. (Malden: Wiley Blackwell, 2016), 93, 273; Dallas Willard, "Discipleship," in *The Oxford Handbook of Evangelical Theology*, ed. Gerald McDermott (New York: Oxford University Press, 2010), 236–46.

[10]I am using *antinomy* in the same way as J. I. Packer, *Evangelism & the Sovereignty of God* (Downers Grove: InterVarsity, 1961), 18–22.

[11]Treier, *IET*, 386.

[12]Peterson, "Holiness," *NDBT*, 549.

[13]Gordon Fee, *God's Empowering Presence* (Peabody: Hendrickson, 1994), 881.

[14]Scorgie, Glen, "Overview of Christian Spirituality," *ZDCS*, 27–8.

[15]For a full discussion of these four terms and their relationship to sanctification see Howard, *Brazos Introduction to Christian Spirituality*, 17–24.

TABLE 6.2 *The Study of Sanctification and Christian Spirituality*

Spirituality	Creation's experience with God in all times and places.
Mysticism	The conscience experience of the manifest presence of God in a particular space.
Spiritual Theology	The study of the Holy Spirit's progressive work in souls from its beginning through full maturity (perfection/glorification/full union/deification).
Spiritual Formation	The study of the specific means used by the Holy Spirit to develop Christlikeness in believers.

Source: Table created by Hank Voss.

under "spirituality" using terms like "deification," "theosis," "Christification," "ascetical theology," "spiritual theology," and "mystical theology." Why so many terms?

In his book *True Spirituality*, Francis Schaeffer identified an important aspect of the answer, noting that while he had heard much in evangelical circles about atonement and justification, he "had heard little about what the Bible says about the meaning of the finished work of Christ for our present lives."[16] Schaeffer had heard much teaching on what Jesus had done in the past, but not on what the Holy Spirit was doing with that work in the present. While evangelicals had developed vocabulary for talking about the practice of sanctification, reflection at the level of models to understand the dynamics of relationship with God was rare.[17] While Schaeffer was writing, Roman Catholics had already for hundreds of years referred to the formal study of experience and models to explain believers' lived experience of life-with-Christ as "spiritual theology," but in Schaeffer's time "there was not even

---

[16]Francis A. Schaeffer, "True Spirituality," in *The Complete Works of Francis Schaeffer: A Christian Worldview; of the Church*, vol. 3 (Wheaton: Crossway, 1982), 196.

[17]Howard, *Brazos Introduction to Christian Spirituality*, 16–17.

a name among Protestants" for second-order reflection on the topic.[18]

Richard Lovelace called the evangelical absence of reflection on spirituality the "sanctification gap" and suggested it has two sources.[19] First, there is always opposition to the church walking in the power of the Holy Spirit from the world, the flesh, and the Devil. Second, "the historical development of Protestant Evangelicalism has predisposed it to lose sight of the central importance of sanctification" and thus sustained reflection has been relatively rare.[20] Although there are a number of schools of thought regarding sanctification and spirituality, the large diversity of views prevalent among evangelicals shows that there is a need for work to identify common ground.[21] Some of the historical reasons for the lack of emphasis on sanctification are similar to those identified in Chapter 4's discussion of conversion, but additional factors are identified below.

John Owen on Dying to Sin and Living in the Spirit

John Owen was passionate about "evangelical holiness," and he longed for God to use him in his own generation.[22] He wrote ten books on the two major emphases of sanctification—dying to sin, or *mortification* (Gal 2:20), and daily walking in the resurrection power of the Holy Spirit, or *vivification* (Rom 8:11).[23] Owen did

---

[18]Richard Lovelace, *Dynamics of Spiritual Life* (Downers Grove: InterVarsity, 1979), 231.

[19]Lovelace, *Dynamics*, 229–37.

[20]Lovelace, *Dynamics*, 233.

[21]See representative "views" books. On some topics, evangelicals only have two or three main positions. At present, one finds at least seven evangelical views. Treier summarizes six: Lutheran, Reformed, Wesleyan, Pentecostal, Keswick, and Contemplative to which we could add Anabaptist. Treier, *Introducing Evangelical Theology*, 283–6; for Anabaptist view see Harold Bender and Owen Alderfer, "Sanctification," *GAMEO*. For views books see *Four Views on Christian Spirituality*, ed. Bruce A. Demarest (Grand Rapids: Zondervan Academic, 2012); *Five Views on Sanctification*, ed. Donald Alexander (Grand Rapids: Zondervan, 1996); *Christian Spirituality: Five Views of Sanctification*, ed. Donald Alexander (Downers Grove: IVP Academic, 1989).

[22]John Owen, *WJO* 3:366–537, esp. 467, 473, 502.

[23]To explore Owen's writings on the resurrection life lived in the power of the Holy Spirit see *Discourse Concerning the Holy Spirit* (*WJO* 3); *Spiritual Mindeness* (*WJO*

not want sin to disqualify him from the Holy Spirit's work in his generation. He lived a fascinating life—he was friend to kings and revolutionaries, prime ministers and paupers (like John Bunyan), but we do not have room to tell more here. Instead, we look at Owen's *The Mortification of Sin* (1656), a book tested and proven by thousands of believers as useful for growing in holiness. John Wesley made it required reading for Methodist leaders. Owen's title was based on Rom 8:13, which in the KJV uses the word "mortify," meaning "to put to death or to kill." Since "mortification" is rarely used today, we could also call the book *Killing Sin*. Owen's text teaches how to apply Rom 8:13b: "If by the Spirit you put to death the deeds of the body, you will live." He knew believers could not say "Yes!" to the Holy Spirit's life without first saying "No!" to sin. Death always precedes resurrection. Owen warned readers: you must "be killing sin or it will be killing you" (*WJO* 6:9).[24] How is this practically done?

Owen first lays out five foundational principles, and then builds on them with five practical steps: (1) Christ's cross provides the power to kill sin, but believers must daily apply this power to their own life, thus "perfecting holiness in the fear of God" (2 Cor 7:1; *WJO* 6:9–16); (2) any effort to kill our sin without the Holy Spirit will fail (*WJO* 6:16); (3) killing sin is rewarding and life-giving, and sin's death releases the Holy Spirit's power and peace (*WJO* 6:21); (4) killing sin is the work of the converted, and conversion is the work of the unconverted. Only one made alive with the power of the Spirit can kill sin, thus Owen is speaking to believers as he explains, "There is no death of sin without the death of Christ" (*WJO* 6:33). (5) Believers must be committed to dealing with *all* their sins, not just a *favorite few* (see Isaiah 58; *WJO* 6:40). God wants his children to obey all the way, right away, with joy!

---

7); *Discourse of the Work of the Holy Spirit in Prayer* (*WJO* 4); *Of Communion with God* (*WJO* 2); and his commentary on Hebrews (*WJO* 18–23). Owen also wrote five volumes on how to deal with sin: *Mortification of Sin* (*WJO* 6); *Temptation: The Nature and Power of It* (*WJO* 6); *The Nature, Power, Deceit, and Prevalency of the Remainders of Indwelling Sin in Believers* (*WJO* 6); *A Practical Exposition upon Psalm 130* (*WJO* 6); and *On the Dominion of Sin and Grace* (*WJO* 7).

[24]Quotes from John Owen's Complete Works (*WJO*) are cited by volume and page number. In this section, chapters refer to Owen's *Mortification of Sin*.

Moving to the more practical action steps, Owen notes sixth, that believers must *analyze the sin's roots* (ch. 9).[25] Inwardness—have you allowed it to remain in you for a long time without dealing with it? Smiling at it—are you telling yourself that the sin is not a big deal and covered by grace anyway? Consequences—are you more concerned about the earthly consequences than the loss of intimacy with God? Seventh, believers must carefully *consider the fruit on sin's tree, and refuse to be comfortable without deliverance* (ch. 10–11). Am I placing my soul in danger? Are the souls of others in danger by continuing in this sin? Is my heart being hardened? Am I missing out on peace and strength? How am I grieving the Holy Spirit by continuing in this sin? How am I hurting Jesus afresh by repeatedly returning to this sin? What kingdom fruit will be missing if I continue in it? Encourage yourself to feel valid guilt, and challenge your conscience to reflect on the holiness of God and his law. How has your sin left you in need of God's mercy afresh? Even if you have not yet experienced deliverance, recognize that the desire, the longing, the panting after freedom is itself the Holy Spirit's grace—a gift bringing transforming freedom.

Moving to Owen's eighth step, he challenges us to know ourselves well—mentally, physically, emotionally, and relationally. Be able to identify *your own body's signature sins and learn to recognize the times and places where you are especially susceptible to sin* (ch. 11). Which of the seven deadly sins (or others) do my temperament and personality, gender and phenotype, intellectual and physical abilities or disabilities especially lead me to embrace?[26] If you swim in an Artic lake, you will likely catch a cold. Our souls operate similarly. Are there particular people, places, or projects often present when you choose a particular sin? Ninth, *never delay, attack sin right away* (ch. 11). Sin is a camel poking its nose into your tent. If you let its nose inside, you will soon find yourself sleeping with the whole camel. Attack the very first impure or envious thought, and deny it a foothold. Finally, we must *remember we are continually in the awesome presence of the living God, and learn to discern the difference between the Holy Spirit's healing and an attempt to*

---

[25]Sin is a soul weed. The deeper the roots the harder to pull up and destroy. What I am calling "roots," Owen calls "symptoms."

[26]For help, see Michael Mangis, *Signature Sins: Taming Our Wayward Hearts* (Downers Grove: InterVarsity, 2008).

fix our own sin (chs. 12–13). When we pause under a starry sky or before a vast ocean, we begin to recognize our finitude. As far as the heavens are above the earth, so far are his thoughts above our own. Walking in the fear of the Lord and humbling ourselves before the greatness of God helps put the foolishness of all sin in proper perspective. There is a vast difference between trying to fix our own sin problem and allowing the Holy Spirit to heal our brokenness.

If we created a "top ten" list by placing Owen's principles together, the result would be Owen's "Ten Preparation Steps for Killing Sin" (see Table 6.3).

TABLE 6.3 *Owen's Ten Preparation Steps for Killing Sin*

Step	Action
1	Choose to apply the power of the cross to your sinful desires every day.
2	Depend upon the Holy Spirit or you will fail to kill sin.
3	Enjoy the rewards of peace and joy that come from killing sin.
4	Return to the cross, because the power to kill sin is only found there.
5	Be committed to dealing with all your sin, not just a favored few.
6	Analyze the sin's roots.
7	Consider the fruit on sin's tree, and refuse to be comfortable without deliverance.
8	Know your body's signature sins and learn to recognize the times and places where you are especially susceptible to sin.
9	Never delay; attack sin right away.
10	Remember you are continually in the awesome presence of the living God, and learn to discern the difference between the Holy Spirit's healing and an attempt to fix your own sin.

Owen's ten preparation steps are followed by the actual killing of sin (ch. 14). If the vital preparatory work is done, then putting sin to death is easy. It simply involves faith in Christ's work on the cross and a clear understanding that "this whole work, which I have described as our duty, is effected, carried on, and accomplished by the power of the Spirit" (*WJO* 6:85). Owen has given us an excellent introduction to the first half of sanctification, "mortification." The second half is "vivification." Vivification means learning to walk in the new life of the Spirit (*Inst.* 3.3.3–9). To understand more, we take a brief tour of how evangelical understandings of sanctification developed.

History: Mystery or Muddled Mess? Sanctification and Christian Spiritualties

Two Ways or One Way?

At the beginning of the church, believers acknowledged a single path to the purity of heart required to see God (Mt 5:8). What Phoebe Palmer called *The Way of Holiness* was simply called "the Way" by the first Christians (Acts 9:2; 19:9; 24:14). Outside of the New Testament, one of the first discipleship manuals for new believers (*The Didache*), most likely written during the first century (60–100 AD), introduces the path to holiness with these words: "There are two ways, one of life and one of death, and there is a great difference between these two ways."[27] The way of holiness leads to life (Jn 14:6). All other paths, no matter how attractive, end in death (Mt 7:13).

In the fourth century, the conversion of the Emperor Constantine was a watershed moment for the doctrine of sanctification. We cannot discuss the reasons here, but as the definition of the word "Christian" changed from "follower of the Way" to "citizen of

---

[27]*Didache* 1:1, *AF*, 345; Alistair C. Stewart, *On the Two Ways* (Yonkers: St. Vladimir's Seminary Press, 2011), 35.

the Roman Empire," the definition of "the Way" also changed.[28] The *Way* (singular) became *"ways"* (plural); the one path for all disciples was split into two different paths for two different kinds of Christians to walk. Eusebius (d. 339) claimed these two ways began at the time of Christ: *"Two ways of living* were given by the law of Christ to his church. The one is [for clergy and monks] ... *the perfect form* of the Christian life. And the other more humble, more human, [is for normal Christians] ... and a kind of *secondary grade of piety* is attributed to them."[29]

Eusebius suggested there was a "normal" Christian life lived by average Christians with a lower level of holiness, and then a "perfect form of the Christian life" lived only by an elite group.[30] Over the next thousand years those making baptismal vows ("ordinary" Christians) were almost completely eclipsed in emphasis by those making ordination and monastic vows (clergy and monks).[31] Baptismal vows involve a public commitment to following Jesus. They require a renunciation of the world, the flesh, and the Devil. Ordination and monastic vows indicate a public commitment to a clerical or spiritual way of life in order to serve the church and the world with a particular spiritual gift (*charism*). Believers who were ordained to church office (referred to as clergy) and those who had taken monastic vows (referred to as "spiritual") were required to live at a different standard of holiness ("perfection") than those simply baptized.[32] Rather than *one* way of discipleship, there

---

[28]See Hank Voss, *The Priesthood of All Believers and the Missio Dei: A Canonical, Catholic, and Contextual Perspective*, Princeton Theological Monographs (Eugene: Pickwick, 2016), 122–5.

[29]Eusebius, *The Proof of the Gospel*, trans. William John Ferrar (1920; repr., Eugene: Wipf and Stock, 2001), 48–50. I adapted Ferrar's translation for readability and added italics for emphasis.

[30]For additional insight, compare Eusebius's idea with the proposals about holiness and "the normal Christian life" found in William Law, *A Serious Call to a Devout and Holy Life: Adapted to the State and Condition of All Orders of Christians* (Grand Rapids: Eerdmans, 1966), 84–7; and Watchman Nee, *The Normal Christian Life* (Wheaton: Tyndale, 1977), 11–12.

[31]Martin Luther, "The Judgment of Martin Luther on Monastic Vows," in *LW* 44 (St. Louis: Concordia, 1966), 573–669.

[32]See, e.g., the essays overviewed by Greg Peters, "Introduction," in *A Companion to Priesthood and Holy Orders in the Middle Ages*, ed. Greg Peters and C. Colt Anderson (Boston: Brill, 2015), 1–3.

became *two ways*: a lower way for "normal" baptized believers and a *second* higher way for serious disciples (the monastic/spiritual and clerical vowed). From AD 500 to AD 1500, discipleship was largely monopolized by a specialized group of Christians made up of clergy and monks with the majority of baptized believers largely ignorant about the way of holiness.[33] Luther democratized holiness by emphasizing the priesthood of all baptized believers.[34]

The Eastern Way: Sanctification as Theosis

The Eastern Orthodox Church views salvation as Christification, deification, or *theosis*.[35] *Theosis* is a Greek word found in 1 Pet 2:4 where Peter describes believers as "partakers of the *divine* nature." Eastern Church leaders emphasized that through God's divine power and promises we can progressively participate more and more in God's own nature (2 Pet 1:3-4). For the Eastern Church, participation with God's work is an important part of *theosis*. While it is God's divine energy that works in believers, we are still called to "make every effort" to grow in godliness (2 Pet 1:3-11). The walk of faith is not easy; opposition from the world, the flesh, and the devil requires constant vigilance and diligence. Christians pursue *theosis* through a developing life of continuous prayer and participation in the church.[36] While evangelicals have some concerns about aspects

---

[33]The problem was not with the elevated commitment of monks (both men and women), but rather with the lowering of the value and expectations related to baptismal commitment. For an explanation of how the wisdom of the monastic tradition is relevant to all believers today see Greg Peters, *Monkhood of All Believers: The Monastic Foundation of Christian Spirituality* (Grand Rapids: Baker Academic, 2018). Cf. Voss, *Priesthood of All Believers*, 122-8.

[34]Much more could be said. See Evan Howard's overview of twelve schools of Christian spirituality that have especially influenced evangelicals. Evan Howard, "The Schools of Christian Spirituality," in *Reading the Christian Spiritual Classics: A Guide for Evangelicals*, ed. Jamin Goggin and Kyle Strobel (Downers Grove: InterVarsity, 2013), 63-78. NWDCS includes articles on more than fifty Christian spirtualties—many of which have had influence on various regional forms of evangelicalism.

[35]Brad Nassif, "Orthodox Spirituality," in *Four Views on Christian Spirituality*, ed. Bruce A. Demarest (Grand Rapids: Zondervan Academic, 2012), 53; Norman Russell, *Fellow Workers with God: Orthodox Thinking on Theosis* (Crestwood: St. Vladimir's Seminary Press, 2009).

[36]For one example, see Olga Savin, trans., *The Way of a Pilgrim and the Pilgrim Continues His Way* (Boston: Shambhala, 2001).

of Orthodoxy's doctrine of *theosis*, we welcome it to the extent that it points to clear biblical teaching. Recent conversations show how Martin Luther may have been influenced by Orthodox ideas related to *theosis* more than was previously realized.[37] There is also evidence that John Wesley's understanding of sanctification was influenced by Eastern theologians like Ephrem the Syrian (d. 373) and John Chrysostom (d. 407).[38]

The Western Way(s): Three Stages, a Spiritual Mountain Climb, and a Love Story

The Western Church birthed the Protestant Reformation, which in turn birthed evangelicalism. With this genealogy, Western understandings of salvation and spirituality are especially important to contemporary evangelical views on sanctification. In the Western church, concepts related to spirituality center around means of grace. How does one receive grace from the Father by the Son through the action of the Holy Spirit today? A story by C. S. Lewis illustrates the Western quest. In Lewis's *Voyage of the Dawn Treader*, a young boy named Eustace is accidently turned into a dragon through lust and greed.[39] After much sorrow, Eustace meets a Christ figure named Aslan. While Eustace is unable to remove his dragon scales by himself, he can choose to position himself near Aslan. Once in Aslan's presence, Eustace accepts Aslan's offer of freedom from his dragon flesh. He lies flat on his back to allow Aslan to "do it"—an activity with a mysterious passivity. Eustace is then raised (through water!) as a new creation—a new boy—even though his external appearance appears largely the same as his pre-dragon self. Like Eustace's transformation through the process (or means) of drawing near to Aslan, the Western tradition emphasizes

---

[37]Tuomo Mannermaa, *Christ Present in Faith: Luther's View of Justification*, ed. Kirsi Irmeli Stjerna (Minneapolis: Fortress, 2005); Jordan Cooper, *Christification: A Lutheran Approach to Theosis* (Eugene: Wipf and Stock, 2014).

[38]Richard P. Heitzenrater, "John Wesley's Reading of and References to the Early Church Fathers," in *Orthodox and Wesleyan Spirituality*, ed. S. T. Kimbrough (Crestwood: St. Vladimir's Seminary Press, 2002), 25–32; and Francis Young, "Inner Struggle: Some Parallels between the Spirituality of John Wesley and the Greek Fathers," in *Orthodox and Wesleyan Spirituality*, ed. S. T. Kimbrough (Crestwood: St. Vladimir's Seminary Press, 2002), 168.

[39]C. S. Lewis, *The Chronicles of Narnia* (New York: Harper Collins, 2001), 473–5.

human growth in holiness through divine gifts received through particular means.

Medieval Christianity made use of at least three models for spirituality and "sanctification" that continue to influence evangelicalism today. These models do not belong exclusively to the Western church, but they shape the tradition's lived reality. Greg Peters introduces them as (1) the triple way, (2) the spiritual ascent, and (3) the spiritual theology of love (a love story).[40] The triple way's (*triplica via*) roots come from biblical texts like 1 John 2:12–14, where spiritual growth is compared to physical growth (cf. Lk 2:52). It was first articulated in Egypt by Clement of Alexandria (d. 215) and Origen (d. 254) and then expanded upon by theologians like Evagrius of Pontis (d. 399), John Cassian (d. 435), and Benedict (d. 547). Origen, for example, taught that King Solomon's canonical writings (Proverbs, Ecclesiastes, and Song of Solomon) provide a three-stage map to spiritual growth. The triple way was expanded by a Franciscan theologian, Bonaventure (d. 1274), who articulated a specific focus for each of the three stages.[41] The first stage focuses on allowing the Holy Spirit to bring conviction and repentance. The second stage focuses on growing in the power of the Holy Spirit, especially through imitating Christ's life. The final stage reflects on Christ as the soul's spouse as a means to understand participation in inter-Trinitarian love through the Holy Spirit. Lutheran pastor Johann Arndt used the triple way as the structure for his spiritual classic *True Christianity*, a work known as the Protestant version of *The Imitation of Christ*.[42] Calvin's theology can also be viewed in relation to the triple way (see Table 6.4).

The second model for understanding evangelical models of sanctification is spiritual ascent—a lifelong mountain climb. John Climacus (d. 649) wrote *Ladder of Divine Ascent*, a book that has been read annually by Orthodox monks during Lent for more than a thousand years; many monks will read this spiritual classic

---

[40]Greg Peters, "Spiritual Theology: A Historical Overview," in *Reading the Christian Spiritual Classics*, 79–94.

[41]St. Bonaventure, *The Triple Way*, ed. Peter Damian M. Fehlner (New Bedford: Academy of the Immaculate Heart, 2012).

[42]In the introduction to book three, Arndt explains his use of the triple way as the organizing structure for his larger project. See Johann Arndt, *True Christianity*, ed. John Wesley (1606; repr., Vancouver: Regent College, 2012), 242.

TABLE 6.4 *Historical Development of the Triple Way*

1 John 2:12–14	Origen and Evagrius	Bonaventure and the Triple Way	Johann Arndt's True Christianity	John Calvin
First Century	Second–Eleventh Century	Eleventh Century –Present	1606–Present	1560–Present
Children	Proverbs Praktikos (Ethics)	Purgation Focus on the Cross and Death to Sin	Book 1: Foundation Stage Repentance	Justification
Youth	Ecclesiastes Gnostikos (Contemplation of Creation)	Illumination Focus on imitating the life of Christ	Book 2: Middle Stage Illumination	Sanctification
Elders	Song of Solomon Kephalaia Gnostica (Contemplation of Trinity)	Perfection Love and Union with the Trinity	Book 3: Perfect Stage Union and Perfect Love	Glorification

Source: Table created by Hank Voss.

fifty or sixty times during their life.[43] Climacus builds on biblical images like Enoch and Elijah's ascents into heaven, Jacob's ladder, Moses's climbing of Mt. Sinai, the Psalms of Ascent (Ps 120–134), and Jesus's growth during his earthly life. Climacus lays out thirty steps for spiritual growth based on the thirty (or so) years Jesus lived on earth prior to his baptism.[44] While Climacus is an Eastern theologian, the model of spiritual journey he illustrates is foundational in the West where we find it in Augustine, Anselm, Teresa of Avila, Dante, and many others.[45] One example of the ascent model influencing evangelicals is in John Bunyan's spiritual classic, *The Pilgrim's Progress*.[46]

A third model for growth in godliness is the "soul's love story." This path finds its roots in the *Shema*—Israel's daily prayer— (Deut 6:5), the Great Commandment (Lk 10:27), and the *Song of Solomon*. The ancient and medieval church universally read the *Song of Solomon* as a love story between Christ and the soul or between Christ and the church (Eph 5:25–32). Some call *Songs* the "Magna Carta, or founding document" for both Jewish and Christian models of spirituality.[47] Most agree that Bernard of Clairvaux's (d. 1153) *On Loving God* is one of the best examples of the love-story model. Martin Luther endorsed Bernard's preaching on the love of Christ, and Puritan authors cite Bernard almost as much as Augustine.[48] Bernard's path to perfect love cannot be explored here, but many evangelical understandings of holiness were shaped by the vision of experiencing perfect love for God and neighbors. Henry Scougal (d. 1657), who died at the young age of 27, wrote a short guide to holiness called *The Life of God in the*

---

[43]Kallistos Ware, "Introduction," in *John Climacus: The Ladder of Divine Ascent*, trans. Colm Luibheid and Norman Russell (New York: Paulist, 1982), 1.

[44]Ware, "Introduction," 11.

[45]Robert McMahon, *Understanding the Medieval Meditative Ascent: Augustine, Anselm, Boethius, & Dante* (Washington, DC: Catholic University of America Press, 2006), 2; Peters, "Spiritual Theology," 86–9.

[46]For an overview of the importance of *Pilgrim's Progress* to evangelical mission work see David Dixon, "The Second Text: Missionary Publishing and Bunyan's Pilgrim's Progress," *International Bulletin of Mission Research* 36 (April 2012): 86–90.

[47]Bernard McGinn, "'One Word Will Contain within Itself a Thousand Mysteries': Teresa of Avila, the First Woman Commentator on the Song of Songs," *Spiritus: A Journal of Christian Spirituality* 16, no. 1 (spring 2016): 21.

[48]James Houston, "Editor's Note and Introduction," in *The Love of God*, by Bernard of Clairvaux, Classics of Faith and Devotion (Vancouver: Regent College, 2018), xx.

Soul of Man.[49] His description of the love of God and neighbor had a powerful transforming impact on John Wesley and the other members of his Oxford Holiness Club.[50] To sum up, Protestant, and then evangelical, approaches to sanctification were shaped by three models: the triple way, the concept of a spiritual ascent, and a theology of love.

The Protestant Way: Sanctification after the Reformation

Sanctification involves a process of becoming holy. Believers grow in holiness through participation in Christ's life and death. The *Westminster Shorter Catechism* (Question 35; 1647) defines sanctification as "the work of God's free grace, whereby we are renewed in the whole man after the image of God, and are enabled more and more to *die unto sin*, and *live unto righteousness*." What does it mean to die to sin and to live unto righteousness? The following section addresses this question by looking at Martin Luther, John Calvin, and John Wesley.

Martin Luther: A Return to One Way for the Priesthood of All Believers

One of Martin Luther's gifts to the church was rediscovering the priesthood of all believers. Known as the "priesthood of the baptized" among the Orthodox and as the "priesthood of the faithful" in the Roman Catholic Church, the doctrine was in dismal condition when Luther nailed his ninety-five theses to the Wittenberg church door (1517). Luther emphasized that the believer is justified by faith in Christ and is already married to Christ (united) as a member of the church. Thus, everything that belongs to Christ—holiness, righteousness, and participation in Christ's royal priesthood—now belong to the believer through faith. Luther argued that believers are temples of the Holy Spirit. Since they are already holy by virtue of the Holy One dwelling in them, they are now called to live holy

---

[49]Henry Scougal, *The Life of God in the Soul of Man*, ed. J. I. Packer (Fearn: Christian Focus, 1996).
[50]Scougal, *Life of God*, 6–7.

lives as members of Christ's royal priesthood. A believer's baptism is their public ordination to service as a member of Christ's royal priesthood to both fellow believers and to creation regardless of whether one's vocation is selling shoes (D. L. Moody), repairing pots (John Bunyan), or milking cows.[51]

Lutherans describe sanctification as "the art of getting used to justification," and emphasize that believers are simultaneously justified and sinners (*simul justus et peccator*). The result is that some Lutherans are ambivalent as to whether believers should "do" things to grow spiritually. They tend to view any talk of human effort as proof of practical Pelagianism. Lutherans often place more emphasis on judicial images and vocabulary like "justification" (think "justice system") than on biological ones like "new birth," "new man," and growing into "spiritual maturity."

As evangelical Protestantism became more diverse, so too did views on sanctification. To help us follow these developments we look at two groups. The first group often places priority on sanctification's participation in the *death of Christ*. The second group emphasizes sanctification's participation in the *life of Jesus* and the present power of the Holy Spirit. Both groups affirm sanctification's participation in Christ's death and life; it is simply a matter of what receives emphasis. Today's globally diverse evangelical family can be categorized in other ways as well, but this strategy focuses on strengths.

John Calvin and Sanctification as Participation in Christ's Death

When John Calvin designed his personal seal, he chose the image of a hand lifting up a heart to heaven with the words "willingly and sincerely" (*prompte et sincere*). His most famous book, *The Institutes of the Christian Religion*, provides instruction for serious Christians who want to learn how to read Scripture in order to grow in holiness (the word "piety" occurs twice in the original title). At the heart of the *Institutes* are five chapters on the Christian life (*Inst.* 3.6–10). Even during Calvin's lifetime, these five chapters were published on their own under the title,

---

[51]As persuasively argued by Peter Leithart, *The Priesthood of the Plebs: A Theology of Baptism* (Eugene: Wipf & Stock, 2003).

The Golden Booklet of the Christian Life. Calvin views the Christian life as a journey where "we travel as pilgrims in this world" (*Inst.* 3.7.3). On this journey, Christians deny ourselves, take up our cross, and follow Jesus. The two longest chapters in the *Golden Booklet* emphasize this theme (*Inst.* 3.7–8). The first chapter describes each believer's responsibility to offer their whole life to God as a "living sacrifice" (Rom 12:1). The second chapter emphasizes that each believer must take up his or her cross and follow Jesus (Matt 16:24).

The word "piety" (*pietas*) occurs repeatedly in Calvin's writing but is rare today. A positive understanding of Christian piety refers to one who is taking personal responsibility for their duty to pursue a humble and holy life lived in the presence and power of the Holy Spirit. Calvin believed that the first step of piety was to die to one's desires and take up the cross of Christ "to the end that they be conformed to Christ" (*Inst.* 3.8.1). As one dies to sin, one begins the process of progressive sanctification. How does one die to sin and progressively grow in sanctification? Calvin provides a number of suggestions (see especially *Inst.* 3.20), but one of the best examples was explored above in Owen's *The Mortification of Sin.* While Owen's text gave us an excellent picture on how to die to sin (mortification), we turn to Wesley for an emphasis on how to live in the Spirit (vivification).

John Wesley and Sanctification as Participation in Christ's Resurrection Life

In the year 1740, John Wesley declared that for the rest of his life (fifty-one more years) he would be "*homo unius libri,* 'a man of one book'" (*WJW* 11:373). Despite his critics calling him a "Bible-moth," his claim cannot be taken too literally, as he edited or wrote some four hundred works. Of special interest to students of sanctification are the fifty volumes he edited for the serious Christians called *The Christian Library.* The *Christian Library* was a full-shelf collection of spiritual classics and spiritual biographies edited by Wesley to equip Methodist leaders to grow toward Christlikeness. Wesley knew that formal theological education would be unavailable for many of his followers, and he published texts helpful for "plain" Christians hungry for holiness. Wesley's own hunger was initially kindled by spiritual classics, and he longed for his friends and coworkers to also burn with this passion.[52]

While *The Christian Library* included Lutheran texts like Johann Arndt's *True Christianity* and Anglican texts like Henry Scougal's *Life of God in the Soul of Man* (both mentioned above), the majority of texts (over one hundred of them) were by or about Puritans.[53] For example, Wesley chose five of John Owen's books for his followers to read including *The Mortification of Sin* (discussed above). Wesley wanted Methodists to read Puritans because Puritans were the best resource he knew on how to practically live the Christian life.

Wesley's chief interest was helping believers learn to walk in "humble, gentle, patient love of God" and neighbor (*WJW* 11:446). When God's love is ruling a believer's emotions, words, and actions, Wesley called it "Christian perfection." Christian perfection is not the perfection experienced in the Garden of Eden (*adamic* perfection) or that angels experience (*angelic* perfection). It does not mean a believer is without sin, weakness, temptation, psychological brokenness, finitude, or forgetfulness (*absolute* perfection). Rather, Christian perfection emphasizes the "new creation" the Holy Spirit creates when regenerating a believer's heart. The Holy Spirit's power "breaks the power of cancelled sin and sets the prisoner free" to love God and neighbor with their whole heart.

Wesley also refers to Christian perfection as entire sanctification (1 Thess 5:23) or as having a "pure heart" (cf. Mt 5:8). Just as one with a pure heart can still grow, so can one who has been "entirely sanctified." However, for Wesley, the possession of a pure heart reflects an intentional choice believers make at some point *after* their initial conversion when they understand more of what it means to follow and love Jesus. The specifics of exactly what entire sanctification looks like are unique to each individual, but after this experience, believers find a new level of power for both holy living and missional service. Diane Leclerc provides an example of how one Wesleyan family of churches (Nazarene) interprets Wesley's teaching today. According to Leclerc, there are four components to a Wesleyan understanding of sanctification: initial, progressive, entire, and final.[54]

---

[52]T. A. Noble, *Holy Trinity, Holy People: The Theology of Christian Perfecting* (Eugene: Cascade, 2013), 76.

[53]Robert C. Monk, *John Wesley: His Puritan Heritage: A Study of the Christian Life* (Nashville: Abingdon, 1966).

[54]Leclerc, *Discovering Christian Holiness*, 178.

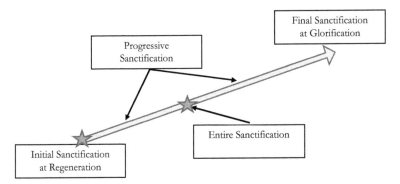

FIGURE 6.1 *Wesleyan understanding of sanctification (adapted from Leclerc,* Discovering Christian Holiness, *178).*

Figure 6.1 illustrates these components' relationship. Wesleyan theology attempts to take seriously the lived experience of the biblical texts found in Table 6.1. What does it mean to "have a pure heart" (Matt 5:8) or to be entirely sanctified (1 Thess 5:23)? Wesleyans would assure the believer that they receive all of the Holy Spirit they will ever have at the moment of regeneration—after all the Holy Spirt is a person and how could one have half a person? When the Spirit enters a believer's life, it is called initial sanctification. After a period of progressive growth, Wesleyans believe that there is often a moment of full consecration or surrender to the Spirit called "entire sanctification." One mark of entire sanctification is that a believer is deeply involved in active service to the body of Christ and intentional witness in the world. Believers who have been entirely sanctified continue to grow and develop until death at which point they receive final sanctification also known as glorification.

In this section we have explored developments in sanctification and spirituality from the *Didache*'s initial emphasis on *the Way* to John Wesley's emphasis on mature Christians walking in *perfect love* for God and others. We now turn to some challenges this doctrine presents.

Challenges to Evangelical Holiness

Applying sanctification is dangerous. The pursuit of holiness can be like climbing Angel's Landing Trail in Utah's Zion National Park, a narrow path with deadly cliffs on either side. As John Bunyan observed in *Pilgrim's Progress*, there are perennial challenges to understanding and applying the truths of sanctification to the Christian life. Many sincere believers have wandered to one side and fallen into the chasm of legalism (also known as moralism or neonomianism) while others have drifted to the other side and perished on the cliff of antinomianism—the belief that Christians have a "license to sin," since laws no longer apply to them.[55] Evangelicals have debated the balance between these two in every generation. Wisdom involves both intellectual knowledge and an understanding of what to do that with that knowledge. Thus, evangelicals will need to think through and then apply biblical truth on holiness to a number of contemporary issues. Consider the following for example.

First, today's rapid changes in neuroscience raise numerous questions for evangelicals concerned with sanctification. New insights are regularly discovered with significant implications for understanding how our mind, body, and soul interact. To give one example, victims of trauma often experience "black outs" or complete memory loss in relation to the traumatic event they experienced. When asked about the trauma, they often do not remember the event and vehemently deny that anything negative took place (e.g., many victims of child sexual abuse). At other times, a behavior that might be considered sinful (e.g., obesity) could actually be a coping mechanism for dealing with a much deeper soul wound.[56] Connected to the contemporary revolution in neuroscience are advances in psychology related to human development, learning, and growth. These discoveries about the human mind and body are often important for students of sanctification. While there is much discussion of these advances among Christian psychologists

---

[55]Martin Luther coined the word "antinomian." See his *Against the Antinomians*. For Wesleyan concerns about Reformed tendencies toward antinomianism see the foundational work of John Fletcher, *Checks to Antinomianism* (New York: Soul and Mason, 1820), https://commons.ptsem.edu/id/checkstoantinomi01flet.

[56]These examples and many more are raised by a careful reading of the research on trauma reported by Bessel A. Van der Kolk, *The Body Keeps the Score: Brain, Mind, and Body in the Healing of Trauma* (New York: Viking, 2014). For further examples, see Thomas M. Crisp, Steven L. Porter, and Gregg A. Ten Elshof, eds., *Psychology and Spiritual Formation in Dialogue: Moral and Spiritual Change in Christian Perspective* (Downers Grove: InterVarsity, 2018).

and Christian educators, the fragmentation and specialization of theology has meant that these discoveries are often not addressed by evangelical theologians.[57]

A second challenge needing consideration is the balance between individual and social holiness. On one hand, some evangelicals have almost exclusively focused on the individual's sanctification process. On the other, evangelicals in the Anabaptist tradition emphasize with John Wesley that the gospel "knows of... no holiness but social holiness."[58] John Woolman (d. 1772) provides one model of careful thought on social holiness. Woolman was a contemporary of Jonathan Edwards. Edwards rationalized his family's slave ownership of an African American woman on the basis of living in a society where everyone was already complicit in the sin.[59] Woolman, in contrast, succeeded in leading his denomination to abolish slavery and refused to buy or use products that were produced by slave labor.[60] Another example come from the contrast between the Confessing Church movement in Nazi Germany and certain Baptist churches whose leaders claimed, "In the third Reich the situation of the Baptists never deteriorated to the point where they felt the government was demanding disobedience to the gospel."[61] Many evangelicals today would suggest this statement reveals a myopic vision of social holiness, yet it is not clear how many of these same evangelicals are ready to address the social logs in their own eye (Matt 7:3). Biblically, Paul wrote about the temple of the Holy Spirit including both the individual believer and the people of God as a whole (1 Cor 3:26; 6:19).[62] A faithful doctrine of sanctification will press into this tension and fully embrace both the individual and social dimensions of holiness.

---

[57]For an introduction to this topic see James Riley Estep and Jonathan H. Kim, eds., *Christian Formation: Integrating Theology & Human Development* (Nashville: B&H Academic, 2010).

[58]Alan Kreider, *Social Holiness: A Way of Living for God's Nation* (Eugene: Wipf & Stock, 2008), 11.

[59]George M. Marsden, *Jonathan Edwards: A Life* (New York: Yale University Press, 2003), 258.

[60]John Woolman, "Introduction," in *The Journal of John Woolman*, ed. Phillips Moulton (Richmond: Friends United, 1989), 11, http://search.ebscohost.com/login. aspx?direct=true&scope=site&db=nlebk&db=nlabk&AN=2008633.

[61]Waldren Scott, *Bring Forth Justice* (Grand Rapids: Eerdmans, 1980), 213.

[62]Nijay Gupta, "Which 'Body' Is a Temple (1 Corinthians 6:19)? Paul beyond the Individual/Communal Divide," *Catholic Biblical Quarterly* 72 (2010): 518–36.

A final challenge centers on the choice of vocabulary to emphasize when describing the believer's lived experience of growing in holiness. As noted above, evangelicals use many terms to describe the sanctification process. Is there a single term that evangelicals could agree to emphasize when describing the growth to which sanctification points? Should a more objective and legal vocabulary be preferred, emphasizing "Christian perfectionism," "depravity," "imparted righteousness," "imputed righteousness," and "positional holiness"? Or, should a more personal and relational vocabulary be used, emphasizing "consecration to God," "covenant," "discipleship," "participation in Christ," and walking in the "power of the Spirit," placing emphasis on a growing relationship with Father, Son, and Holy Spirit?[63] The former is the traditional language used in Protestant systematic theology, the latter the traditional language of spiritual theology. Whatever terminology is chosen, it needs to draw attention to the centrality of Jesus to both sanctification and spirituality! In the next section, we meet a recent evangelical writer who has proposed use of the term "discipleship" as a possible way forward.

Forward: Dallas Willard's Theology of Discipleship

In 1961, the Motilone-Bari tribe in the jungles of Columbia was facing extinction as a result of exploitation, wars, disease, and hunger. The situation changed, however, after the tribe decided to "walk in the footsteps of Jesus on the trail of life's experience."[64] Dallas Willard (1935–2013), an important North American evangelical, would agree with the tribe's description of the Christian life. For clarity, he would explain that walking in Jesus's footsteps is only possible through the Spirit's power as Christ's kingdom becomes present on

---

[63]Deprivity (in contrast to depravity) is a Wesleyan perspective on sin that emphasizes humanity's main problem as a broken relationship with God rather than internal pollution. Consecration usually refers to intentional human action in contrast with sanctification as a monergistic action of the Holy Spirit. For more on these terms see glossaries and discussions in Leclerc, *Discovering Christian Holiness*; Horton, *The Christian Faith*; Treier, *IET*.

[64]For the story of the conversion of the Motilone-Bari tribe, see Bruce Olson, *Bruchko* (Lake Mary: Charisma, 2006).

earth as it is in heaven.[65] Willard taught that the best vocabulary to describe spiritual formation is the language of discipleship. He was concerned that evangelicalism lacked and desperately needed to develop "a theology of discipleship."[66] For Willard, sanctification is irreducibly personal as it begins and ends with a person—Jesus.[67] The Christian life is thus a Spirit-empowered walk of obedience to Jesus's command, "you follow me" (Jn 21:15–22).

Willard describes our participation in sanctification with the acronym VIM: *Vision, Intention, Means*. Willard uses the examples of learning Arabic or participating in an Alcoholics Anonymous (AA) group to show how many human changes follow the same reliable VIM pattern. He explains, "If this VIM pattern is not put in place properly and held there, Christ simply will not be formed in us."[68] What is this VIM pattern in Christian spiritual formation? Believers must have a clear *vision* of Christlikeness. They must make a conscious decision of the will to pursue that vision (*intention*). And they must understand the *means* God has chosen for growth as disciples. The pursuit of a clear vision of God has traditionally been known as contemplation or the beatific vision.[69] Once a vision of God, especially as seen in the image of Christ, is clearly held before us, we must make a conscious decision of the will (*intention*) to pursue this vision through the Holy Spirit's power. As Cassian (d. 435) explains, "There is no arrival unless there is a definite plan to go."[70]

---

[65]For an example see Dallas Willard, *The Divine Conspiracy: Rediscovering Our Hidden Life in God* (San Francisco: HarperSanFrancisco, 1998).

[66]Willard, "Discipleship," 245.

[67]Willard was part of the philosophical school known as personalism. This school emphasizes the centrality of personhood. In *The Disciple*, James Houston builds on Kierkegaard to explain the personal nature of discipleship. Willard writes the foreword to this text. See James M. Houston, *The Disciple: Following the True Mentor*, Soul's Longing Series (Colorado Springs: Cook, 2007), 144.

[68]Dallas Willard, *Renovation of the Heart: Putting on the Character of Christ* (Colorado Springs: NavPress, 2002), 85.

[69]See Hans Boersma, *Seeing God: The Beatific Vision in Christian Tradition* (Grand Rapids: Eerdmans, 2018); and the collection of essays in John Coe and Kyle Strobel, eds., *Embracing Contemplation: Reclaiming a Christian Spiritual Practice* (Downers Grove: IVP Academic, 2019).

[70]Cited in Simon Chan, *Spiritual Theology: A Systematic Study of the Christian Life* (Downers Grove: IVP Academic, 1998), 18. Cf. Cassian, *Conferences*, ACW 2.26, 104.

Finally, for Christian spiritual formation, there must also be a use of appropriate *means* of grace. A relational theology of discipleship embraces the truth that sanctification is opposed to earning, not to effort. Growth in holiness and relational intimacy with God requires our participation in spiritual disciplines and practices—the *means* used by the Holy Spirit in sanctification. J. I. Packer explains, "Habit forming is the Spirit's ordinary way of leading us on in holiness."[71] Throughout church history, seven *means* central to helping believers become conformed to the image of Christ (or reaching spiritual maturity) are baptism, prayer, Scripture engagement, participation in the ministry of the body of Christ, engaging in proclamation, embracing the accountability of church discipline, and a regular practice of the Lord's Supper.[72] These means include participation in small groups, Christian friendship, Christian marriage, and the parenting of children. Through the Holy Spirit's power and presence, these means help believers grow in love, leading to greater holiness and conformity to Jesus in mind, heart, and behavior.

This chapter has explored the doctrine of sanctification and the Spirit's work in bringing believers into Christ-like maturity (perfection). After exploring John Owen's *The Mortification of Sin*, we took a brief tour of the streams that feed the evangelical vision of the church. We then looked at six challenges facing evangelicals as they seek to grow in spiritual maturity. Finally, we looked to the future and asked whether discipleship might be a fruitful concept for articulating truths related to sanctification moving forward.

Will evangelicals in this generation take up Willard's challenge to develop a theology of discipleship? What about the challenge to embrace John Owen's evangelical holiness? Evangelicals hope that what was said at Owen's funeral might be said of them: our "aim in life was to promote holiness."[73]

---

[71]J. I. Packer, *Keep in Step with the Spirit: Finding Fullness in Our Walk with God* (Old Tappan: Revell, 1984), 109–10.

[72]For a defense of these seven practices in conversation with Martin Luther, Karl Barth, James Howard Yoder, and Alasdair MacIntyre, see Voss, *Priesthood of All Believers*, 209–39. Note that what is called Scripture engagement here is there called *lectio divina*. For examples of Scripture engagement, see resources developed by Taylor University's Center for Scripture Engagement at www.biblegateway.com/resources/scripture-engagement/.

[73]Stated by David Clarkson at the funeral sermon for John Owen. Cited in Sinclair B. Ferguson, "The Reformed View," in *Christian Spirituality: Five Views of Sanctification*, ed. Donald Alexander (Downers Grove: IVP Academic, 1989), 48.

Recommended Reading

Michael Allen, *Sanctification*, New Studies in Dogmatics (Grand Rapids: Zondervan, 2017).

Simon Chan, *Spiritual Theology: A Systematic Study of the Christian Life* (Downers Grove: IVP Academic, 1998).

John Owen, *The Mortification of Sin*, Puritan Paperbacks (Carlisle: Banner of Truth, 2004).

Phoebe Palmer, *Phoebe Palmer: Selected Writings*, ed. Thomas Oden, vol. 59, Sources of American Spirituality (New York: Paulist, 1988).

A. W. Tozer, *The Pursuit of God* (Camp Hill: Christian Publications, 1993).

John Wesley, *A Plain Account of Christian Perfection* (Kansas City: Beacon Hill, 1978).

Dallas Willard, *Renovation of the Heart: Putting on the Character of Christ* (Colorado Springs: NavPress, 2002).

Developments

7

"You Will Receive Power": The Holy Spirit

We love the Holy Spirit within the unity of the Trinity, along with God the Father and God the Son. He is the missionary Spirit sent by the missionary Father and the missionary Son, breathing life and power into God's missionary Church. We love and pray for the presence of the Holy Spirit because without the witness of the Spirit to Christ, our own witness is futile. Without the convicting work of the Spirit, our preaching is in vain. Without the gifts, guidance and power of the Spirit, our mission is mere human effort. And without the fruit of the Spirit, our unattractive lives cannot reflect the beauty of the gospel.

THE CAPE TOWN CONFESSION §5, LAUSANNE MOVEMENT[1]

Evangelicals focus much attention on Jesus, but we have often neglected the significance of the Holy Spirit. Some evangelicals might respond to questions about the Spirit like believers in Ephesus who told Paul, "We have not even heard there is a Holy Spirit" (Acts 19:2). Conversely, other evangelicals place more emphasis on the Holy Spirit than appropriate. The formal study of the Holy Spirit is

---

[1]Julia Cameron, ed., *The Lausanne Legacy: Landmarks in Global Mission* (Peabody: Hendrickson, 2016), 113.

known as pneumatology; the term itself helps explain why the Spirit sometimes remains in the background. The Greek word *pneuma* means spirit, wind, or breath. As Jesus reminded his disciples, the Holy Spirit, like the wind, is not seen, but the effects of the Spirit (i.e., fruit), like the effects of the wind, are easily discernable (John 3:8). Even though pneumatology comes toward the end in this book's discussion of evangelical doctrine, it is not least. In fact, we have already discussed the doctrine in a number of places: Scripture—especially relating to inspiration and illumination; salvation including conversion, adoption, sanctification, and glorification; and especially in discussions of the Trinity and mission.

So why treat the Holy Spirit now—in the book's final section? For one reason, there has been a "pneumatological renaissance" of late in evangelical reflection on the Holy Spirit.[2] Christians of all kinds are talking more about the Holy Spirit, but especially evangelicals since a significant global majority of evangelicals now fall into "charismatic" or "Pentecostal" churches.[3] Thus, our treatment of pneumatology comes last not because it is least important, but because it is especially important to where evangelicalism is going. We agree with Karl Barth's observation that pneumatology is "the future of Christian Theology," or at the least, we affirm with Orthodox theologian Nikolay Berdyaev that pneumatology is one of the "last unexplored theological frontier[s]."[4] Recall the Puritan pastor John Robinson, who reminded his Pilgrim congregation, "There is yet fresh truth and light to break forth from God's Word." As evangelicals continue to read Scripture, they continue to find fresh wind and fire in their experience and encounters with the Holy Spirit.[5]

This chapter explores a conciliar evangelical statement on the Holy Spirit from the 2010 Cape Town Commitment. This statement,

---

[2]Veli-Matti Kärkkäinen, *Pneumatology: The Holy Spirit in Ecumenical, International, and Contextual Perspective* (Grand Rapids: Baker Academic, 2002), 11.

[3]The global Pentecostal and charismatic movements number nearly six hundred million members. Pew Research Center, "The Size and Distribution of the World's Christian Population," *Pew Research Center's Religion & Public Life Project* (blog), 2011, https://www.pewforum.org/2011/12/19/global-christianity-exec.

[4]Kärkkäinen, *Pneumatology*, 13.

[5]For two North American examples, see Jim Cymbala, *Fresh Wind, Fresh Fire: What Happens When God's Spirit Invades the Hearts of His People*, rev. ed. (Grand Rapids: Zondervan, 2018); Jack Deere, *Surprised by the Power of the Spirit* (Grand Rapids: Zondervan Academic, 1996).

signed by evangelicals from more nations than are in the United Nations, provides a global window into evangelical emphasis on the Holy Spirit. The history section looks at two evangelical thinkers who made significant contributions to evangelical pneumatology. John Owen's thinking has significantly impacted many evangelical streams. In a similar way, Phoebe Palmer's teaching has helped to shape the Wesleyan, Holiness, Pentecostal, and Charismatic movements. Her contributions are thus also important for evangelical thinking about the Holy Spirit. Finally, the chapter ends with identifying challenges and opportunities facing evangelicals moving forward.

Doctrine: "We Love the Holy Spirit"

Chapter 2 introduced the global evangelical Lausanne Movement, one that continues into the present. On October 16–25, 2010, some 4,200 Christian leaders from 198 countries gathered in Cape Town, South Africa, to commit themselves to one another and to shared participation in God's global mission. Fruit from this congress included the Cape Town Commitment, a document with two parts: a call to love (Part 1) and a call to serve (Part 2). Part 1, entitled "For the Lord we Love: The Cape Town Confession of Faith," consists of ten sections focused on shared doctrine. It continues the Lausanne Covenant's aim of "doctrinal breadth within boundaries" by pursuing unity in essentials and charity in "non-essentials."[6] The Confession acknowledges the presence of many sincere followers of Jesus in other Christian traditions (e.g., Roman Catholic and Orthodox churches), but aims to identify and emphasize the central doctrines of the global evangelical community.

Part 2, entitled "For the World We Serve: The Cape Town Call to Action," consists of six areas where the congress discerned the Holy Spirit leading the church into active mission. Space constraints only permit examination of Section 5 from the Confession (hereafter CTC §5) titled, "We Love God the Holy Spirit." The entirety of Section 5 is printed above as the chapter's epigraph.

---

[6]Cameron, *Lausanne Legacy*, 103.

The Holy Spirit Is a Person in Relationship with the Father and the Son

Doctrinally, evangelicals affirm the Nicene Creed's Trinitarian confession. But just as Stephen Charnock (d. 1680) noted in his day that many Christians were living as "practical atheists," so today many evangelicals live as "practical binitarians"—operating in conscious communion with only two of the three persons of the Trinity. The neglected divine person has usually been the Holy Spirit.[7] To address this concern, the Cape Town Confession affirms, "We love the Holy Spirit" (*CTC* §5). One hundred years before Cape Town, the evangelist and teacher R. A. Torrey noted, "Before one can correctly understand the work of the Holy Spirit, he must first of all know the Spirit Himself."[8] Who then is the Holy Spirit that the Confession calls believers to love? Scripture provides a clear answer.

First, the Holy Spirit is a person like the Father and the Son. Jesus refers to the Spirit as a person (Jn 16:13) who is like Jesus (Jn 14:16). Jesus promises that the Spirit will be a *paraclete* like he has been to his disciples (cf. 1 Jn 2:1). Jesus who was a friend, teacher, guide, comforter, advocate, and counselor to his disciples while on earth has now sent his Spirit to do this same personal work in the present (Lk 12:12; Jn 14:26; 16:13–15; Acts 8:29). The Spirit helps believers understand Scripture and how it relates to Jesus (1 Cor 2:9–14; cf. Lk 24:25). The Spirit reminds believers of what God has said (Jn 14:25; Isa 59:21). The Spirit can be grieved and lied to like Jesus or a human person (Eph 4:30; Heb 10:29; Acts 5:3). Thus, the Spirit is a person, not an impersonal power (Acts 10:28, 1 Cor 2:4). Scripture clarifies that the Holy Spirit is not only a person but also a divine person. Paul explains that the Lord (*Yahweh*) is the Spirit (2 Cor 3:17–18). The angel Gabriel reveals that the Holy Spirit is God while talking with Mary (Lk 1:35). Peter calls the Spirit, "God," when speaking with Ananias (Acts 5:3–4). Throughout Scripture, the Holy Spirit shares the nature of God (omniscience, omnipresence, omnipotence, eternality), does the divine work of

---

[7]Francis Chan and Danae Yankoski, *Forgotten God: Reversing Our Tragic Neglect of the Holy Spirit* (Colorado Springs: Cook, 2009).

[8]R. A. Torrey, *The Person and Work of the Holy Spirit* (1910; repr., Grand Rapids: Zondervan, 1974), 1.

God (sanctifies, raises the dead, leads the church), and receives God's divine names (Eph 4:30; Rom 1:4; 8:9; Mic 2:7; 1 Pet 4:14).[9]

Second, the Holy Spirit is "within the unity of the Trinity, along with God the Father and God the Son" (*CTC* §5). When permitted a window into heaven, believers hear a threefold cry from those surrounding God's throne, "Holy, Holy, Holy" (Isa 6:3; Rev 4:8). When granted a vision of heaven, believers see God revealed in threefold theophany. The clearest and most evident theophany is seen at the turning point in the life of Jesus of Nazareth when he is baptized in the Jordan River. As Jesus is baptized "he saw the Holy Spirit of God descending like a dove and … a voice from heaven said, 'this is my beloved Son, with whom I am well pleased'" (Mt 3:16–17). Church leaders throughout history have also seen the three "men" who appeared to Abraham at the Oaks of Mamre as a theophany that reveals the Trinity (Gen 18:2–10). Not only what believers hear and see but also what they do and speak gives evidence to the threeness in God's oneness. While obeying Jesus's command to baptize, evangelicals do so in the threefold name of "the Father, the Son, and the Holy Spirit" (Mt 28:19). When speaking blessings over one another and the world, a threefold blessing is used, "the Grace of the Lord Jesus Christ and the love of God and the fellowship of the Holy Spirit be with you all" (2 Cor 13:14; 1 Pet 1:2; Num 6:24–26).[10]

The evangelist and evangelical theologian R. A. Torrey (a founding leader of both Moody Bible Institute and Biola University) loved the Holy Spirit. He preached and taught about the personality of the Holy Spirit because he was concerned that if believers thought of the Spirit simply as a power to be used, they would seek the wrong goal and ask the wrong questions. Believers who think of the Holy Spirit simply as power, ask, "How can I get more of the Holy Spirit?" In contrast, those who understand that the Holy Spirit is the omniscient and omnipotent Lord, the Giver of Life, ask different questions, such as, "How can the Holy Spirit have more of me? How can I surrender more of my life to the Spirit's guidance and counsel?"[11] Once the focus turns to what the Holy Spirit wants

---

[9]Terry Cornett, *God the Holy Spirit*, vol. 14, 16 vols. (Wichita: Urban Ministry Institute, 2005), 21. Torrey lists twenty-five distinct divine names for the Holy Spirit found in Scripture (*Person and Work of the Holy Spirit*, 35–65).

[10]Nathan MacDonald, "A Trinitarian Palimpsest: Luther's Reading of the Priestly Blessing (Num 6:24–26)," *Pro Ecclesia* 21 (2012): 299–313.

[11]Torrey, *Person and Work of the Holy Spirit*, 10.

to do with me, rather than what I can do with the Holy Spirit, a new perspective emerges. The Cape Town Confession captures this perspective as it focuses on the Holy Spirit witnessing *through* us, walking *with* us, and working *in* us.

The Holy Spirit Witnesses through Us

The Holy Spirit "is the missionary Spirit sent by the missionary Father and the missionary Son" (*CTC* §5). If creation is a divine work especially appropriated to the Father, and redemption a divine work especially appropriated to the Son, then the mission of God—the reconciliation of all things to the Father through the Son—is a divine work especially appropriated to the Holy Spirit.[12] The fundamental task of mission is simply to witness in word and deed to the truth that God has revealed in the person and work of Jesus Christ. In the Old Testament this task of witness was also known as prophecy. At its core, prophecy and witness both refer to truth directly revealed by God, which is then spoken by a person or community to God's people (Israel, the church) and to the world (Gentiles, nations, ethnic groups).[13] The essence of prophecy is seen in Jeremiah's witness, "The LORD put out his hand and touched my mouth. And the LORD said to me, 'Behold, I have put my words in your mouth'" (Jer 1:9). The words were not to sit in Jeremiah's mouth; rather, he was to speak them to whomever he was sent. Jeremiah was not responsible for how people responded to God's message; he was simply called to faithfully witness to God's revelation.

There are some misconceptions floating around about what it means to participate with the missionary Spirit of God as a witness or prophet today. First, prophetic witness to God's truth does not usually mean standing with a sign claiming the end of the world is coming soon. Even in the Old Testament, less than 10 percent of the prophecy has to do with the future.[14] Most prophecy is about God's

---

[12]For explanation on the doctrine of appropriation especially in relation to mission and the Holy Spirit see Hank Voss, *The Priesthood of All Believers and the Missio Dei: A Canonical, Catholic, and Contextual Perspective* (Eugene: Pickwick, 2016), 187–99.

[13]Gary Tyra, *Holy Spirit in Mission: Prophetic Speech and Action in Christian Witness* (Downers Grove: IVP Academic, 2011).

[14]Gordon Fee and Douglas Stuart, *How to Read the Bible for All Its Worth*, 2nd ed. (Grand Rapids: Zondervan Academic, 2014), 166.

character, about his calling and concern for his people, or about God confronting something wrong. Second, prophetic witness is for every believer since the last days have come and the Holy Spirit has been poured out on all people (Acts 2).[15] One long suppressed implication is that both men and women are called to witness to Christ within their sphere of influence.[16] While there were female prophets prior to the day of Pentecost like Miriam (Exod 15:20), Deborah (Judg 4:4), Huldah (2 Chr 34:22), and Anna (Lk 2:36; cf. Acts 21:9), the situation changed radically with the eschatological day of the Lord arriving at Pentecost (Acts 2). Even if the full experience of the benefits of the New Covenant will not be complete until the *Parousia* (second coming) of Christ, the first fruit is here now for every believer to enjoy. The Old Testament prophets clearly testify that in the last days what was once the privilege of a few can now be the experience of all of God's servants (Isa 56–66).[17] Joel's prophecy, that God would pour out his Holy Spirit on both men and women so that all would prophesy (witness), came to fulfillment at Pentecost (Joel 2:28–29; Acts 2:17–18).

The Cape Town Confession also states that the Holy Spirit breathes "life and power into God's missionary Church" (*CTC* §5). The Holy Spirit is Lord and Life-Giver. In the Old Testament, this life-giving work resulted in the Holy Spirit often being described as the powerful breath of God. We see the Spirit's power at work during creation (Gen 1:1–2; 2:7), and when the Holy Spirit is described as sustainer of life in the present (Ps 104:29–30; Isa 32:14–15; Jn 6:63; Rom 8:2–11). The Spirit's power comes in many forms, but it is always power for service, first to the body of Christ, and then to the world.

The Holy Spirit Walks with Us

The Holy Spirit goes before us, inviting believers to participate in the life, light, and love of Jesus. Thus, the Cape Town Confession

---

[15]R. Stronstad, "The Prophethood of All Believers: A Study in Luke's Charismatic Theology," in *Pentecostalism in Context: Essays in Honor of William W. Menzies*, ed. Wonsuk Ma and Robert P. Menzies (Sheffield: Sheffield Academic, 1997), 60–77.
[16]Phoebe Palmer, *Promise of the Father* (Boston: Degan, 1859).
[17]The eschatological seeds of the Suffering Servant (Isaiah 53) are the primary actors in Isaiah 56–66. They share in the Servant's royal and priestly privileges and include representatives from all peoples. See Voss, *Priesthood of All Believers*, 51–71.

states, "We love and pray for the presence of the Holy Spirit" (*CTC* §5). When Jesus spoke to his disciples in the upper room, he promised them the continual presence of the Holy Spirit: "He dwells with you and will be in you" (Jn 14:17). The Holy Spirit is always with us, for as God he is omnipresent (Psalm 139). Yet there are times when the Holy Spirit makes his manifest presence known in a special and powerful way. Jonathan Edwards called these unique seasons "visitations," describing them as times when believers "are suddenly roused from a state of torpor and lethargy by a new and overwhelming awareness of the reality of spiritual things, and of God. They are like sleepers shaken awake."[18] Traditionally, the formal study of this special sense of God's manifest presence is called "mysticism," often defined as all "that concerns the preparation for, the consciousness of, and the reaction to ... the immediate or direct presence of God."[19] The Spirit desires believers to live a with-God life—a life growing more aware and dependent upon the Holy Spirit.

The Holy Spirit Works in Us

The Holy Spirit works *through* us and walks *with* us, but he also makes his home *in* us (Jn 14:17).[20] From within, the Spirit convicts, provides gifts, guidance, and power, and produces the fruit of righteousness. First, the Spirit performs a "convicting work" within believers (*CTC* §5). The Holy Spirit is a sanctifying Spirit and a purifying fire. In the Old Testament, fire was used for purifying garbage (Lev 8:17), disease (Lev 13:47–59), stains (Isa 4:4), and metals (Mal 3:2–3). In the New Testament, John the Baptist speaks about the Holy Spirit coming as fire (Mt 3:11–12), and when the Spirit appears, he takes the form of fire (Acts 2:3–4). If sin is a disease within the body of Christ, then the fire of the Holy Spirit is what burns the sickness from the body. Even if this conviction

---

[18]J. I. Packer, cited in Michael Griffiths, "The Power of the Holy Spirit," in *The New Face of Evangelicalism: An International Symposium on the Lausanne Covenant*, ed. C. René Padilla (Downers Grove: InterVarsity, 1976), 245.

[19]Bernard McGinn, *The Foundations of Mysticism* (New York: Crossroad, 1991), 1: xvii.

[20]Recognize that the "us" in the sentence above, like the "us" in the Lord's Prayer, has both an individual and corporate sense.

is painful, believers are warned not to quench the Spirit's fire (1 Thess 5:19).

Second, the Spirit's work within a believer provides "gifts, guidance and power" (*CTC* §5). This work is necessary for vocational holiness and fruitful lives.[21] The gifts of the Spirit are diverse and delightful (Isa 11:1–5; Rom 12:1–8; 1 Cor 12; Eph 4:11–16; 1 Pet 4:10–12). They include gifts of service, speaking, power, and leadership.[22] The Spirit speaks to believers and illumines their eyes and ears to help them understand how Scripture testifies to Jesus.[23] Finally, the Spirit produces fruit so that believers' lives "reflect the beauty of the gospel" (*CTC* §5). As shown in Chapter 6, the Spirit works in believers to help them conform to the image of Christ. Conformity to Christ does not mean conformity to one another, for the doctrine of the incarnation reveals that each of us will reflect Christ's image in a unique way. Jesus revealed God as a first-century Jewish male. When we reflect Jesus's image in our sphere of influence, we also do it in a unique way. While there will be commonality—love, joy, peace, patience, kindness, repentance, justice, and so forth (Gal 5:22–23; Mt 3:8; Acts 26:20; Lk 13:1–9; Phil 1:11)—there is also a diversity unique as human fingerprints when the Spirit's fruit is tasted and seen in individual believers, cultures, and churches.

History: Two Evangelicals on the Holy Spirit

The previous section reviewed the work of the Holy Spirit through us, with us, and in us. In this section we look at a few snapshots of how the Holy Spirit has been talked about in the evangelical church. Too often, teaching about the Holy Spirit has been a cause for division among evangelicals. Yet, it is helpful to recognize that divisions over the doctrine of the Holy Spirit are not only an evangelical problem. One of the biggest splits in church history took place over

---

[21]Eugene Peterson, *Under the Unpredictable Plant: An Exploration in Vocational Holiness* (Grand Rapids, MI: Eerdmans, 1992).

[22]Cornett, *God the Holy Spirit*, 14:123–4.

[23]Norman Geisler, *To Understand the Bible Look for Jesus: The Bible Student's Guide to the Bible's Central Theme* (Eugene: Wipf & Stock, 2002).

the doctrine of the Holy Spirit. Like any church split, there were many underlying issues, but the official reason was that the Western church (centered in Rome) and the Eastern church (centered in Constantinople) could not agree on how the Holy Spirit related to God the Son. In 1054, Christians in the West and East officially excommunicated each other in a theological fistfight known as the *filioque* controversy.[24] Eastern theologians felt that the church in the West was neglecting the Holy Spirit. Almost one thousand years later, some Eastern Orthodox theologians still think evangelicals are too Jesus-centric, a problem they call "christomonism."[25] There is certainly validity in the concern of Eastern Orthodox Christians. For a variety of reasons, the Holy Spirit has tended to be hidden, working behind the scenes to draw people to Christ and to bring glory to the Father. But this self-emptying of the Holy Spirit does not mean the Spirit should be ignored, nor is the Spirit any less worthy of worship and adoration than the Father or the Son.

While pneumatology has often been a doctrine that divides, the Cape Town Confession's section on the Holy Spirit illustrates that evangelical understandings of the Spirit agree in many important areas. In the historical section below, we return to two evangelical theologians met in previous chapters, John Owen and Phoebe Palmer. John Owen is an important figure to evangelicals, and his teaching on the Holy Spirit is worthy of far greater attention than it has yet received. First, Owen is one of the first in Christian history to attempt a comprehensive study of the person and work of the Holy Spirit. He wrote about the Holy Spirit in a number of works— his most famous work entitled *Discourse on the Holy Spirit*. This monograph consists of nine books and runs over 1,100 pages. He did not know of anyone before him who had attempted to lay out a complete "economy of the Holy Spirit" like he set out to do in his massive project.[26] Second, Owen's work on the Spirit has influenced many streams of evangelicalism. Evangelical branches connected to the Puritan roots honor him as an important figure.

Wesleyan, Holiness, and Pentecostal churches also honor Owen as an important forbear and teacher on the Holy Spirit. John

---

[24]The disagreement has yet to be reconciled. See Myk Habets, *Ecumenical Perspectives on the Filioque for the 21st Century* (London: Bloomsbury T&T Clark, 2014).
[25]Orthodox theologians confront the whole Western church with this concern, not just evangelicals. See Kärkkäinen, *Pneumatology*, 15.
[26]*WJO* 3:7.

Wesley asked all Methodist leaders, lay and ordained, to read five of Owen's books, one of which was *Of Communion with God the Father, Son, and Holy Ghost*. Wesley edited a series of books for his followers called *The Christian Library*, and included five of Owen's spiritual classics there.[27] Wesley chose texts that had been especially influential on him and that he wanted to see influence his followers. One of Wesley's followers influenced by Owen was Phoebe Palmer. Palmer's father converted in England after hearing Wesley preach. As such, Palmer was proud to be a spiritual granddaughter of Wesley. She also grew up in a home where Wesley's teaching on the Holy Spirit as well as his recommendations of Owen and other Puritan writers were taken quite seriously.[28] As a theological grandmother to today's Pentecostal churches, her teaching on the Holy Spirit will also be explored below.

John Owen (d. 1683): Attentive Awareness to Each Person of the Trinity

To explore Owen's pneumatological contribution, we start with a Trinitarian concern raised more recently by missionary theologian Lesslie Newbigin (d. 1998). Newbigin observed that in his experience the average Western Christian, when hearing the word "God," likely does not think of the three Trinitarian Persons, but rather of a "supreme monad ... shaped more by the combination of Greek philosophy and Islamic theology that was powerfully injected into the thought of Christendom at the beginning of the High Middle Ages than by the thought of the fathers of the first four centuries."[29] What do we make of Newbigin's claim?

John Owen provides one way to address Newbigin's concern. In another of Owen's works, *Communion with God*, he teaches that believers should come to know God through the way he has revealed himself in history. Reflection on the work of the Trinity in light

---

[27]See further, Robert Monk, *John Wesley: His Puritan Heritage*, 2nd ed. (Lanham: Scarecrow, 1999).
[28]The best overall introduction to Palmer's thought remains Charles White, *The Beauty of Holiness: Phoebe Palmer as Theologian, Revivalist, Feminist, and Humanitarian* (Grand Rapids: Zondervan, 1986).
[29]Lesslie Newbigin, *The Open Secret: An Introduction to the Theology of Mission* (Grand Rapids: Eerdmans, 1995), 27–8.

of the doctrine of appropriation helped Owen think through what was especially emphasized about each person in the Godhead.[30] Appropriation can be defined as "a way of speaking about God in which an attribute, action, or effect of an action is assigned to a particular divine person. This appropriation is founded on the distinctive properties of each person and its explicit goal is to better manifest the divine persons to the mind of believers."[31]

Once believers are clear on what work is especially associated with each person of the Trinity, it becomes possible to think through the type of response each believer should give to each individual person of the Trinity. Owen was concerned that believers exercise "distinct communion with each Person of the Trinity." As part of that communion, he observed that "there is no ... duty or obedience performed, but they are distinctly directed unto Father, Son, and Spirit."[32] For Owen, Paul's exhortation in 1 Cor 10:31—"Whether you eat or drink, or whatever you do, do all to the glory of God"— could be applied specifically by attending to the specific glory of an individual act in relation to the Father, the Son, or the Holy Spirit. For example, while preparing to write a letter to someone who did not know Christ, Phoebe Palmer would ask the Holy Spirit who was already at work in that person's life, to lead her to the right words to say.[33] The doctrine of appropriation helps believers recognize that the act of proclaiming the good news about Jesus in the world today is especially a work appropriated to the Holy Spirit. Thus, before a believer engages in evangelism, it is especially appropriate to ask the Holy Spirit for guidance, wisdom, and boldness. Participation in the divine work of witness through evangelism and proclamation,

---

[30]John Owen, *Communion with the Triune God*, ed. Kelly M. Kapic and Justin Taylor (Wheaton: Crossway, 2007), 95; Kevin J. Vanhoozer, "Triune Discourse: Theological Reflections on the Claim That God Speaks," in *Trinitarian Theology for the Church: Scripture, Community, Worship*, ed. Daniel J. Treier and David Lauber (Downers Grove: InterVarsity, 2009), 60-1; Colin E. Gunton, "The Community. The Trinity and the Being of the Church," in *The Promise of Trinitarian Theology* (Edinburgh: T&T Clark, 1991), 75-7; J. I. Packer, "A Puritan Perspective: Trinitarian Godliness According to John Owen," in *God the Holy Trinity: Reflections on Christian Faith and Practice*, ed. Timothy George (Grand Rapids: Baker Academic, 2006), 108.

[31]Voss, *Priesthood of All Believers*, 187.

[32]Owen, *Communion*, 101.

[33]White, *Beauty of Holiness*, 148, 119, 123.

whether in word or deed, is an activity of the Holy Spirit at work in and through believers.

Another example of the close relationship between the Holy Spirit and the work of mission can be seen in Acts where the main human actors are the apostles, but the main divine actor is the Holy Spirit. Ajith Fernando, who has spent over fifty years as a missional theologian in Sri Lanka, testifies to this truth. Fernando spent the first fifteen years of his evangelistic work studying the book of Acts, which "became like a textbook" for his ministry.[34] According to Fernando, the book of Acts has two main themes: "the Holy Spirit and witness" (Acts 1:8).[35] Given the high regard for the book of Acts among evangelicals, it is no surprise to learn that it has often become a starting place for pneumatical reflection.[36] Much of the evangelical reflection has not only come in formal treatises and textbooks but also in narratives describing the Holy Spirit's work as experienced in mission. Thus, one preferred method for exposition of the Holy Spirit's person and work has been hagiography—literally "writing about the holy"—in the form of missionary biography.[37] Over the last four hundred years, examples of this genre come from Jonathan Edwards (whose most frequently republished book is a missionary biography, *Life of David Brainerd*, 1749), John Woolman (*Journal of John Woolman*, 1774), Amanda Smith (*An Autobiography: The Story of the Lord's Dealings with Mrs. Amanda Smith*, 1893), and Howard and Geraldine Taylor (*Hudson Taylor's Spiritual Secret*, 1932). Chapter 3 introduced Phoebe Palmer, who also wrote an influential missionary autobiography, *Four Years in the Old World* (1867). We turn to Palmer's life and teaching for additional insight into how evangelicals have come to think about the Holy Spirit.

---

[34]Ajith Fernando, *Acts* (Grand Rapids: Zondervan Academic, 1998), 15.

[35]Fernando, *Acts*, 29; Ajith Fernando, "Grounding Our Reflections in Scripture: Biblical Trinitarianism and Mission," in *Global Missiology for the 21st Century: The Iguassu Dialogue*, ed. William David Taylor (Grand Rapids: Baker Academic, 2000), 191-256.

[36]Craig Keener, *Gift & Giver: The Holy Spirit for Today* (Grand Rapids: Baker Academic, 2001), 209-13.

[37]Thomas Herrernan, "Hagiography," *NWDCS*, 332-3; Anthony Gitton, "Mission and Spirituality," *NWDCS*, 442-4.

Phoebe Palmer (1807–1874): Holy Spirit Power for Witness

Thomas Oden describes Phoebe Palmer as an "original, clear, extraordinarily influential, and spiritually vital" theologian, noting that her theological influence has "deeply affected" four global evangelical traditions (Wesleyan, Holiness, Pentecostal, and Charismatic).[38] Charles White agrees, calling Palmer mother to the Holiness movement and "grandmother" to the modern Pentecostal movement.[39] Palmer's theological contributions are especially rooted in her appreciation and proclamation of a lived experience with the Holy Spirit rooted in Scripture. William Abraham calls her Methodism's "great mystic," and Elaine Heath describes her as the evangelical equivalent of "Catherine of Siena, Teresa of Avila, or Thérèse of Lisieux."[40]

While Palmer did not consider herself an academic theologian, she was certainly a practical theologian of the Christian life.[41] She wrote eighteen books and helped to found and edit one of the most influential religious periodicals of her generation.[42] Her most influential theological book, *The Way of Holiness* (1843), addressed the process of sanctification and passed through over fifty editions in her lifetime.[43] Her four-hundred-page book on the importance of women participating in the Holy Spirit's mission, *Promise of the Father* (1859), is, according to Tom Oden, "the most important treatise written by a male or female in the Christian tradition from the first to the nineteenth century" on this topic.[44] Theologically,

---

[38]Thomas Oden, "Introduction," in *Phoebe Palmer: Selected Writings* (New York: Paulist, 1988), 8, 14.

[39]Charles Edward White, "Phoebe Palmer and the Development of Pentecostal Pneumatology," *Wesleyan Theological Journal* 23 (1988): 208. For a more recent study of Palmer's influence, see Justin A. Davis, *Schleiermacher and Palmer: The Father and Mother of the Modern Protestant Mindset* (Eugene: Pickwick, 2019).

[40]Abraham, "Foreword," in *Naked Faith: The Mystical Theology of Phoebe Palmer*, by Elaine Heath (Eugene: Wipf & Stock, 2009); Heath, *Naked Faith*, 2.

[41]White, *Beauty of Holiness*, 105.

[42]White, "Phoebe Palmer and the Development of Pentecostal Pneumatology," 92–94, 233. Other important works include *Entire Devotion to God* (1845, rev. ed. 1855) and *Faith and Its Effects* (1848).

[43]Harold E. Raser, "Palmer, Phoebe," in *Biographical Dictionary of Evangelicals*, ed. Timothy Larsen, D. W. Bebbington, and Mark Noll (Leicester: InterVarsity, 2003), 501.

[44]Oden, "Introduction," 5.

her primary contribution is in pneumatology, specifically the Holy Spirit's presence (spirituality), power (sanctification), and mission (sentness) in relation to the church.

Palmer's life was characterized by her twin commitments to Scripture and mission. She placed clear emphasis on the relationship between Scripture and living a life pleasing to the Holy Spirit. For Palmer, a life of holiness is the natural outcome of being a "Bible Christian," and holiness is characterized by participation in the Holy Spirit's missionary work in the world. Palmer wished to be known first and foremost as a "Bible Christian." As an 11-year old child, Palmer authored a poem and copied it in the flyleaf of her New Testament. The poem gives good insight into both the intellectual gifts and the high value she placed on Scripture from an early age.[45]

This Revelation—holy, just, and true—
Though oft I read, it seems forever new;
While light from heaven upon its pages rest,
I feel its power, and with it I am blest.
To this blest treasure, O my soul, attend,
Here find a firm and everlasting friend—
A friend in all life's varied changes sure,
Which shall to all eternity endure.
Henceforth, I take thee as my future guide,
Let naught from thee my youthful heart divide
And then, if late or early death be mine,
All will be well, since I, O Lord, am thine![46]

As an adult, Palmer continued the strong emphasis on Scripture she inherited from her parents. Family devotions consisted of an hour in both the morning and the evening. Meal times were often spent discussing biblical passages facilitated by a systematic program for household Scripture memorization. Palmer's own practice was to rise at 4:00 a.m. each morning to spend two hours in prayer

---

[45]Phoebe Palmer, *Phoebe Palmer: Selected Writings*, vol. 56, ed. Thomas Oden, Sources of American Spirituality (New York: Paulist, 1988), 57–65.

[46]The poem contained additional stanzas. Richard Wheatley, *The Life and Letters of Mrs. Phoebe Palmer (1876)* (New York: Self-Published), 18. See also a similarly themed poem in Phoebe Palmer, *The Way of Holiness: With Notes by the Way: Being a Narrative of Religious Experience Resulting from a Determination to Be a Bible Christian* (New York: Piercy and Reed, 1843), 69.

and Scripture reading. She aimed to spend thirty minutes around noon in intercession and a final hour with God in the evening before going to bed whenever possible.[47] She pursued a "systematic course" of reading from the Old Testament in the morning, the Gospels at noon, and the Epistles in the evening.[48] When Palmer died in 1874, some forty years after penning the poem above, she had succeeded in her goal of helping many come to know and love the Spirit who speaks in Scripture. At her death, a leading pastor remarked that Phoebe Palmer was "the Priscilla who taught many an Apollos the way of the Lord more perfectly."[49]

How does Palmer's emphasis on Scripture relate to the Holy Spirit? The simple answer is found in Palmer's often repeated saying, "The voice of the Scriptures is the voice of the Holy Spirit."[50] A longer answer requires us to go back to Wesley and the first generation of Methodists to whom Palmer looked for inspiration and guidance. First, remember that Wesley and his followers embraced John Owen's understanding of triune communion—a communion that was attentive to each person of the Trinity. Second, her theological vision and imagination were shaped by biographies of the lives of the first Methodists, especially the published diaries of Lady Maxwell, Mary Bosanquet Fletcher, and Hester Ann Rogers.[51] Lady Maxwell reported a "conscious union" with God where she was able to "distinguish the approach of the three separate persons of the Trinity."[52] On September 9, 1838, Palmer also claimed that she experienced "near communion and distinctness of perception of the persons of the Trinity."[53] Hester Rogers wrote that it was important to not simply believe biblical promises as abstract truths. Rather she urged Wesleyans to say to God, "I now take Thee at Thy word."[54] The focus was to be on trusting the person of the Holy Spirit who is speaking rather than focusing simply on the words themselves. Palmer was most well known for her teaching about the

---

[47]Palmer, *Way of Holiness*, 133; Heath, *Naked Faith*, 45:6.

[48]Phoebe Palmer, *The Way of Holiness: With Notes by the Way*, 2nd ed. (New York: Lane and Scott, 1849), 124; Heath, *Naked Faith*, 45:6; White, *Beauty of Holiness*, 147.

[49]Timothy Smith, "Foreword," in White, *Beauty of Holiness*, xiii.

[50]White, *Beauty of Holiness*, 107.

[51]White, *Beauty of Holiness*, 118.

[52]White, *Beauty of Holiness*, 119.

[53]White, *Beauty of Holiness*, 117.

[54]White, *Beauty of Holiness*, 123.

Spirit's work of sanctification, and the heart of this teaching rested on Rogers's insight of trusting the person of the Holy Spirit who is doing the work of sanctification as declared in the Word of God. The Word and the Spirit work together to sanctify, but it is the Spirit who is living and gives the power to the Word.

In addition to Palmer's emphasis on the Holy Spirit speaking and shaping believers through Scripture, she also placed great emphasis on the "sentness" of every believer. By "sentness" I refer to Palmer's belief that just as the Holy Spirit was sent from the Father and the Son, so "it is the duty of every believer" to embrace a holy life that includes a responsibility to publicly testify to the grace one has received.[55] Rom 10:9–10 was important to Palmer who taught that public testimony was an essential fruit of inward heart change. For Palmer, "Not to tell others is to withhold the honor due to Christ," as well as to reveal a heart of ingratitude.[56] As Palmer began to experience powerful workings of the Holy Spirit, she spoke more and more about "the baptism of the Holy Spirit." Her emphasis upon the baptism of the Holy Spirit and Pentecostal power became a dominant characteristic of her teaching. Contemporaries like Charles Finney also spoke about the importance of the baptism of the Holy Spirit, but it was Palmer whose teaching first placed a major emphasis on power for mission and ministry as a result of the baptism of the Holy Spirit.[57] This connection between baptism of the Holy Spirit with power for mission and ministry would become a major emphasis for Pentecostals and Charismatic Christians.[58] Yet before the Pentecostals, preaching on the baptism of the Holy Spirit as a source of power for evangelistic ministry was a central theme for Palmer's theological heirs, evangelicals like William and Catherine Booth, A. B. Simpson, Charles Blanchard, D. L. Moody, and R. A. Torrey. Torrey, for example, writes,

> The baptism with the Holy Spirit is the birthright of every believer ... primarily for the purpose of testimony and service ... while the power may be one kind in one person and of another kind

---

[55]Palmer, *Select Writings*, 188.

[56]White, "Phoebe Palmer and the Development of Pentecostal Pneumatology," 206.

[57]White, "Phoebe Palmer and the Development of Pentecostal Pneumatology," 207.

[58]See John Wimber and Kevin Springer, *Power Evangelism* (San Francisco: Harper & Row, 1986); J. P. Moreland, *Kingdom Triangle: Recover the Christian Mind, Renovate the Soul, Restore the Spirit's Power* (Grand Rapids: Zondervan, 2017).

in another person, there will be power, the very power of God, when one is baptized with the Holy Spirit … [It] is absolutely necessary in every Christian for the service that Christ demands and expects of him … for all Christians are called to ministry of some kind.[59]

Some will agree with Palmer and her theological descendants that this power comes in a subsequent experience to salvation; others will see the power as latent in the believer from the moment of conversion. Nevertheless, all evangelicals agree that the Holy Spirit provides the power necessary for mission and ministry in the Christian life. This recognition of the importance of a believer's continual dependence upon the Holy Spirit for supernatural power (grace) is one of Palmer's legacies to all evangelicals.

Challenges: Pneumatology and the Future of Evangelicalism

Readers will have noticed that the historical discussion so far has only hinted at the majority of evangelicals now living in the global South. If Palmer planted the seeds of Pentecostalism, those seeds have now flowered on every inhabited continent. Since at least the 1990s, global evangelicals have pointed to pneumatology as foundational to future doctrinal reflection. Singaporean Simon Chan has invested significant effort into thinking through implications of the Holy Spirit for the Christian Life and for ecclesiology, especially in light of an Asian context where Christians are almost always a significant minority.[60] Malaysian American Amos Yong has reflected on the role of the Holy Spirit in conversation with other religions.[61] Wonsuk Ma warns of Western

---

[59]Torrey, *Person and Work of the Holy Spirit*, 151, 153, 162, 173.
[60]Simon Chan, *Spiritual Theology: A Systematic Study of the Christian Life* (Downers Grove: IVP Academic, 1998); Simon Chan, *Pentecostal Ecclesiology: An Essay on the Development of Doctrine* (Two Gates: Deo, 2011); Simon Chan, *Grassroots Asian Theology: Thinking the Faith from the Ground Up* (Downers Grove: IVP Academic, 2014).
[61]Amos Yong, *The Spirit Poured Out on All Flesh: Pentecostalism and the Possibility of Global Theology* (Grand Rapids: Baker, 2005).

evangelicals' neglect of the Holy Spirit's relation to the world of evil spirits and spiritual warfare.[62] African theologians like Erhard Kamphausen and Igor Kopytoff have called attention to both the presence of the Holy Spirit and the reality of evil spiritual powers connected to everyday market commodities.[63] These and other issues will be explored further as we move to pneumatical challenges and future opportunities.

The Cape Town Confession (2010) declares that the Holy Spirit is a missionary Spirit. Some thirty-five years earlier, the Lausanne Congress affirmed "that Christ sends his redeemed people into the world as the Father sent him, and that this calls for a similar deep and costly penetration of the world." Evangelicals find God's missionary nature revealed in Scripture's story, and we recognize that God's people are called to participate in God's mission.[64] A challenge faced by evangelicals in North America is the lack of urgency for participation in the Spirit's missionary work. Despite near universal recognition of the Spirit's missionary nature and the need for a missionary ecclesiology, there remains a serious dearth of leaders equipped to lead the church into her missionary vocation. Leith Anderson, former president of the National Association of Evangelicals, reported on a 2011 meeting of the presidents of numerous evangelical seminaries and Bible schools. "Participants bemoaned the epidemic shortage of a sense of mission, a theology of mission, and especially the leadership of mission in North American congregations."[65] Missional leaders are women and men who have explored theologically and experientially what it means to walk in the power of the Holy Spirit. There is much need for serious exploration on the relationship between Christian spirituality and missional theology.

---

[62]Timoteo D. Gener, Stephen T. Pardue, and Wonsuk Ma, eds., "Lord and Giver of Life: The Holy Spirit among the Spirits in Asia," in *Asian Christian Theology: Evangelical Perspectives* (Cumbria: Langham, 2019), 132.

[63]Kärkkäinen, *Pneumatology*, 173.

[64]"World mission is thus the first and most obvious feature of early Christian praxis" (N. T. Wright, *The New Testament and the People of God*, vol. 1 (Minneapolis: Fortress, 1992), 362). See also Christopher Wright, *Mission of God* (Downers Grove: IVP Academic, 2006), 224–5, 239, 250–1, 255–7, 329–33, 369–75.

[65]Leith Anderson, "New Churches for a New Millennium: The Holy Spirit Does It Again," in *Created and Led by the Spirit*, ed. Mary Sue Dehmlow Dreier (Grand Rapids: Eerdmans, 2013), 72.

A second challenge for pneumatology in the twenty-first century is a perennial one. Since the book of Acts, there has been a temptation to use the Holy Spirit as an instrument for making money and increasing one's reputation and place in the world. Simon the magician wanted to use the power of the Holy Spirit to make money (Acts 8:9–24). Thus, throughout church history, those who attempt to use the Holy Spirit for their own profit are in grave spiritual danger. In some contexts, the spirituality of simony looks like televangelism and promises of economic prosperity. In other contexts, it looks like an embrace of the status quo so that materialistic goods and consumeristic vices can remain unrebuked by the Spirit's prophetic voice. The materialism of Western evangelicals have left many blind to this latter danger.[66]

Renewed reflection on the role of the Holy Spirit leads to renewed reflection on the nature of the church. Thus, a third challenge to pneumatology is a rethinking of ecclesiology from the perspective of the Holy Spirit. If within the divine economy it is recognized that the Holy Spirit is leading the church into mission, then evangelicals, especially in the West, must replace a Christocentric ecclesiology with what Michael Goheen called a "Christocentric-Trinitarian" ecclesiology.[67] The missionary ecclesiology of Lesslie Newbigin is often held up as a model for evangelicals serious about engaging the work of the kingdom in the power of the Holy Spirit.[68] Other evangelicals, like Myk Habets, call for a "Third Article" theology, meaning thinking about theological topics from the perspective of the Holy Spirit—the focus of the third section of the Nicene-Constantinopolitan Creed.[69]

---

[66]C. René Padilla, "Spiritual Conflict," in *The New Face of Evangelicalism: An International Symposium on the Lausanne Covenant*, ed. C. René Padilla (Downers Grove: InterVarsity, 1976), 205–21; "Lausanne Occasional Paper 20: An Evangelical Commitment to Simple Life-Style" (Hoddesdon: Lausanne Committee for World Evangelization, 1980).

[67]Michael Goheen, *"As the Father Has Sent Me, I Am Sending You": Lesslie Newbigin's Missionary Ecclesiology* (Zoetermeer: Boekencentrum, 2000), 117; Voss, *Priesthood of All Believers*, 183–5.

[68]Michael Goheen, *The Church and Its Vocation: Lesslie Newbigin's Missionary Ecclesiology* (Grand Rapids: Baker Academic, 2018), 51–4.

[69]Myk Habets, *The Anointed Son: A Trinitarian Spirit Christology* (Eugene: Pickwick, 2010), 231.

Forward: Come Holy Spirit—with Us, in Us, through Us

Looking forward, there are three broad areas for evangelicals to explore via continued pneumatological research. These areas relate to spirituality (the Spirit with us), sanctification (the Spirit in us), and sentness (the Spirit through us). First, the Holy Spirit is always seeking to draw people to Christ. Jesus invites those who are thirsty to come to him (Jn 7:37; Rev 22:17). James declares, "Draw near to God, and he will draw near to you" (Jas 4:8). Some have observed that the Holy Spirit seems to go where he is wanted. Students of evangelical awakenings have noted that the pouring out of the Holy Spirit is often connected to individuals and groups like the early Christians in Acts who were committed to "extraordinary praying and preaching."[70] Those who are interested in the theology of the Holy Spirit will watch for "signs of the Spirit," for evidence of God's people seeking him for conviction in the church and conversion of the lost.[71] Thus, one area for evangelicals to pursue in coming decades is a deeper commitment to prayer and intimacy with God.

A closely related area is the formal study of the Spirit's indwelling presence in believers. Chapter 6's exploration of the doctrine of sanctification touched on this topic. Sanctification is the study of how the Spirit works within believers—as individuals and as a corporate body—to conform us to Christ's image. Yet to understand what the Spirit is doing in Christians we must also attend to who the Spirit is as he comes to work within us. The formal study of the believer's relationship with God in general, but more specifically with the Holy Spirit in particular, is known as spiritual theology.[72] In general, evangelicals have emphasized the formal study of spirituality less than Roman Catholic and Orthodox traditions. The neglect of the person of the Holy Spirit and his indwelling work in believers is

---

[70]J. Edwin Orr, *The Fervent Prayer: The Worldwide Impact of the Great Awakening of 1858* (Chicago: Moody, 1974), ix.

[71]Sam Storms, *Signs of the Spirit: An Interpretation of Jonathan Edwards's "Religious Affections"* (Wheaton: Crossway, 2007).

[72]The newer understanding of spiritual theology "acknowledges that the Christian life must be understood relationally, especially in relation to its divine source" (Chan, "Spiritual Theology," ZDCS, 53).

cause for repentance.[73] For example, prayer is an important aspect of how the Spirit works to sanctify believers. Yet as Gordon Fee notes, "One of the remarkable incongruities in Pauline studies is that thousands of books exist that search every aspect of Paul's 'thinking' while only very few seek to come to terms with his life of prayer."[74] There are signs that the neglect of formal attentiveness to spirituality among evangelicals is beginning to change, but much work remains.

Finally, future work on understanding the person and work of the Holy Spirit must take seriously the sentness of the Spirit. Just as the Spirit led Jesus from the Jordan to battle spiritual forces and engage in a ministry of word and deed, so the Holy Spirit leads God's people into the world on mission today. Lesslie Newbigin identified the need for believers to engage their communities as a priesthood in the world. There is a pressing need for theological reflection on what it means for Christians to participate through the Holy Spirit in Christ's royal priesthood in the midst of daily life and "in the secular business of the world." Related to this is the recognition by many global evangelicals that mission and spiritual warfare are closely related. In short, the challenging observation of Henry Martyn (1781–1812), pioneer missionary to Persia, remains as needed now as when it was spoken some two hundred years ago: "The Spirit of Christ is a missionary Spirit, and the nearer we get to him, the more intensely missionary we must become."[75]

Recommended Reading

Simon Chan, *Spiritual Theology: A Systematic Study of the Christian Life* (Downers Grove: IVP Academic, 1998).

Gordon Fee, *God's Empowering Presence: The Holy Spirit in the Letters of Paul* (Peabody: Hendrickson, 1994).

Craig Keener, *Gift Giver: The Holy Spirit for Today* (Grand Rapids: Baker Academic, 2001).

---

[73]Thomas Oden, *Classic Christianity: A Systematic Theology* (New York: HarperOne, 2009), 501.

[74]Gordon Fee, *God's Empowering Presence: The Holy Spirit in the Letters of Paul* (Peabody: Hendrickson, 1994), 866.

[75]Cited in Fernando, *Acts*, 57.

John Owen, *Discourse on the Holy Spirit*, vols. 3 and 4
(Edinburgh: Banner of Truth, 2013).
J. I. Packer, *Keep in Step with the Spirit: Finding Fullness in Our Walk
with God*, rev. ed. (Grand Rapids: Baker, 2005).
R. A. Torrey, *The Person and Work of the Holy Spirit* (Grand
Rapids: Zondervan, 1974).

8

"In the Name of the Father, Son, and Holy Spirit": Trinitarian Theology

We affirm our belief in the one eternal God, Creator and
Lord of the world, Father, Son and Holy Spirit.
LAUSANNE COVENANT §7

The Trinity is at the center of evangelical life. But, for many evangelicals, the *doctrine* of the Trinity lives somewhere out at the edges of our awareness. We are deeply trinitarian in practice, but often only shallowly trinitarian in theology. As evangelicals, we are a practical people. We like to get stuff done. We feel the urgency of sharing the good news, serving the church, growing in holiness, and caring for the poor, the orphan, and the widow. Studying theology can seem a distraction from the real business of Christianity. What evangelicals are finding, however, is that the doctrine of the Trinity is surprisingly practical. Knowing God as the Triune explains and energizes our busy life as his children. The renewed interest in trinitarian theology among evangelicals draws much of its excitement from seeing how the Trinity changes everything.

This development in trinitarian theology can be overheard in an excited crowd of recent books.[1] Prominent among these, and

---

[1]Tim Chester, *Delighting in the Trinity: Just Why Are Father, Son and Spirit Such Good News?* (Oxford: Monarch, 2005); Andreas J. Köstenberger and Scott R.

spanning the range from scholarly treatises to *Dr. Doctrine's Christian Comix*, are the works of Wesleyan theologian Fred Sanders.[2] Officially, Sanders is professor of theology at the Torrey Honors Institute at Biola University. Unofficially, he has been moonlighting for twenty years as a Trinity salesman.[3] Sanders is one of the leading evangelical theologians working on the doctrine of the Trinity today, and his works will help guide this chapter.

Doctrine: The Triune God

This section surveys the way in which Christian worship and the joining of the Old and New Testaments press us to think in trinitarian

---

Swain, *Father, Son and Spirit: The Trinity and John's Gospel* (Downers Grove: IVP Academic, 2008); Donald Fairbairn, *Life in the Trinity: An Introduction to Theology with the Help of the Church Fathers* (Downers Grove: IVP Academic, 2009); Thomas McCall, *Which Trinity? Whose Monotheism? Philosophical and Systematic Theologians on the Metaphysics of Trinitarian Theology* (Grand Rapids: Eerdmans, 2010); Michael Reeves, *Delighting in the Trinity: An Introduction to the Christian Faith* (Downers Grove: IVP Academic, 2012); Stephen R. Holmes, *The Quest for the Trinity: The Doctrine of God in Scripture, History and Modernity* (Downers Grove: IVP Academic, 2012); Gene L. Green, Stephen T. Pardue, and K. K. Yeo, eds., *The Trinity among the Nations: The Doctrine of God in the Majority World* (Grand Rapids: Eerdmans, 2015); Malcolm B. Yarnell III, *God the Trinity: Biblical Portraits* (Nashville: B&H Academic, 2016); Brandon D. Crowe and Carl R. Truman, eds., *The Essential Trinity: New Testament Foundations and Practical Relevance* (Phillipsburg: P&R, 2017); Robert Letham, *The Holy Trinity: In Scripture, History, Theology, and Worship*, rev. ed. (Phillipsburg: P&R, 2019); Michael Bird and Scott Harrower, eds., *Trinity without Hierarchy: Reclaiming Nicene Orthodoxy in Evangelical Theology* (Grand Rapids: Kregel, 2019); Scott R. Swain, *The Trinity: An Introduction* (Wheaton: Crossway, 2020).

[2]Fred Sanders, *Dr. Doctrine's Christian Comix*, vol. 3, *On the Trinity* (Downers Grove: InterVarsity, 1999); *The Image of the Immanent Trinity: Rahner's Rule and the Theological Interpretation of Scripture* (New York: Peter Lang, 2004). With Klaus Issler, eds., *Jesus in Trinitarian Perspective: An Intermediate Christology* (Nashville: B&H Academic, 2007); *The Deep Things of God: How the Trinity Changes Everything* (Wheaton: Crossway, 2010; Korean trans. 2016; 2nd ed. 2017). With Oliver D. Crisp, eds., *Advancing Trinitarian Theology: Explorations in Constructive Dogmatics* (Grand Rapids: Zondervan, 2014); *The Triune God* (Grand Rapids: Zondervan, 2016). With Scott R. Swain, eds., *Retrieving Eternal Generation* (Grand Rapids: Zondervan, 2017).

[3]Fred Sanders, "Evangelical Trinitarianism and the Unity of the Theological Disciplines," *Journal of the Evangelical Theological Society* 60, no.1 (March 2017): 65–80.

categories. It then turns to the heart of trinitarian theology: what the incarnation of the Son and the outpouring of the Spirit show us about the one eternal life of the triune God.

"Praise Father, Son, and Holy Ghost"

The doctrine of the Trinity begins in praise. "Blessed be the God and Father of our Lord Jesus Christ," says Paul. Why? Because the Father has blessed us in Christ with every spiritual blessing, chosen us in Christ before the foundation of the world, and predestined us in Christ for adoption as sons—all to the praise of his glorious grace (Eph 1:3–6). The praise of the Father overflows to include praise of his beloved Son, Jesus Christ, who brings us "redemption through his blood, the forgiveness of our trespasses," knowledge of the Father's plan of salvation, and a glorious inheritance—again to the praise of the Father's glory (Eph. 1:6–12). Such praise cannot rest until it also embraces the Holy Spirit, who seals our faith in Jesus and guarantees our inheritance—once again, to the praise of the Father's glory (Eph 1:13–14).[4]

When Christians go to praise the one God of Israel, we find ourselves magnifying Father, Son, and Holy Spirit. When Christians then go on to explain how Father, Son, and Holy Spirit are the one God of Israel, we find ourselves speaking the doctrine of the Trinity. Praise comes first. Doctrine follows.

At the center of Christian praise stands Jesus. At the Great Commission, the disciples "worshiped" the risen Lord Jesus (Mt 28:17). It was while the disciples "were worshiping the Lord"—that is, the Lord Jesus—that the Holy Spirit tells the church at Antioch to send out Paul and Barnabas (Acts 13:2). In John's vision, God the Father (the one "who was seated on the throne," Rev 5:1) and the ascended Lord Jesus ("a Lamb standing, as though it had been slain," Rev 5:6)—together with the Holy Spirit ("the seven spirits of God," Rev 5:6)—receive the worship of "every creature in heaven and on earth": "To him who sits on the throne and to the Lamb be blessing and honor and glory and might forever and ever!" (Rev 5:13). Amen!

What could explain this most peculiar aspect of the Christian religion? How could first-century Jews, of all people, worship an

---

[4]Sanders, *Triune God*, 25–35.

executed rabbi as Lord? In the Old Testament, God shows a fierce jealousy for his people's exclusive loyalty. Again and again he insists, "I am the LORD, and there is no other, besides me there is no God" (Isa 45:5, 6, 18). "There is no other god besides me, a righteous God and a Savior; there is none besides me" (Isa 45:21). Then in the New Testament, Jesus appears, and the apostles summon us to an exclusive loyalty to him. "There is salvation in no one else, for there is no other name under heaven given among men by which we must be saved" (Acts 4:12). In light of the Old Testament, how does Christian praise of Jesus make sense? How do we explain our praise?

When Old Testament Israelites wanted to praise God and proclaim their faith in him, they would start by saying, "Hear, O Israel: The LORD our God, the LORD is one" (Deut 6:4). One of the most wonderful things about God is that he is unique, totally unlike the gods of the nations and supreme over them. This explains why God requires Israel's total and undivided worship: "You shall love the LORD your God with all your heart and with all your soul and with all your might" (Deut 6:5). Jesus himself quotes these verses to affirm that God is incomparable and exalted and therefore worthy of our wholehearted devotion (Mt 22:37; Mk 12:29–30). In doing so, Jesus even seems to deflect attention away from himself. How then did he become the center Christian attention?

Rising from the dead can have that effect. When the disciples meet the risen Lord Jesus, they finally understand what it means to confess him as "the Christ, the Son of the living God" (Mt 16:16), or as "the Christ, who is God over all, blessed forever" (Rom 9:5). It means that Jesus, along with God the Father, is included in the Old Testament confession, "The LORD our God, the LORD is one." The one God actually includes both Father and Son! We hear stunned echoes of this Old Testament confession when no-longer-doubting Thomas exclaims to the risen Jesus, "My Lord and my God!" (Jn 20:28). Paul too recalls this confession, "We know ... that 'there is no God but one'" (1 Cor 8:4). Then he explains how Christians have come to understand it: "For although there may be so-called gods in heaven or on earth ... yet for us there is one God, the Father, from whom are all things and for whom we exist, and one Lord, Jesus Christ, through whom are all things and through whom we exist" (1 Cor 8:5–6). The central confession of Old Testament monotheism actually includes the identity of Jesus and therefore explains Christian worship of Jesus.[5] With the coming of Jesus and the triumph of his resurrection, there is more about God for Israel to hear.

The New Testament worship of Jesus is a recognition that the creating and saving work of the one God of Israel has always involved Father, Son, and Holy Spirit. Jesus Christ is the one "through whom are all things" (1 Cor 8:6), by whom "all things were created" (Col 1:16). He is the Word who was with God in the beginning and who made all things (Jn 1:1–3). Astonishingly, Jude mentions almost in passing that it was "Jesus, who saved a people out of the land of Egypt" (Jude 1:5)! The New Testament also helps us realize that it is "the eternal Spirit" (Heb 9:14) who hovers over the waters at the beginning of Genesis. It is this "Spirit who gives life" (Jn 6:63; Rom 8:11; 2 Cor 3:6) who is sent forth to create and to renew (Ps 104:30) and to give resurrection life to "an exceedingly great army" of dry bones (Ezek 37:10).

One of the most stunning flashes of mutual illumination between the Old and New Testaments occurs between Isaiah 45 and Philippians 2.[6] Isaiah 45 is one of the sharpest assertions of strict monotheism in the entire Old Testament. In it the Lord says, "Turn to me and be saved, all the ends of the earth! For I am God, and there is no other. By myself I have sworn; from my mouth has gone out in righteousness a word that shall not return: 'To me every knee shall bow, every tongue shall swear allegiance'" (Isa 45:21–22). It is clearly to the Lord, and to no other, that every knee will bow and every tongue confess. Philippians 2 tells us that this Lord is actually Jesus! Because Jesus humbled himself in becoming human and in enduring the cross, "God has highly exalted him and bestowed on him the name that is above every name, so that at the name of Jesus every knee should bow, in heaven and on earth and under the earth, and every tongue confess that Jesus Christ is Lord, to the glory of God the Father" (Phil 2:9–11). When Isaiah writes, "To *me* every knee shall bow," Paul hears the voice of Jesus. And when Jesus receives the worship of

---

[5]Richard Bauckham, "God Crucified," in *Jesus and the God of Israel: God Crucified and Other Studies on the New Testament's Christology of Divine Identity* (Grand Rapids: Eerdmans, 2008), 26–30.

[6]David S. Yeago, "The New Testament and the Nicene Dogma: A Contribution to the Recovery of Theological Exegesis," *Pro Ecclesia* 3, no. 2 (spring 1994): 152–64.

the nations, the Father's glory does not go to another god, but to his own Son, and so to himself.

The Missions of Son and Spirit

This brings us to the heart of trinitarian theology. At the turn of the ages, God the Father sent his Son to redeem us and his Spirit to empower us, and Christianity emerged baptizing disciples of all nations "in the name of the Father and of the Son and of the Holy Spirit" (Mt 28:20). God reveals his triunity to us first and foremost not by speaking, but by entering human history in person and in a way that he never had before. There are many hints of God's triunity in the Old Testament, and ample witness to God's triunity in the New Testament. But it was not *in* the two Testaments, but in actual historical events *between* the Testaments, that the Trinity publicly and openly entered the stage of human history. The baptism of Jesus is a particularly clear example of this. As the incarnate Son is being baptized, the voice of the Father sounds from heaven and the Spirit descends as a dove. Christianity has no gospel unless, in actual history, a dead man burst out of a tomb. Likewise, Christianity has no doctrine of the Trinity unless, in actual history, the Son became a man and the Spirit entered human hearts.

The historical appearances of the Son and the Spirit are known as their "missions." A mission is a task that you are sent to accomplish, and the task God sends his Son and Spirit to accomplish is our salvation.

> When the fullness of time had come, God sent forth his Son, born of woman, born under the law, to redeem those who were under the law, so that we might receive adoption as sons. And because you are sons, God has sent the Spirit of his Son into our hearts, crying, "Abba! Father!" (Gal 4:4–6)

The doctrine of the Trinity is anchored in God's sending his Son to redeem us and in God's sending his Spirit to transform us into sons and daughters. God reveals his triunity in these missions. The Old Testament perfectly anticipates this revelation. The New Testament perfectly reflects this revelation. But the revelation itself comes in actual history. The central question is, what exactly about God's triunity do these historical missions reveal? They reveal that, within

God's own eternal triune life, God the Son and God the Spirit somehow come from God the Father. The Father is somehow the eternal origin of the Son and the Spirit. That is, God the Father somehow eternally gives being and life to the Son and the Spirit. The Father's eternal origination of the Son and his eternal origination of the Spirit are called the divine "processions." Missions reveal processions.

What this means is that God the Father gives the Son and the Spirit their being in eternity (the divine processions) and he gives them their tasks in time (the historical missions). The eternal processions of Son and Spirit correspond to the temporal missions they execute in our salvation. Who God is eternally as Father, Son, and Spirit is the basis for what God does temporally for us and for our salvation. And what Father, Son, and Spirit do temporally for us and our salvation reveals who God is in his own eternal triune life. If we know a tree by its fruits, then gospel fruit hangs only from the Trinity tree.

Where do we find this in Scripture? It should not surprise us to find it in one of our favorite gospel verses, John 3:16. "For God so loved the world that he gave his only begotten Son."[7] What does it mean to say that the Father "gave" his Son? Certainly that the Father gave the Son as a sacrifice for sins. But the Father's giving of the Son begins before the cross. It begins in the Son's incarnation and includes all of his saving work. The Father gives the Son by sending him to do his work of salvation. Notice also that it is the "only begotten Son" who is given. The Father did not give the Son to *become* the only begotten. The Son is not only begotten because he was born as a man. He was already the only begotten when the Father gave him. The Son was already "only begotten" because of his eternal relationship to the Father. The Father is (eternally) the origin of the Son. The Son is (eternally) from the Father. This is what is called the Son's eternal generation from the Father. Though it might sound a little odd, we could also call it the Son's eternal begottenness from the Father. This is the Son's procession. John 3:16 tells us to see in the saving work of the Son (his mission) a reflection of the eternal generation of the Son (his procession).

---

[7]The King James Bible had "only begotten" right. See Charles Lee Irons, "A Lexical Defense of the Johannine 'Only Begotten'," in Sanders and Swain, *Retrieving Eternal Generation*, 98–116.

Consider how John 15:26 speaks of the Holy Spirit. Jesus says, "When the Helper comes, whom I will send to you from the Father, the Spirit of truth, who proceeds from the Father, he will bear witness about me." Jesus sends the Spirit in breathing him out on the disciples (Jn 20:22) and in pouring him out at Pentecost (Acts 2:33) and in indwelling every individual Christian (Jn 14:23). This is the saving mission of the Spirit. Notice also that, as with the Son, the Spirit who will be sent "from the Father" is the one who already "proceeds from the Father." When the Spirit is sent to bear witness and bring life and power and adoption (his mission), Jesus wants his disciples (and us) to realize that this Spirit is the one who eternally proceeds from the Father (his procession).

Missions reveal processions. In the fullness of time, the Father sent his Son and his Spirit. Through these saving missions, God opens to us the eternal depths of his own triune being. Long before we were here, long before anyone was here, "within the happy land of the Trinity above all worlds," Father, Son, and Spirit were enjoying a perfect blessedness in the giving and receiving of life and love and glory beyond all our imagining.[8] To this eternal blessedness of the triune God, we are latecomers, and we are rebels. But that does not mean we are left out. By the Spirit of adoption, the Father offers to bring us, sanctified and renewed, into the blessedness he shares with his eternal Son. The doctrine of the Trinity explains these gladdest of gospel tidings: "The triune God is a love infinitely high above you, eternally preceding you, and welcoming you in."[9]

History: The Development of Trinitarian Doctrine

The heart of evangelicalism is the gospel. The *evangel* of *evangel-icalism* means "gospel." What we gospel-folk are realizing is that the gospel we hold dear is itself deeply trinitarian. The doctrine of the Trinity is helping us make better sense of truths we already believe and things we already do. If explicit teaching about the triune God sounds suspiciously novel to our ears, it also feels strangely familiar.

---

[8]Sanders, *Deep Things*, 67–88 (86).
[9]Sanders, *Deep Things*, 101.

We quickly warm to the doctrine of the Trinity because it makes the gospel bigger. And it makes the gospel bigger by making God bigger.

But why are we recognizing this only now? Should we not have known this all along? When did we forget? While the severity of the amnesia varies widely across congregations and denominations and nations, why would all of us find ourselves nourished to better spiritual health by more carefully attending to the trinitarian teaching of Scripture?[10] This section diagnoses our condition first by surveying the fourth-century debates that clarified the basic teaching about the triune God that all Christians share. Because evangelicalism traces its lineage back through the sixteenth-century Reformation, we will also note how early Protestants approached the doctrine of the Trinity. We will then identify two causes of recent evangelical trinitarian forgetfulness, followed by one particularly effective reminder of our evangelical trinitarian heritage.

Classic Trinitarianism

Everything was going fine. Christians from the beginning had been worshiping Jesus, confessing Jesus to be Lord and God, praying and healing and casting out demons in Jesus's name, and embracing martyrdom rather than denying the Lord Jesus who bought them. For the early Christians, the praise and practice of Jesus's divinity was not a problem. The problem was to explain it.

How can Jesus and the Father be one God? Various suggestions were made and then discarded as inadequate. A respected priest named Arius eventually came up with what would become Christianity's besetting heresy.[11] He said that the Son is goddish, but not God. So, technically, only the Father is the one God. However, according to Arius, at some point God the Father was not Father at all, because there was no Son. The not-yet Father was just the one God all alone by himself. But then he became Father by creating the Son. Arius thought that this Son was an incredibly exalted

---

[10]Leopoldo Cervantes-Ortiz, "God, the Trinity, and Latin America Today," *Journal of Reformed Theology* 3, no. 2 (January 2009): 157–73; Samuel Waje Kunhiyop, "The Trinity in Africa: Trends and Trajectories," in *The Trinity among the Nations: The Doctrine of God in the Majority World*, ed. Gene L. Green, Stephen T. Pardue, and K. K. Yeo (Grand Rapids: Eerdmans, 2015), 55–68.

[11]Holmes, *Quest for the Trinity*, 83–7. Mark Noll, *Turning Points: Decisive Moments in the History of Christianity*, 3rd ed. (Grand Rapids: Baker Academic, 2012), 39–57.

being, a super-mega archangel of sorts, but a creature nonetheless. And it was this Son who became incarnate as Jesus. Arius solved the problem of divine unity at the expense of the full deity of the Son. Though a "Christian" priest, Arius was theologically a fourth-century Jehovah's Witness.

The church now had some serious explaining to do. It needed a clear, precise, and above all biblical explanation of how Jesus and the Father are the one God. How do we identify the unity of Father and Son and also the distinction between them? It took the church most of the fourth century to sort out these questions. But in the process it produced statements of such luminous biblical and spiritual insight that Christians ever since have recognized them as the truth about who God is.

Though it is hard to imagine the entire Roman Empire getting worked up over theology, it did. Jesus was at stake. The ecclesiastical tensions between Arians and Trinitarians threatened to exacerbate existing political tensions. So, to settle the controversy, Emperor Constantine summoned a council of bishops and attended it himself. This was the Council of Nicaea, which met in AD 325. If there was a single mastermind behind the church's response at Nicaea, it was the daring and brilliant Egyptian bishop Athanasius.

Athanasius liked John 3:16. When his opponent Arius read in this verse that God gave his "only begotten" Son, Arius thought this proved his point that the Son is just a creature. For God to "beget" a Son is to make a Son. According to Arius, John 3:16 shows that God is the Creator, while the Son is a creature. Athanasius argued the exact opposite. Being only begotten does not mean the Son is less than the Father. It means he is equal. Even Jesus's own opponents had recognized this. They saw that, by "calling God his own Father," Jesus was "making himself equal with God" (Jn 5:18). A son is not a lesser being than his father, but equal in being, the same kind of being. A Homo sapiens father does not have a Neanderthal son, nor vice versa. And if the Father is an eternal being, somehow he must also beget an eternal Son.

But what about Scriptures that speak of the Son as being less than the Father? Jesus himself says, "The Father is greater than I" (Jn 14:28). Certainly Jesus Christ in his humanity is less than the Father. But if the Son's mission as man in time reflects his existence beyond time, what does the less-ness of his mission reflect? Athanasius's most profound theological achievement was to show that the lowliness of the Son's mission reflects his eternal generation. The

Son eternally receives his being from the Father, and so the Son historically executes the plan of the Father. The Son is less than the Father in time because he is from the Father in eternity. In his saving mission, Jesus brings the Father's message, obeys the Father's will, prays for the Father's direction, gives thanks for the Father's provision, and works for the Father's glory. The Father is the origin of the mission of the Son in time because the Father is the origin of the person of the Son in eternity. This same ordered relation is expressed in Scripture's descriptions of the Son as the Word of the Father, the Wisdom of the Father, the image of the Father, and the radiance of the Father. Word, wisdom, image, and radiance are all relational terms. They express an eternal relation. Jesus's sonship in time reflects his sonship in eternity. Less-ness reflects from-ness. Mission reveals procession.

In the words of the Creed of Nicaea, Jesus Christ is "God from God, light from light, true God from true God, begotten not made, consubstantial with the Father." That is, the Son is God, but he is so only "from … from … from" the Father. Eternal "fromness" is a big deal. Thus, when Scripture calls the Son "only begotten," it does not mean that God made the Son, as Arius taught. The Son is "begotten not made," that is, eternally from the Father, not created. In eternity, the Father gives to the Son all that he is. "As the Father has life in himself, so he has granted the Son also to have life in himself" (Jn 5:26).[12] Finally, the Son is "consubstantial" with the Father. With this famous term (Greek *homoousion*) Nicaea affirms, with as much philosophical clarity as it can muster, that the Son shares the exact same essence or substance or being as the Father. The Son is not goddish. He is just as much God as the Father is God.[13] But even here, in a word that emphasizes the metaphysical equality of Son and Father, the idea of fromness is included.[14] "For Athanasius, the very term that was the watchword of the Son's equality with the Father was simultaneously the term that marked the Son's relationship of origin from the Father."[15] Historically, the

---

[12]D. A. Carson, "John 5:26: *Crux Interpretum* for Eternal Generation," in Sanders and Swain, *Retrieving Eternal Generation*, 79–97.

[13]Fred Sanders, "Chalcedonian Categories for the Gospel Narrative," in Sanders and Issler, *Jesus in Trinitarian Perspective*, 18–19.

[14]Lewis Ayres, *Nicaea and Its Legacy: An Approach to Fourth-Century Trinitarian Theology* (Oxford: Oxford University Press, 2004), 95–96, 140–2.

[15]Sanders, *Triune God*, 116.

great achievement of the Council of Nicaea is in giving a biblically convincing explanation of the full deity of Jesus Christ in terms of his eternal generation from the Father.[16]

What about the Holy Spirit? The church's next major gathering of bishops framed its statement about the Holy Spirit around the Spirit's "procession" from the Father (Jn 15:26). At the Council of Constantinople (AD 381), the Holy Spirit was confessed to be "the Lord and Giver of Life, who proceeds from the Father, who with the Father and the Son together is worshiped and glorified." The Spirit is bearer of the divine name ("Lord"), creator ("Giver of Life"), and God ("worshiped and glorified"). But he is so as one who eternally "proceeds from the Father."[17]

With the creeds of the fourth century, the Christian church finally achieved consensus around a biblical explanation of its trinitarian life that has lasted for over 1,600 years. Even at the time of the Protestant Reformation, when many aspects of the medieval church were rejected, the Nicene doctrine of the Trinity was warmly embraced.[18] From the simple affirmations of his *Small Catechism* to the profound reasoning of his *Treatise on the Last Words of David*, Martin Luther was fully committed to the doctrine of the Trinity. "This article of faith remained pure in the papacy and among the scholastic theologians, and we have no quarrel with them on that score."[19] John Calvin includes a major chapter on the doctrine of the Trinity in his *Institutes* (1.13).[20] Evangelicals ever since have been firmly committed trinitarians. The works of the great English

---

[16]Nicaea is also famous for having been attended by Saint Nicholas, revered in legend both for slapping the heretic Arius in the face and for being the ancestor of Santa Claus.

[17]Western versions of the creed confess that the Spirit "proceeds from the Father and the Son."

[18]Scott R. Swain, "The Trinity in the Reformers," in *The Oxford Handbook of the Trinity*, ed. Gilles Emery, OP, and Matthew Levering (Oxford: Oxford University Press, 2011), 227–39.

[19]Martin Luther, *Treatise on the Last Words of David (2 Samuel 23:1–7)*, in *LW* 15:265–352 (310).

[20]Calvin also wrote an entire book on the Trinity, giving the doctrine what has been called "a more thoroughgoing biblical documentation than it had received since the patristic era." See Jaroslav Pelikan, *Reformation of Church and Dogma (1300–1700)*, vol. 4 of *The Christian Tradition: A History of the Development of Doctrine* (Chicago: University of Chicago Press, 1984), 322, referring to Calvin's 260-page *Defense of the Orthodox Faith in the Holy Trinity*.

Puritan John Owen, for example, are full of deeply trinitarian reflection, especially his magnificent *Communion with the Triune God* (1657).[21] Sanders surveys an international parade of major evangelical theologians from the late nineteenth and early twentieth centuries, and he concludes, "Everything that is routinely praised as belonging to the excitement of the trinitarian revival of recent times is fairly easy to find in those older sources, and there does not seem to be any chronological gap during which serious theological voices were not holding forth on the doctrine of the Trinity with faithfulness and creativity."[22]

Puzzling over the Trinity

What went wrong in the twentieth century? Actually, not much. It would be too much to call for a "trinitarian revival" or congratulate ourselves for being in the midst of one.[23] But if evangelical hearts remained warm with the praise of Father, Son, and Spirit, why did some, particularly in America, begin to puzzle intellectually over the doctrine of the Trinity? If our practical trinitarianism was in good working order, why were repairs needed in our theological reflection on the triune God? At one level, opposition to liberal theology kept evangelical attention fixed on other core doctrines of classical Christianity: the trustworthiness of Scripture and Jesus's deity, virgin birth, atoning death, and bodily resurrection. Beyond this, two factors seem chiefly to blame. Under various pressures, evangelicals resorted to narrower views of the gospel and to narrower views of the Bible. As a result, the doctrine of the Trinity seemed to drift away from these two centers of evangelical affection.

First, evangelicals reduced the gospel message from "adoption as sons" (Gal 4:5) to the moment of conversion.[24] The gospel, in all its "breadth and length and height and depth" (Eph 3:14–19),

---

[21]John Owen, *Communion with the Triune God*, ed. Kelly M. Kapic and Justin Taylor (Wheaton: Crossway, 2007).

[22]Fred Sanders, "The Trinity," in *Mapping Modern Theology: A Thematic and Historical Introduction*, ed. Kelly M. Kapic and Bruce L. McCormack (Grand Rapids: Baker Academic, 2012), 42.

[23]Fred Sanders, "Back to the Trinity," in *Theologies of Retrieval: An Exploration and Appraisal*, ed. Darren Sarisky (London: Bloomsbury T&T Clark, 2017), 213–28.

[24]Sanders, *Deep Things*, 13–25.

is adoption.[25] To be adopted is to share by the Spirit in the Son's relationship to the Father. "You have received the Spirit of adoption as sons, by whom we cry, 'Abba! Father!' The Spirit himself bears witness with our spirit that we are children of God, and if children, then heirs—heirs of God and fellow heirs with Christ" (Rom 8:15–17). The good news, in its widest New Testament scope, is that the Spirit of adoption makes us coheirs with the Son and children of the Father. Salvation as adoption presupposes God as Trinity. On the other hand, salvation as something less than adoption presupposes a less-than-trinitarian God. In the twentieth century evangelicals sometimes preached salvation as mere forgiveness. It was a less-than-adoption gospel, one that was aimed narrowly at conversion.[26] Evangelicals found that they did not need the doctrine of the Trinity in order to explain mere conversion. So we began to wonder why the doctrine of the Trinity matters. It began to feel more like a theological puzzle to solve, a distraction from the serious business of getting people saved.

Second, critical biblical scholarship made it harder to see how the doctrine of the Trinity is taught in Scripture.[27] Enlightenment critics resented what they considered the oppressive authority of traditional Christianity. They wanted instead a more reasonable Christianity, one that any clear-thinking person could approve. So they sought to reinterpret the source of Christianity's authority: the Bible. If they could strip the Bible of miracle, mystery, and authority—and especially the doctrine of the Trinity—Christianity could be remade and society freed from the tyranny of priests.[28] Their strategy was to divide and conquer. Critics divided the Bible from history, claiming that the Bible has many historical errors. They divided the New Testament from the Old Testament, claiming that the New Testament was merely one of many possible developments of ancient Israelite religion. They even divided the New Testament from itself, claiming that the apostles themselves had distorted the simple teachings

---

[25]See chapter 19, "Sons of God," in J. I. Packer's magnificent *Knowing God* (Downers Grove: InterVarsity, 1973).

[26]See John Stott's careful critique of Everett Harrison, "Must Christ Be Lord to be Savior?" *Eternity* 10, no. 9 (September 1959): 13–18, 36–7, 48.

[27]Sanders, *Triune God*, 161–71.

[28]Jaroslav Pelikan, *Christian Doctrine and Modern Culture (since 1700)*, vol. 5 of *The Christian Tradition: A History of the Development of Doctrine* (Chicago: University of Chicago Press, 1991), 60–74.

of Jesus. The critics saw correctly that traditional Christianity cannot stand on a dismembered Bible. The doctrine of the Trinity in particular assumes that the Bible gives a true account of God's wondrous deeds in history, that the God of the Old Testament is the same as Father, Son, and Spirit in the New, and that the apostles have faithfully transmitted to us what Jesus did and taught. None of these assumptions is shared by critical biblical scholarship.[29] From the mid-nineteenth century to today, critics came to dominate Western universities, making them increasingly hostile to traditional Christian beliefs about Scripture.[30] Evangelicals trained in these universities have often struggled to see Scripture once again as a unified whole in its testimony to the triune God.

A narrow gospel and a fragmented Bible. These cannot sustain a vigorous commitment to the doctrine of the Trinity. Without a big gospel and a whole Bible, many twentieth-century evangelicals began to wonder whether certain aspects of the doctrine of the Trinity were really necessary. What was it, then, that brought about the revival of evangelical interest in classical trinitarianism? It should come as no surprise that the gospel had something to do with it. The surprise is where the reminder of this gospel-Trinity connection came from: Karl Barth.

Recognizing the Trinity

In April 2000 *Christianity Today* ran a piece on "Books of the Century." Of the one hundred top nominations, third place overall went to Karl Barth's massive *Church Dogmatics*, published in multiple volumes from 1932 to 1967. J. I. Packer explained that Barth's work "opened a new era in theology in which the Bible, Christ, and saving grace were taken seriously once more."[31] Packer

---

[29]Sanders, *Triune God*, 170–1: "Many of the major strategic decisions about how to read the Bible in the academy—decisions that still guide the field of academic biblical studies today—were made early in the Enlightenment period and were made by antitrinitarians motivated by their unorthodox doctrinal commitments."

[30]David F. Wells, *No Place for Truth: Or, Whatever Happened to Evangelical Theology* (Grand Rapids: Eerdmans, 1993), 122–7; Mark A. Noll, *The Scandal of the Evangelical Mind* (Grand Rapids: Eerdmans, 1994), 100–14.

[31]"Books of the Century: Leaders and Thinkers Weigh in on Classics That Have Shaped Contemporary Religious Thought," *Christianity Today* 44, no. 5 (April 24, 2000), 92, https://www.christianitytoday.com/ct/2000/april24/5.92.html.

is not suggesting that evangelicals did not take the gospel seriously until Barth taught it to them. It was liberal theologians who had trivialized the gospel, and it was for them that Barth opened a new era. But evangelicals were watching.

One of the central strategies in Barth's theological revolution was his retrieval of the doctrine of the Trinity. Barth took up the classical Christian insight that the Trinity and the gospel go together. The saving, gospel work of Father, Son, and Holy Spirit in history is a revelation of who God is in eternity.[32] Barth expounded this insight with such biblical depth, historical awareness, and conceptual elegance that the scholarly world took notice.[33] The doctrine of the Trinity was back on the academic agenda. When evangelicals caught wind of this excitement and were reminded of the trinitarian depths of the gospel, we began to see that a bolder trinitarianism was exactly what we had been missing.

The Challenge for Evangelical Trinitarianism

What about the fragmented Bible? If evangelicals are finding it easier to see the Trinity in the gospel, we still struggle to see the Trinity in the Bible. In fact, we struggle mightily. Sanders warns, "The doctrine of the Trinity stands today at a point of crisis with regard to its ability to demonstrate its exegetical foundation."[34] This is the biggest challenge facing evangelical trinitarianism today.

There is a sort of minimal biblical trinitarianism that evangelicals have remained confident in. In this approach, the doctrine of the Trinity is broken down into some of its parts, and then each part is proven from Scripture.[35] There is one God; Father, Son, Spirit are each God; and Father, Son, and Spirit are each distinct from the others. These pieces are clearly taught in Scripture. Many excellent

---

[32]Karl Barth, *Church Dogmatics* I/1, ed. G. W. Bromiley and T. F. Torrance (Edinburgh: T&T Clark, 1975), 304–5.

[33]Sanders, "The Trinity," in *Mapping Modern Theology*, 41: "Barth put the Trinity back on the agenda of self-consciously modern theology, specifically among the liberal mainstream of academic theology in Europe and America."

[34]Sanders, *Triune God*, 162.

[35]Sanders, *Triune God*, 171–6; "Evangelical Trinitarianism," 75–8.

evangelical biblical commentaries and works of theology affirm these pieces of the doctrine of the Trinity, but say nothing about the entire missions-processions correlation. The tragic flaw in this minimalist approach is that it obscures the connection between the gospel and the Trinity, between God's external work in salvation history and his internal life as Father, Son, and Spirit.[36] The good news of salvation is not required in order to speak only of the unity, equality, and distinctions of the three persons.

To make the gospel connection obvious, the classic missions-processions approach to the doctrine of the Trinity starts not with the pieces, but with the whole. In the fullness of time, God sent his Son to redeem us and his Spirit to indwell us (Gal 4:4–6). "The doctrine of the Trinity is a large doctrine, and its formulation and defense have always required a certain ampleness of reflection on the revealed data."[37] It takes the whole Bible to help us understand what these missions reveal, and understanding what these missions reveal helps us understand the whole Bible. "The most holistic interpretive move in the history of biblical theology took place when the early church discerned that these missions reveal divine processions, and that in this way the identity of the triune God of the gospel is made known. This was the insight that manifested most clearly the relation of divine act (salvation) to divine being (triunity)."[38] The challenge of seeing the doctrine of the Trinity in Scripture will be met as we attend to the big picture of Scripture, salvation history as a unified whole, and to what this shows us about the God behind it all.

Forward: Reading the Trinity

The doctrine of the Trinity is a confession of biblical teaching. For evangelicals, making this confession confidently once again will involve retrieving for our own day practices of reading Scripture that were common in the past. In some ways, this retrieval has already begun.

---

[36]Sanders, "Evangelical Trinitarianism," 77–8.
[37]Sanders, *Triune God*, 179.
[38]Sanders, *Triune God*, 113.

The fragmenting tendencies in academic biblical studies have given rise to a countertrend. Instead of analyzing merely isolated passages or individual books of the Bible, more scholars are looking at the narrative and theological unity of collections of books of the Bible.[39] Old Testament scholars are documenting the remarkable ways in which the Pentateuch as a whole—not just, say, Exodus or Deuteronomy on its own, but the entire five-book series—functions as a coherent collection, with a carefully crafted, overarching narrative and a profound theological unity. Others are analyzing the minor prophets as a unified twelve-book collection. Still others are examining the structure of the book of Psalms. New Testament scholars are doing likewise with the fourfold Gospel collection and the General Epistles. There is renewed interest in the fascinating ways in which the New Testament interprets the Old Testament. All of these attempts to examine larger sections of Scripture and broader swaths of salvation history hold promise for illuminating the biblical basis of trinitarian doctrine.

One neglected reading strategy that holds particular promise is known as person-centered exegesis.[40] Person-centered exegesis is the attempt to discern what dramatic persona is speaking the words of any given passage of Scripture. This attentiveness to who is speaking to whom uncovers one of the most striking ways in which the Trinity appears in the Old Testament: in conversation. Specifically, person-centered exegesis hears in the Old Testament Spirit-inspired accounts of conversations between the person of the Father and the person of the Son. This is not a reading strategy invented by the church fathers, though they used it extensively. It is found directly in the New Testament. Jesus himself uses it (e.g., Mk 12:35–37 quoting Ps 110:1). And by spanning the two Testaments, it draws attention to the big picture of God's mighty works of salvation.[41]

Psalm 2, for example, is one of the great messianic passages of the Old Testament. It is quoted or alluded to over a dozen times in the New Testament, from the Gospels to Revelation, as a luminous

---

[39]Sanders, *Triune God*, 101–8.
[40]Matthew W. Bates, *The Birth of the Trinity: Jesus, God, and Spirit in New Testament and Early Christian Interpretations of the Old Testament* (Oxford: Oxford University Press, 2015).
[41]Sanders, *Triune God*, 226–35.

portrait of the identity of Jesus. Hebrews 1, a chapter filled with person-centered exegesis, identifies God the Father as the one who says in Ps 2:7, "You are my Son, today I have begotten you." The question immediately arises as to when this "today" takes place. When is the Son begotten? Some have thought that the "today" of the Son's begetting is the day of his ascension, or of his resurrection, or of his baptism, or of his incarnation. Person-centered exegesis draws attention to the first half of the verse. "*I* will tell of the decree: The LORD said *to me*, 'You are my Son.'" It is the person of the Son who speaks these words. In direct anticipation of Jesus's ministry, the Son in Psalm 2 does not make his claim to sonship on his own authority. He merely reports what the Father has decreed concerning him (Jn 12:49–50). Such attentiveness to the persons who are speaking immediately makes clear that the Son is recalling what the Father had said to him previously. It was at some point in the past that the Father said to the Son, "You are my Son." So the "today" of Ps 2:7 cannot be restricted to a prophecy of something that would take place in the future. It must also refer to a Father-Son conversation that had already taken place long ago, before Psalm 2 was written. This observation on its own is not enough to establish that Ps 2:7 is referring to the eternal generation of the Son. In Hebrews, however, Ps 2:7 explains how it is that the Son is "the radiance of the glory of God and the exact imprint of his nature" (Heb 1:3). In light of the person-centered exegesis of Hebrews, we see that Ps 2:7 "is not just a claim about Jesus reaching an exalted status. It is a declaration of his eternal relationship with the Father that is always in effect."[42]

It is this eternal relationship between Father and Son, in the Holy Spirit, that is the heart of the triune God. Person-centered exegesis lives in this relationship. It extends our canonical vision, as the New Testament looks back on the Old Testament, and enables us to take in the whole of Scripture in its testimony to Father, Son, and Spirit. It also lets us listen in on conversations between the Father and the Son that we may never have realized are there in our Bibles. And as the Father adopts us by his Spirit to share in the sonship of the Son, we find ourselves drawn in to this conversation, crying out, "Abba! Father!" And we pray all the more earnestly that others may

---

[42]Madison N. Pierce, "Hebrews 1 and the Son Begotten 'Today'," in Sanders and Swain, *Retrieving Eternal Generation*, 117–31 (131).

be drawn in too: "May the grace of the Lord Jesus Christ, and the love of God, and the fellowship of the Holy Spirit be with you all" (2 Cor 13:14). Amen.

Recommended Reading

Donald Fairbairn, *Life in the Trinity: An Introduction to Theology with the Help of the Church Fathers* (Downers Grove: IVP Academic, 2009).
Gene L. Green, Stephen T. Pardue, and K. K. Yeo, eds., *The Trinity among the Nations: The Doctrine of God in the Majority World* (Grand Rapids: Eerdmans, 2015).
Robert Letham, *The Holy Trinity: In Scripture, History, Theology, and Worship*, rev. ed. (Phillipsburg: P&R, 2019).
Michael Reeves, *Delighting in the Trinity: An Introduction to the Christian Faith* (Downers Grove: IVP Academic, 2012).
Fred Sanders, *The Deep Things of God: How the Trinity Changes Everything*, 2nd ed. (Wheaton: Crossway, 2017).
Scott R. Swain, *The Trinity: An Introduction* (Wheaton: Crossway, 2020).

Conclusion—*Quo Vadis?* The Promise of Evangelical Theology

As evangelicals writing about evangelical theology, we have sought to take neither a defensive nor triumphalistic posture. It is our conviction that evangelicalism is a vibrant theological tradition in its own right, with its particular convictions, emphases, and guiding principles. As in any tradition with its own peculiar emphases, there are areas that remain underdeveloped and, thus, represent opportunities for growth. There are also singular contributions the evangelical theological tradition makes to the broader world of theology, which are expressions of its peculiarities. Traditions do a disservice by blunting their leading edges. We make no attempt to do that here. Rather, this final chapter will focus on the unique opportunities for growth and contributions of evangelical theology as we consider its future prospects.

A More Catholic Ecclesiology: Opportunities

Perhaps one of the more conspicuous absences among the loci covered in this book is the doctrine of the church. We made this decision because we wanted to emphasize those elements that characterize evangelical *theology* historically. While there are some discernible threads of commonality among evangelical ecclesiologies, and while the topic has received increased attention in recent years, our judgment was that other loci deserved more focused attention and that ecclesiological reflection is not something that characterizes or unites this particular tradition.[1] In fact, as we ponder opportunities for growth within evangelical theology, it would seem that some of the key areas revolve around ecclesiology. We will highlight three.

The Theater of the Gospel: The Nature of the Church

The strengths and contributions of evangelical theology are undoubtedly correlated to the paucity of evangelical ecclesiologies. The emphasis on the basics of having a relationship with God (both our missional and pastoral impulse) has sometimes inclined evangelicals away from reflection on the *ecclesia*, an allergy perhaps connected to the church's potential for overreach in terms of an individual's salvation and actual underreach in terms of mission effectiveness. One of the obvious complexities facing evangelical ecclesiology is that there is no one historical root to anchor it. Our ecclesiologies are essentially Lutheran, Reformed, Wesleyan, or Anglican, with free church, Anabaptist, and congregationalist elements mixed in.[2] In order to facilitate cooperation and "focus on the main things," we have sometimes downplayed ecclesiological differences or even the importance of articulating a coherent ecclesiology, especially among free church evangelicals (which may now dominate the landscape). Yet, gospel and church are bound together. John Webster writes, "[The gospel] generates an assembly, a social space. ... In that space, the converting power of the gospel of reconciliation becomes visible in creaturely relations and actions. ... The Christian faith is thus ecclesial because it is evangelical."[3] Thus, if salvation and our experience of God are somehow mediated by the church, then it is incumbent upon evangelical theologians to

---

[1] We are aware of the various treatments of ecclesiology in textbooks like Grudem, Erickson, and other whole theologies. Furthermore, there has been recent evangelical reflection on the church in volumes by Husbands/Treier, Allison, Harper/Metzger, Stackhouse, and so on.

[2] Ephraim Radner, "Church and Sacraments," in *The Oxford Handbook of Evangelical Theology*, ed. Gerald R. McDermott (New York: Oxford University Press, 2010), 279.

[3] John Webster, *Confessing God: Essays in Christian Dogmatics II*, 2nd ed. (London: Bloomsbury T&T Clark, 2016), 153–4.

develop a robust ecclesiology to match their (at least historically) nuanced accounts of soteriology. What is the church? How do and how will evangelical theologians answer this question?

Ephraim Radner characterizes evangelical ecclesiology by several emphases:

- *It is Bible-based*: The reading and studying of Scripture by individual believers is central in church life. It may even be characterized as a "mark" of the church.
- *It requires individual assent*: The church is largely constituted by the act of individual choosing.
- *It foregrounds believer baptism*: Baptism is a sign that one has chosen a life that requires repeated individual choices, rather than seeing baptism as once-for-all work of God initiating one into the church.
- *It focuses on the Lord's Supper as primarily a memorial*: The meal is a regular reminder of Christ's work and our individual faith commitment.
- *It is evangelistic*: The church itself is called to promote and aid in the task of evangelism.[4]

Undoubtedly, theological as well as practical commitments drive evangelical ecclesiology. In fact, what is most salient about Radner's description is that it captures the main evangelical themes, but views them through an ecclesiological lens. He, however, cautions that the emphasis on individual choice and the lack of rootedness in an ecclesiological tradition make evangelical doctrines of the church vulnerable to the changing tides of consumerist culture.[5] As the culture shifts, so our ecclesial self-understanding morphs. The common evangelical emphases—Bible, mission, experience—need not be jettisoned or muted, but might there be better ways to integrate them with ecclesiological concerns?

Evangelical ecclesiology will be most fruitful and gain the most traction among evangelicals themselves if it is able to chart a course between treating ecclesiology as entirely extrinsic to the gospel and treating ecclesiology as first theology. As Webster insightfully notes, our task is "to lay bare both the necessary character of the church

---

[4]Radner, "Church and Sacraments," 287–91.
[5]Radner, "Church and Sacraments," 291.

and its necessarily derivative character."[6] One of the good instincts of communion ecclesiologies over the past thirty or so years has been the conviction that the being of the church, or an account of the nature of the church, must begin with first principles, which means it must begin with God. Some fairly recent accounts focus on the intra-Trinitarian relations as providing the grounds for a vision of the church as a communion of persons.[7] Perhaps a better way of relating theology proper to ecclesiology is to map how the *works* of the triune God relate to the being of the church.[8] We can weather cultural and doctrinal fads by clarifying the church's place in the economy of all that God is doing in Christ and by the Spirit. "What we need, if we are going to understand the church's nature," writes J. I. Packer, "is insight into the person and work of Christ and of the Spirit."[9] In other words, an evangelical ecclesiology must be one governed by the evangel. We must give account of the church as the "theater of the gospel."[10] What difference would it make for evangelical ecclesiology to take seriously the Word made flesh, accounting for both the full deity and full humanity of Christ? How would the ministry of Jesus in the Spirit inform our doctrine of the church? What about the inauguration and consummation of the kingdom in Christ? What is the ecclesial significance of the resurrection and ascension?[11] The point here is simply that an evangelical doctrine of the church can be more than an inchoate and piecemeal collection of affirmations and practices. Evangelical theology has the exciting opportunity to find coherence and unity in its ecclesiology as it unpacks the riches of the evangel and builds from its gospel center outward. The gospel is its organizing and

---

[6]See Webster, *Confessing God*, 154–5.

[7]For example, see Colin E. Gunton, The *Promise of Trinitarian Theology*, 2nd ed. (Edinburgh: T&T Clark, 1997), 56–82.

[8]See John Webster, *God without Measure*, vol. 1, *God and the Works of God* (London: Bloomsbury T&T Clark, 2016), 182.

[9]J. I. Packer, *Serving the People of God*, vol. 2 (Carlisle: Paternoster, 1998), 3.

[10]Kevin J. Vanhoozer, *The Drama of Doctrine: A Canonical Linguistic Approach to Christian Doctrine* (Louisville: Westminster John Knox, 2005), 400.

[11]For example, a proper focus on the resurrection and ascension of Christ chastens overly inflated accounts of the church being the body of Christ, his hands and feet, his ongoing incarnation. Writers like John Webster, Colin Gunton, and Douglas Farrow have sought to make these rich gospel connections to ecclesiology. See, e.g., Douglas B. Farrow, *Ascension and Ecclesia: On the Significance of the Doctrine of the Ascension for Ecclesiology and Christian Cosmology* (Grand Rapids: Eerdmans, 1999).

life principle. Polities will differ, but every difference will find its rationale in the history of the triune God's work of redeeming his covenant people.

The Unity and Catholicity of the Church

When we confess the church as "one" and "catholic," we are acknowledging two forms of oneness and universality—diachronic and synchronic. The church is one and catholic throughout history, and it is one and catholic around the world. A continuing opportunity for evangelical theology is to take seriously and give expression to what we would call the long view (the tradition) and wide view (worldwide nature) of the one church.[12]

For decades, evangelicals have been challenged to retrieve the great tradition, for their own good.[13] To a significant degree, evangelical theologians have sought to show a greater acknowledgment of the tradition. This can be seen in the wave of books and commentaries seeking to retrieve the theological interpretation of Scripture, dissertations on patristic, medieval, Reformation, and post-Reformation writers, and several significant works that defend the indispensability and value of tradition for evangelical theology.[14] It is commonly recognized that not only is tradition unavoidable, it is also valuable. At the very least, it liberates us from our own thoughts, our own cultural ways of thinking, and the limitations of our own traditions.[15] Perhaps most importantly for evangelicals, tradition leads us into the proper interpretation of Scripture. Many decades ago, Packer wrote,

The history of the Church's labour to understand the Bible forms a commentary on the Bible which we cannot despise or ignore

---

[12]We are using the term "tradition" loosely here to refer to interpretations of Scripture, practices, significant creedal and confessional statements, doctors of the church, and so forth.

[13]See the various works of D. H. Williams, Robert Webber, and Thomas Oden.

[14]For a recent example, see Gavin Ortlund, *Theological Retrieval for Evangelicals: Why We Need Our Past to Have a Future* (Wheaton: Crossway, 2019).

[15]This is McGrath's summary of Packer's view of tradition. See Alister E. McGrath, "The Great Tradition: J. I. Packer on Engaging with the Past to Enrich the Present," in *J. I. Packer and the Evangelical Future: The Impact of His Life and Thought*, ed. Timothy George (Grand Rapids: Baker Academic, 2009), 26–7.

without dishonouring the Holy Ghost. To treat the principle of biblical authority as a prohibition against reading and learning from the book of Church history is not an evangelical, but an anabaptist mistake ... Tradition may not be so lightly dismissed.[16]

What was said in the 1950s is echoed by Vanhoozer almost sixty year later:

Mere Protestant interpreters do well to consult and be guided by the theological judgments of earlier generations of Christians and of Christian communities in other parts of the world: Protestants who affirm *sola scriptura* ought also to affirm *prima facie* the catholic tradition as *a Spirit-guided embodiment of right biblical understanding* ... Hence, counterintuitive though it may be, "Catholicity is the *only* option for a Protestantism that takes *sola scriptura* seriously."[17]

Evangelical identity, as people of the Book, is now seen to depend somewhat on our attentiveness to the tradition.

Vanhoozer's statement also forms a bridge to an area of increased attention but with much room for growth—the role of the global evangelical community in doing evangelical theology. According to Cyril of Jerusalem, the church is called catholic "because it extends over all the world, from one end of the earth to the other ... and because it brings into subjection to godliness the whole race of mankind, governors and governed, learned and unlearned."[18] Cyril captures the global, multicultural, and trans-socioeconomic nature of the church's catholicity. The catholicity of the church needs to be taken seriously by theologians especially since the center of gravity of Christianity is now in the majority world, outside the West where most written theology has been produced for the past several hundred years. It is not enough to acknowledge the growth of global

[16]J. I. Packer, *"Fundamentalism" and the Word of God* (Grand Rapids: Eerdmans, 1958), 48.

[17]Kevin J. Vanhoozer, *Biblical Authority after Babel: Retrieving the Solas in the Spirit of Mere Protestant Christianity* (Grand Rapids: Brazos, 2016), 146. The final quotation is taken from Peter J. Leithart, "Sola Scriptura, Una Ecclesia," Theopolis, May 1, 2014, https://theopolisinstitute.com/leithart_post/sola-scriptura-una-ecclesia/.

[18]Cyril of Jerusalem, *Catechetical Lectures* 18:23, accessed Mar 25, 2020, http://www.newadvent.org/fathers/310118.htm.

Christianity as a matter of fact. The question is what ramifications this has for the practice of evangelical theology.

One approach is to treat non-Western theologies as quaint, local theologies whose value is in its service to its local culture. In this case, Western theologies are considered more objective, universal, and normative. Another approach is to use non-Western theologies as part of a larger strategy to destabilize and relativize trenchant evangelical commitments. If all theologies are contextual, so it is said, what makes regnant (Western) evangelical accounts of doctrine any more universal than other accounts, Western or non-Western? A better way is through the motif of *conversation*. We are responsible to engage the global church in conversation for some of the same reasons we would engage the historical church: to correct our myopia, strengthen our reading of Scripture, and enrich our doctrinal understanding. To ignore the majority world is likewise, as Packer put it, to dishonor the Holy Ghost. Thus, along with a study of the tradition, reading the theology emerging from the majority world should be a standard part of all (Western) evangelical theological education.[19]

Three Anchors: Contributions

Throughout this volume we have sought to highlight evangelicalism's defining orientation toward Scripture and mission, while also pointing to its concern for the personal experience of salvation. These commitments, each of which shape the ethos and pathos of evangelical theologizing, are the very things evangelical theology has to offer the wider world.

One of evangelical theology's great strengths is its commitment to have doctrine anchored in Scripture. By "anchoring" we mean that evangelicals do not simply desire their theology to have some *loose* relation to the Bible, to be authorized in *some way* by Scripture, but rather to have strong, *evident* roots in it. Reminiscent of our Reformation and post-Reformation past, we, like our forebears, flit back and forth between biblical exegesis and theological

---

[19]See Timothy C. Tennent, *Theology in the Context of World Christianity: How the Global Church Is Influencing the Way We Think about and Discuss Theology* (Grand Rapids: Zondervan Academic, 2009), 15–16.

formulation, always corroborating the latter with the former. This is not meant to imply that other traditions do not have their own ways of and concern for relating Scripture to theology. Evangelical theologians, however, are particularly attuned to drawing a more direct line from Scripture to doctrine. This is our biblicism put to work. While, admittedly, it is not always straightforward to discern what it means for a theology to be biblical, evangelical theology contributes to the practice of theology by calling theologians to "show their work," that is, demonstrate how their proposal is authorized meaningfully by Scripture. Theology is responsible to the prophetic and apostolic writings, which give it its shape and transmit its *raison d'être*. It is a response to a word God has spoken and continues to speak. Even though there are disagreements within and without evangelicalism on the nature of Scripture, a key role of our theology is to call the church and academy back to Scripture. We are the voice of one crying in the wilderness, "Where did you find that in the Bible?"

Closely related is the evangelical concern that theology be anchored to the gospel and mission. How does what one writes contribute to the furtherance of the gospel and the advancement of God's kingdom purposes? In other words, theology, even in its more academic forms, must always have a missional end. John Stott, in trying to articulate the nature of Christian mission, addresses four interrelated areas that are integral to mission: evangelism, dialogue, salvation, and conversion.[20] In some sense, even evangelical *theology* asks how it contributes to the proclamation of the gospel, how it addresses other worldviews or perspectives, how it helps foster the fullness of the salvation, and how it aids the conversion of the whole person to Christ. What Walter Kasper says about Catholic dogma is characteristic of the evangelical mood: "Its dogmas and interpretations of Scripture are not ends in themselves; their purpose is to serve the worldwide mission of the Church."[21] Apologetics in the twentieth and twenty-first centuries is one typically evangelical manifestation of this public, missional concern. But calling theology to be missional involves more a frame of mind, or better, a reframing of ends, than a particular mode or style. It is not about making

---

[20]John R. W. Stott, *Christian Mission in the Modern World* (Downers Grove: InterVarsity, 1975).
[21]Walter Kasper, *The Methods of Dogmatic Theology* (Glen Rock: Paulist, 1969), 29.

all theology populist versus academic in tone. Rather, evangelical theologians ask themselves and their nonevangelical compatriots what the point of their work is if it is not an aid in fulfilling Jesus's commission to make disciples, preach forgiveness, love neighbor, and teach the obedience of faith. Theology hears from and speaks to two publics—the church and world—and it is oriented around the gospel proclamation. Theologians speak as those *in* the world *to* the world *for the sake of* the world.

Finally, evangelical theology is a theology oriented around and anchored to the *personal*—personal faith, personal conversion, personal experience. These concerns animate and often delimit evangelical theological reflection. A question often asked, for good or bad, is: how does this "apply" to me? By this question, evangelicals are inquiring into the experiential payoff of any particular theological proposal. Does this strengthen my faith? Does this help bring someone to Christ? Does this enhance my experience of God? Does this foster love for God or neighbor? The value of the proposal is closely correlated to potential spiritual benefits attained, whether individual or corporate. This instinct sometimes results in a premature dismissal of some academic theologies because they, prima facie, do not affect our experience of God. Yet, this instinct, in its better forms, is a vital corrective to some arid, detached theologies. It was Augustine who said, "So anyone who thinks that he has understood the divine scriptures or any part of them, but cannot by his understanding build up this double love of God and neighbour, has not yet succeeded in understanding them."[22] Christian theology is meant to produce virtue. This is what Ellen Charry calls the "salutarity"—the good-producing or character-forming end—of theology. She writes of the great theologians of the past:

> The theologians who shaped the tradition believed that God was working with us to teach us something, to get our attention through the Christian story, including those elements of the story that make the least sense to us. They were interested in forming us as excellent persons. Christian doctrines aim to be good for us by forming or reforming our character; they aim to be salutary.

---

[22]Augustine, *On Christian Teaching*, trans. R. P. H. Green (Oxford: Oxford University Press, 2008), 27.

They seek to form excellent persons with God as model ... The great theologians of the past were also moralists in the best sense of the term. They were striving not only to articulate the meaning of the doctrines but also their pastoral value or salutarity—how they are good for us ... For these theologians, beauty, truth, and goodness—the foundation of human happiness—come from knowing and loving God and nowhere else.[23]

Even the most conceptually challenging theologies of the past were aimed at the spiritual well-being of the church. This is an impulse found in Puritan writers like John Owen, early evangelicals like Wesley and Edwards, and in their contemporary progeny, both academic and nonacademic. Theological precision and pastoral sensibility are never to be divorced. The value of a theological proposal is tied to its salutarity. Theology cannot avoid the scrutiny of the practical or experiential, and we should not want it to. As evangelicals continue to lean into this instinct, they are doing the church and academy a service, and we are (sometimes unbeknownst to us) calling theologians back to former, more classical ways of doing theology.

* * * * * * * *

Evangelical theology is poised to be a significant voice in theological discourse in the years to come. Its missional edge, calling of the church back to the sources, and rapidly expanding global presence—not to mention the increasing sophistication and nuance in its prominent and younger voices—render it a force not to be relegated to the margins of popular or academic theology.

---

[23]Ellen T. Charry, *By the Renewing of Your Minds: The Pastoral Function of Christian Doctrine* (New York: Oxford University Press, 1999), vii.

INDEX

Algonquin tribe 52
Alleine, Joseph 105–6
Anderson, Leith 195
Anselm 78–80
Arius 209–12
Athanasius 210–12
atonement 71–94
  Christus Victor 89–90
  mystery 76–7
  governmental theory 85–6
  kaleidoscopic view 90–1
  non-Western accounts 90
  retribution 74–5
  solidarity 75–6
  penal substitution 73–4, 91–3
Augustine 3, 18–21, 23
Azariah, Samuel 59–60

baptism 99–101, 104, 114–16
Barth, Karl 33–4, 215–16
Bernard of Clairvaux 162
Boersma, Hans 93
Bonaventure 160
Bosch, David 43
Bunyan, John 121, 162, 168

Calvin, John 80–2, 103–4, 131–2
  on sanctification 164–5
  on the Trinity 212
charismatic movement 6
Charry, Ellen 229–30
Chao, Jonathan 44
church *see* ecclesiology
Confessing Church movement 169
concurrence 149–50

Constantine 156–8
conversion 95–120
  and baptism 114–16
  as a decision 112–14
  as a process 118–19
  new birth 97–100
  preparationism 108–9
  second-generation
    Christians 116
  sinner's prayer 111
Council of Constantinople 212
Council of Nicaea 209–12
Council of Trent 132–3
Cyril of Jerusalem 226

discipleship *see* sanctification
Dunn, James 138–9

ecclesiology 221–7
Edinburgh World Missionary
  Conference 5, 59
Edwards, Jonathan 83–5,
  106 9, 169
Eliot, John 52
Eusebius 157
evangelical theology 1–8, 221-30
*Evangelicals and Catholics
  Together* 140–2
experience 229–30

Finney, Charles Grandison 110–11
Four Spiritual Laws 113–14

globalization 64
God 14–15, 36–7, 201–20

doctrine of appropriation 187–8
and love 77
missions and processions
    206–8, 216–17
and worship 203–6
Graham, Billy 40–2
Great Awakening 4–5

Henry, Carl 33–4
holiness *see* sanctification
Holy Spirit 57, 177–99
and the church 196
filioque controversy 186
gifts of the Spirit 185
and mission 182–3, 188–9,
    193–5, 198
in relation to Father and
    Son 180–1
spiritual theology 197–8

image of God 97–100

Jesus Christ 203–6 (*see also*
    atonement, God, justification)
John Climacus 160–2
Joshua Project 47
Jowett, Benjamin, 28–9
justification 121–44
and adoption 128
antinomianism 135–5
as a gift 122–5, 142
and identity 143–4
imputation 127
and law 125–6
and obedience 126, 130–4
and sanctification 128–9
union with Christ 127–8

Kasper, Walter 228
Keswick movement 58

Lausanne Movement 7–8, 41–50,
    59–62, 65–6
Cape Town Commitment 60–1,
    178–85, 195

Lewis, C. S. 159–60
Lloyd-Jones, D. M. 96
Lovelace, Richard 152
Luther, Martin 17, 22–3, 51–2,
    102, 129–31
on sanctification 159, 163–4
on the Trinity 212

McKnight, Scot 117–18
mission 5–7, 39–67, 228–9
colonialism 48–9
early Protestant 50–1
and Holy Spirit 182–3, 193–4
Moravians 52–4
unreached people groups
    46–8, 65–6

narrative theology 30–1
Ndukuba, Henry C. 18–19
New Perspective on Paul 138–40
Newbigin, Lesslie 187

Owen, John 152–6, 186–9
on the Trinity 212–13

Packer, J. I. 15, 72–8, 105, 112,
    215–16, 224–6
Padilla, René 40, 46–9
Palmer, Phoebe 55–9, 156, 187
on the Holy Spirit 190–4
on Scripture 191–2
Peters, Greg 160
Pietism 3–4, 52–4, 105–6, 133–4
Piper, John 122–9, 139–40
persecution 63
postmodernism 29–30
poverty 46–7, 66
prayer 65
Protten, Rebecca 54
Puritanism 105, 134–5

Radner, Ephraim 223
Ramachandra, Vinoth 63–4
Ramm, Bernard 44
Rowling, J. K. 27–8

sanctification 100, 128–9, 145–73
  and discipleship 170–2
  human participation in
    147–50, 171–2
  individual and social 169
  and justification 145–6
  and means of grace 172
  in medieval western
    Christianity 160
  and modern science 168–9
  mortification and
    vivification 152–3
  and spirituality 150–2
  theosis 158–9
Sanders, Fred 201–8, 213, 216
Scripture 13–38, 227–8
  authority 15–17
  clarity 37–8
  general hermeneutics 26–9
  grammatical-historical
    exegesis 35
  historical criticism 24–6, 214–15
  and the Holy Spirit 191–3
  interpretation 21–31, 217–20
  literal sense 37
  person-centered exegesis 218–19
  truthfulness 17–21
Second Great Awakening 110
Simons, Menno 104
Smith, Amanda 58
Spener, Philipp Jakob 4
Stott, John 39–50, 66

Taylor, William 58
Thomas Aquinas 18
Torrey, R. A. 180–1, 193–4
tradition 35–6, 225–6
Treat, Jeremy 92–3
Trinity *see* God

Ulrich, Antwon 53–4

Vanhoozer, Kevin 45, 87–9,
    93, 226

Warfield, B. B. 13–21, 86–7
Webster, John 222–4
Wesley, John 4–5, 82–3,
    96–102, 135–7
  on sanctification 159, 165–7
*Westminster Confession of
    Faith* 16
*Westminster Larger
    Catechism* 99–100
*Westminster Shorter
    Catechism* 163
Whitefield, George 4, 54, 56, 83,
    85, 107, 110, 114
Willard, Dallas 170–2
Woodberry, Robert 40
Woolman, John 169
World Council of Churches 60
Wright, N. T. 43

Zinzendorf, Nickolaus von 53